Tales
from the
Road

Also by Neil Zurcher:

Ohio Oddities

Strange Tales from Ohio

Ohio Road Trips

Neil Zurcher

Tales *from the* Road

Memoirs from a Lifetime of Ohio Travel, Television, and More

GRAY & COMPANY, PUBLISHERS
CLEVELAND

Gray & Company, Publishers
www.grayco.com

Library of Congress Cataloging-in-Publication Data
Zurcher, Neil.
Tales from the road / Neil Zurcher.
p. cm.
ISBN 978-1-59851-064-5
1. Zurcher, Neil. 2. Travel writers—Ohio—Biography.
3. Journalists—Ohio—Biography. 4. Television journal-
ists—Ohio—Biography. 5. WJW-TV (Television station :
Cleveland, Ohio)—Biography. 6. Cleveland (Ohio)—Biogra-
phy. 7. Zurcher, Neil—Travel—Ohio—Anecdotes. 8. Ohio—
Description and travel—Anecdotes. I. Title.
F496.4.Z87A3 2010
070.92—dc22
   [B]   2010006728

Printed in the United States of America
10 9 8 7 6 5 4 3 2 1

This book is dedicated to my family:
My wife and best friend,
Bonnie Adamson Zurcher;
My daughters and their husbands,
Melody and Ernie McCallister,
Melissa and Peter Luttmann;
My son, Craig William Zurcher ;
My grandchildren,
Allison R. McCallister
Bryan McCallister
Ryan Luttmann
Jason Luttmann;
and to
future generations

Contents

Preface

This is not a biography. For the record, I have been married twice and divorced once. I have two daughters from my first marriage and one son from my second. It is also not a "tell-all" book. It's a collection of memories—stories that I have been telling family and friends for years. I simply wanted to write them down for my grandchildren and their children's children.

As I have gotten older, I've found myself thinking frequently about my grandparents and how little I knew about them. Some vague family stories and old photos, their names, where and when they were born, and when they died—that was it.

Finding a high school diary that my mother, Grace Currier Zurcher, kept in pen and pencil was part of the inspiration for this book. Reading my mother's day-to-day thoughts as a teenage girl in the late 1920s gave me some real insights into who she was and what her life had been like.

There were no great secrets, just her daily thoughts, a record of places she had been, and the people she interacted with. It was a window on a time I never knew.

I hope this book will be a window on time for the folks who used to watch me on WJW-TV, a place where I can share some of my favorite destinations as well as some behind-the-scenes events. For my descendants, who someday might be curious about my life, I hope this book will also provide a glimpse of who and what I was. These are stories from my life that made me laugh and a few that made me cry. It is also a look back at places and things that have, in some cases, just become memories and even history. Perhaps its greatest lesson is how our lives interact with the people we come in contact with.

There's no great message here. I'm just an ordinary person fortunate to live in extraordinary times; my wonderful job allowed me to wander through many people's lives, to explore our state from top to bottom, and even to witness some history-making events.

These are tales from the road.

Tales *from the* Road

CHAPTER 1

The Hill

Most folks around Henrietta simply called it "The Hill." Everyone knew what they were talking about: Zurcher's Henrietta Service, a combination gasoline station, country store, and, at one time, a truck-stop restaurant operated by my father and mother. At various times it stocked groceries and a cooler with meat, cheese, milk, and eggs. A small lunch counter offered Page's Ice Cream, homemade soups and sandwiches. Out front were two gasoline pumps and a cooler filled with iced bottles of soda pop. Our staples were newspapers, milk, bread, cigarettes, pipe and chewing tobacco, potato chips, and candy. We sometimes had fresh oranges, watermelons, and other produce, depending on the season. We were a convenience store before such a term was coined.

But it was much more: When there was a death or an accident in our small crossroads community, our little store was the unofficial headquarters where money from neighbors was collected to buy flowers, or where a cigar box might be placed to pick up donations to aid a family facing hardship. Being the only store in the community, it was a sort of unofficial community center where farmers or their farm families would meet to leave messages and trade gossip and the latest scandal while comparing prices of apples, potatoes, milk, and other commodities they produced. And then upstairs over the store were three rooms that served as my family's home as I entered junior high school. We were there literally by accident.

Have you noticed that life can be so promising one minute and then, in a split second, everything can change?

The first ten years of my life were spent growing up on my grandfather Currier's farm in Henrietta. It was an idyllic life with fields to roam, creeks to play and fish in, cows and horses to care for. No one played a greater role in shaping my life than my mother's parents, Canarius and Caroline Currier. In the last years of the Great Depression and during World War II they were the rock in my life. They gave me and my parents, Oscar and Grace Zurcher, love and shelter.

My father was an insurance company executive for twelve years. He started at the height of the Great Depression with the Town and Village Insurance Service of Columbus. By the early 1940s he was traveling Ohio in charge of recruiting new agents for the independent company.

Living with my mother's parents wasn't unusual for a family during the depression. But with the start of 1945, as World War II was winding down, my parents had finally been able to save enough money to purchase a former one-room schoolhouse that had been converted into a home on Garfield Road, just across the pasture from my grandfather's barn.

My father hired a carpenter to do some modernization to the building, which had no electricity or running water. We were able to dig out a basement underneath the building, and the tall ceilings allowed us to install a second floor with bedrooms and a modern bath. We were all looking forward to the job being finished by the end of the year so we could spend Christmas in our own home.

On Halloween 1945 my father was scheduled to go on a trip to central Ohio. He stopped at the new home to check on the work the carpenter was doing. Since the war had ended in August, it was much easier to get building supplies, and the job was moving along ahead of schedule.

The carpenter had just finished installing window dormers on the second floor. He asked my father to climb up onto the scaffolding to inspect the work on the roof. Dad was walking along the wooden scaffolding along the roofline when he lost his balance. He made a desperate lunge at the edge of the roof but toppled off the scaffolding and fell nearly fifteen feet, momentarily catching his right foot in the cross-members of the scaffolding. His weight nearly tore the foot from his body. Only an Achilles tendon kept his right foot attached to his leg. He hit the ground with a thud and was mercifully knocked unconscious.

The carpenter scurried down the ladder and had to drive to nearby Henrietta School for a telephone to call for an ambulance. He then drove frantically back to the house, where he found that my father had come to, but was in great pain and was losing blood from his badly injured foot. The carpenter managed to tie a tourniquet around Dad's lower leg to slow the bleeding until the ambulance arrived and rushed him to Oberlin's Allen Memorial Hospital.

Family doctor Lester Trufant, who was also a surgeon, happened to be on duty when the ambulance arrived, and he took my father directly into surgery. He told Dad that the injury was so severe that he would probably have to amputate the foot. My father pleaded with him to try to save it. Against his better judgment, Dr. Trufant spent several hours reattaching the foot. What followed were weeks and months in and out of hospitals as my father fought infections and had more surgery to try to restore some use to the foot.

Ironically, although my father worked in the insurance industry, his company had no benefits, and he carried no hospitalization coverage. The bills mounted as the long hospital stays continued, and my mother and father realized that the dream of their own home was slipping away. The final straw came in the spring of 1946, when my father received word from Town and Village Insurance that, because he was unable to work, they were stopping his pay and severing his employment. With no job and with more medical expenses still ahead, my parents sold the unfinished home.

It was a frightening time. There were very few jobs since the massive war effort was being powered down, and returning war veterans had first shot at those that were available. So when we learned that the operator of the store at Henrietta Hill had passed away and his widow wanted to sell the business, my father and mother talked long into the night and decided to gamble their remaining savings by purchasing the small country store. That spring, when I was ten years old and my brother, Noel, was just four, and my father was still on crutches and facing more surgery, we moved our family into the three small rooms above the store that was now Zurcher's Henrietta Service.

Henrietta in the late 1940s and early 1950s was a conservative little northern Ohio farming community. My high school class had only eight students. Our store was miles from the nearest sizeable town or supermarket.

Henrietta Hill was nine miles south of Lake Erie. It froze in the winter as lake winds swept in from the north. Frost would coat the windows of our tiny business as farmers came in out of the cold, their boots leaving an earthy-smelling residue of manure on the linoleum floor.

As cold as it was in the winters, we melted in the summer as golden acres of wheat and green fields of corn sprouted in the soggy heat. A large roaring fan in front of an open window or door would push the muggy air over the counters of our store as the motors on the coolers worked nonstop to overcome the humidity. Yet, there were spring nights when the soft perfume of lilacs and apple blossoms from the many orchards that surrounded Henrietta Hill wafted through open doors and windows.

And, finally, there was autumn. It was when our fields and orchards turned Technicolor, and our woods took on the gold of the sun. Farmers offered fresh produce at small stands in front of their homes. The senses came alive with the smell of burning leaves and smoke from wood fires, all the odors intertwined with the fragrance of ripe apples. In the evenings a few regular customers, mostly farmers, would gather on wooden soft drink cases under the portico of our store, bathed in the flickering light of our Sohio sign, to watch traffic go by on State Route 113 while drinking an RC Cola or smoking and talking quietly with their neighbors at the end of a long day.

Our number-one best seller was chili. My father always had a big pot of it cooking on the back of the stove. I cannot ever remember the pot being empty—my father, in fact, called it "never-ending chili"—and for the life of me, I cannot remember the recipe.

You have probably heard the old saying, "If you knew what they made hot dogs from, you probably would never eat one." The same went for the chili we served at Zurcher's Henrietta Service. My father would toss in things like a cup of coffee grounds, apple cider, and onions fresh from the garden once in a while. When the contents dipped below a certain spot on the pot's chili-encrusted innards, we would also dump in tomato soup, kidney beans, and a couple of pounds of hamburger, adding pepper until someone sneezed—preferably not into the pot. I suspect some other things got in, too. My father's ever-present cigarette was known to occasionally drop its ashes into the chili. Also, being a teenager at the time, when I was called on to refill the chili pot, I might have just come in the door from changing the oil in a car and didn't take time to wash my hands before scooping up a couple of handfuls of fresh ground meat to toss in. I am also sure that perspiration from our foreheads dripped into the kettle on the broiling summer nights when we'd stir the chili with a large spoon. It never won any awards, but we sold barrels of it. In spite of this—or maybe because of it—I have never been exactly crazy about chili.

* * *

The late 1940s were a time of hope. The young men who had become soldiers and sailors and interrupted their lives to fight World War II were home. They were again working in garages, farms, small businesses, and factories. Some were headed off to college. Memories from the whirlwind of the Great Depression and from the ashes of world war were fading. The future beckoned with the bright light of optimism.

It was against this backdrop that I grew from a boy into a man. I was living in a time when the world was finally offering hope. Thoughts of vacations and travel had been few for more than a decade, but the world was putting itself back together. For veterans and their families, a new era was at hand that would provide time to relax and to discover beaches, parks, forests, and other attractions, some just a short trip from home. The road beckoned. It called me, too.

As a teenager I was expected to run the store after school, cook food, wait on grocery customers, and pump gasoline for an eight-hour shift, sometimes all by myself. Before the coming of turnpikes and the Interstate Highway System, rural communities like Henrietta were isolated. Business was slow in the evening after dinnertime.

I would often walk back and forth on the gravel driveway in front of our store, wistfully watching the occasional truck or car hurrying past us on the state highway that connected Elyria, thirteen miles to the east, with Milan, twenty-five miles to the west. I would often fantasize about the people I saw in those vehicles. I saw them as salesmen, hurrying to their customers; young men heading out for an evening of fun with a pretty girlfriend; mysterious strangers off on adventures that would carry them far across our state, perhaps into faraway cities I had only read about.

I longed to travel with them, but I saw only a blur of faces, and the dust whipped around me by the speed of their passing vehicles. The illuminated red and white gasoline sign and the 150-watt bulbs that illuminated our gasoline pumps were my key lights; the dusty gravel-filled parking lot was my stage. I longed to walk away from this tiny community. To raise my thumb and jump into the first car that would stop and offer me a ride, not caring where I was headed. Just to see what was at the end of the road that ran in front of my country store.

With my father's permission, I did it a couple of times. Once I hitchhiked from Henrietta to Columbus to see the state fair. Another time, a friendly customer, a truck driver, gave me a lift to Cleveland before dawn. I watched the sun rise over the Terminal Tower and felt the hustle and bustle of the morning rush hour as we waited for a warehouse along the Cuyahoga River to unload his truck. After breakfast at a roadside diner, we headed back west. By afternoon I was again on the gravel parking lot of Henrietta Service, my thirst to travel only temporarily sated.

THE NIGHT OF FLAMES

Henrietta didn't lack its occasional action or excitement, however. I recall an evening when motors thundered and a high-flying cloud of dust spread over the county fairgrounds as Lucky Lott and his Hell Drivers had just completed their big finale: a jump by a man on a motorcycle, through a wall doused with gasoline and set ablaze, over the tops of three parked cars, and onto a ramp, where he landed safely.

During the ride from Wellington all the way back to Henrietta Hill that night, I imagined it was me the crowd had cheered and whistled for, that I was the motorcyclist who roared around the racetrack, slid to a stop, and calmly stepped off the sliding bike to wave and acknowledge the homage.

The next day I rode my bicycle around and around our dusty parking lot, jumping it over small potholes and skidding to awkward, dusty stops to wave to an imaginary cheering crowd. As the day went on, the pothole jumping got boring, and I began to develop a new plan. With my friend Joe Cucco, I would do a real fire act with my bicycle!

I asked Joe to join me in the backyard that evening near the blackened ring on the ground where we burned our store's rubbish each night. I had piled up several large, empty cardboard cartons. I also had a six-foot length of barn siding, my Flexible Flyer sled, an empty wooden pop case, and a two-gallon can of kerosene.

I explained my plan. We would saturate the empty cardboard

cases and put them in the rubbish area. Half of the barn siding would serve as a short ramp to the top of the empty pop cases on one side of the fire ring. The Flexible Flyer would prop up the remaining three feet of board that would be our escape ramp on the other side of the fire ring. Joe didn't like my use of the word "our." Actually, he went so far as to tell me that I was crazy and that he wouldn't have any part in such a stupid stunt. It was obvious that Joe had not heard the cheers at the fairgrounds. It also was obvious that if I was to duplicate the Hell Driver's bravery, I would have to do it alone.

Though Joe wasn't interested in achieving immortality as the world's youngest fire-crashing bicycle daredevil, he was willing to help me do so. He would light the fire and stand by with a bucket of water, in case anything went wrong.

It was nearly 9 p.m. by the time we had sawed the board in two, made our rickety ramps, piled the cardboard boxes nearly twelve feet high, and soaked the pile with kerosene. I handed Joe a box of wooden matches. The air filled with the pungent odor of fuel oil as I strapped on the war surplus leather aviator's helmet I bought for the occasion, pulled down the goggles, and nervously nodded that I was ready.

I rode my bicycle across the darkened lawn, ducking under my mother's clothesline and making a mental note to duck again when I started my run. Near the highway I turned and faced the backyard. At that moment, flames shot fifty feet in the air with a giant *whoosh!* as Joe scrambled away from the inferno he had touched off. Orange light filled the backyard, casting tall shadows on the back wall of our store. I could hear voices inside and knew my parents would be coming to investigate any minute. My moment was now!

I leaned forward and started pumping. My legs were going like pistons, trying to get up enough speed to carry me through the fire and onto the back of the Flexible Flyer, twenty feet on the other side of the fire ring.

I remembered to duck as I approached the clothesline, but not far enough. It caught the top of my helmet, ripping the goggles off my head. I barely managed to stay upright on the bicycle as I flashed by Joe, his mouth open in a giant "O." Somewhere in the darkness I could hear my mother yelling to my father, "Something's on fire in the backyard!"

I felt, more than saw, my bicycle hit the ramp to the top of the pop case. Suddenly I was surrounded by flames and sparks and heat as my bike smashed into the crumbling tower of cardboard boxes, scattering them in every direction. The bicycle missed the Flexible Flyer, and the front wheel collapsed as it hit the ground five feet in front of the escape ramp. I flew off the seat headfirst, over the handlebars and onto the ground, where I slid through my mother's flower bed like a human bulldozer. When I raised my head, I found myself staring at the startled face of the owner of that flower bed.

My mother, calming herself enough to make sure that I was still alive, ran to help my father put out the numerous fires created by the scattered, burning boxes. Hearing the anger in her voice as she scurried around the backyard stamping out burning bits of cardboard, and realizing that I was alive and well, Joe escaped on his bike and headed home, leaving me to face the music alone.

Aside from a few minor gravel burns on my forehead, belly, and knees, I walked away from my adventure intact. Sure, my parents were upset. My bicycle was impounded for a month. (It took me that long to earn the money to repair it.) And I was grounded for a month. But, truthfully, I didn't hear any of their words that night. All I could hear was the cheering of the crowd at the county fair. Lucky Lott's Hell Drivers' newest star had just made his first successful stunt run.

Well, almost.

THE BREAD RUN

It was not uncommon for kids in our community to start driving trucks, tractors, and cars by the time they were twelve or thirteen. Henrietta was still a farming community. If a kid could reach the pedals of a tractor, and if parents needed an extra hand in the field, the child learned to drive—first by sitting on his father's lap as they plowed the fields or dragged wagons through orchards, later by helping to steer, and eventually driving by himself.

I had learned to drive our old Case tractor on my grandfather Currier's farm. I was expected to move vehicles that had been left at our garage for a tire change or oil change. I didn't even have a driver's license when I spotted an opportunity to drive myself to school each day. In my mind, it became a huge status symbol that I just had to have.

After Grandfather Currier died in 1951, when I was fifteen, I would frequently spend the night with my grandmother, who now lived alone on the farm on Vermilion Road about two miles from our store. My father at that time had a contract with Henrietta School, also on Vermilion Road, to furnish fresh bread to its cafeteria each schoolday. The Model Bakery in Lorain would deliver trays of still-warm bread to our store every morning before dawn, and my father would drive them to the school when it opened.

I started lobbying him to allow me to use a 1939 Buick four-door sedan that he had purchased and was rehabilitating as an extra vehicle for the family. I pointed out that if he would let me take the car to my grandmother's each night, I could get up early, drive to the store at the Hill, pick up the bread, and deliver it to school before my classes started. It was a win-win situation, I noted. He wouldn't have to get up early to drive the bread to school, and the responsibility of the bread run would ensure that I was on time for school every day.

My father was reluctant. My mother was totally opposed. While it was one thing for me to drive around the parking lot of our store, it was quite another for me to be out on a public highway. They both pointed out that I was still not sixteen years old, the legal age for a driver's license. The car had no license plates and was not insured. They had not planned to spend that money until the car was completely roadworthy.

I countered that we lived in a small rural community with no police department. The sheriff's department was fifteen miles away and rarely patrolled our peaceful area. I would only be driving two miles, on a side road with very little traffic. Then I tossed out my strongest point: that we frequently saw youngsters my age driving their family tractors up and down the same road, going from one field to another. Were they breaking the law?

Apparently my point hit home. Late that evening, as we were closing the store and I was preparing for my father to drive me to my grandmother's home, he suddenly handed me the keys to the old Buick.

"We're going to try this tomorrow," he said. "You take the car to Grandma's tonight and then be here at 7:30 to pick up the bread. Drive slow. Be careful and remember we still haven't put new brake shoes on that car, so give yourself plenty of time when you stop."

I was giddy with excitement as I drove south on Vermilion Road through the autumn night, carefully watching each approaching headlight in fear that it might be a police car.

In bed that night, thinking about my new adventure the next morning, I began to worry. It was dark when I had driven down the road that night, but this would be in broad daylight. What if I was spotted by neighbors who knew I wasn't old enough to drive? What if this was the day the sheriff's department decided to patrol the rural roads? Anyone who saw my smooth, round face would know I was just a kid. It would be like driving down the road with a huge sign plastered on the side of the Buick that said "Illegal, underage driver inside!" I needed a disguise.

Bright and early the next morning while my grandmother made breakfast, I was upstairs rummaging through an old trunk that held costumes and clothes from many years ago. I came down to breakfast wearing a Santa Claus wig and beard and a stained and crumpled cowboy hat, peering over a pair of wire-rimmed glasses that probably had belonged to my great-grandfather.

"My goodness!" my grandmother exclaimed. "Are you getting ready for Halloween?"

I mumbled something about a project in school that required a costume, quickly ate my breakfast, and ran out of the house to the car.

I was barely tall enough to see over the steering wheel. To a passerby, I must have resembled a scraggly, white-haired, near-sighted gnome as I roared north along the country highway. I was probably traveling at fifty miles per hour as I approached the intersection of State Route 113 and Vermilion Road and stepped on the brake to slow down. The pedal went all the way to the floor. No brakes! I frantically started down-shifting, hoping the gears might slow the car as it sped closer and closer to the intersection.

What happened next is still ingrained in my memory like a kaleidoscope of thoughts. The speedometer read 35 miles per hour. Large trucks were rolling from both directions on the fast- approaching highway. Across the highway was our store, and waiting with the stack of freshly baked bread was my mother.

At the last second, when it appeared that I was about to become the hamburger in a truck sandwich, I desperately turned the wheel sharply to the left to avoid the intersection. With a great squealing of tires, the old Buick responded. I lost control as the car spun sideways into a large gravel parking lot across from our store. It was my good fortune that no trucks were parked there that morning as the car, now lost in a cloud of dust, spun around once more before coming to a stop, its front end pointed towards Otto Knoble's orchard.

This was long before seat belts, and I had been knocked across the front seat. The cowboy hat was on the floor, the wig was underneath me, the beard hung askew, and the glasses hung from one ear. I was still shaking when the car door was ripped open and my nearly hysterical mother started shouting and tugging at me. She was shouting so loudly and fast that it was hard to make out what she was saying. I caught the words "knew we should never have trusted you to drive."

"But Mom, the brakes . . ." I tried to explain, but she was in full scared-mother-righteous-indignation mode, and not in any mood to listen to my side.

She yanked me out of the car and stuck her finger in my face as she shouted, "I'm going to park this car, young man, and it's the last time you're going to see the keys!"

Before I could stop her she got into the car, started it up, and slammed it into first gear. I was still stammering about the brakes failing as she stomped the accelerator, did a three-sixty turn and shot across the highway into the parking lot of our store. Through the open window of the car I could hear her surprised scream, "THERE'S NO BRAKES!" as the car missed the side of the store, crashed through her small garden of rose bushes, and came to rest against the outhouse that served our customers' needs for a bathroom.

My mother was not hurt, but the outhouse had to be reset on its foundation.

UNEASY RIDER

During my later teenage years at Henrietta Hill, I often bought and traded cars that would best be described as junkers. Most were retrieved from auto salvage yards and probably were not really road safe, but to my teenage eyes they were beautiful. Most importantly, they were mine.

In one memorable deal I traded a fire-engine red 1940 Plymouth convertible with yellow plaid seat covers, green fender skirts, and two 100-inch-long antennas complete with hanging foxtails, for two vehicles: a 1942 Oldsmobile with automatic transmission and a war-surplus Indian motorcycle, still clad in olive-drab paint.

World War II veteran Jerry Leimbach operated a garage in an abandoned old church across from our store. Jerry had been an Army Air Force mechanic in England, keeping fighter planes and bombers in the air, and he was the man you took things to, from tractors to automobiles, to be fixed. If Jerry didn't have the part, he could fashion something out of baling wire and electrical tape that would probably keep the vehicle going for a few more weeks or months.

He was a good friend. At the end of the day, even though I am mechanically challenged, he would often allow me to bring my junkers into his garage and use the lift to work on them. He usually would watch me struggle to install a gas line or a brake shoe before eventually shoving me aside and saying, "Here, let me show you how to do it." And he would end up doing the job. Jerry always said he liked a challenge, and I gave him plenty with my various orphans from the junkyard.

The day I arrived home towing the '42 Oldsmobile with the disassembled Indian motorcycle stuffed in the backseat and trunk, my father was just coming out of the store. He stopped, stared at my proud new purchase, shook his head in disbelief at the rusting hulk of a car, and, without a word, turned and went back inside.

Jerry spent several hours working to start the Oldsmobile without success. When he dropped the transmission and found it packed with sawdust, he finally threw up his hands in surrender and suggested I get a wheelbarrow and take it back to the junkyard.

The Indian was something else. Although it was in pieces and parts, they appeared little used. It took several weeks of part-time evening tinkering for Jerry and me to reassemble the bike and motor. When we fueled it up, however, it would not start.

Jerry tweaked and tuned the motor in spare moments over the next couple of days. Finally, late one afternoon, he stood on the kick-pedal starter. After nearly two dozen tries, the motorcycle suddenly surprised both of us by giving a belch of smoke and roaring to life.

I was excited. Since it was my motorcycle, I claimed the right to its first spin, despite Jerry's warnings that we should make sure it would continue to run. I was already climbing onto the saddle, twisting the throttle, exulting in the throaty roar it gave.

The noise attracted Dad's attention across the street. He had just made his way to the edge of the road when I shoved the gearshift into low and started to let out the clutch while twisting the accelerator.

It should be noted here that, while I had ridden on several motorcycles as passenger, this was the very first time I had ever driven one.

My foot slipped off the clutch, and the cycle did what motorcyclists today like to call a "wheelie." It reared up on the back wheel and went charging across the driveway into the road, with me clinging to the handlebars. I managed to get the front wheel back on to the road at just about the time I realized the throttle no longer responded to my twists and turns. It was stuck, wide open.

I opened my mouth to scream as the speedometer climbed to forty miles per hour. I plowed through a cloud of mosquitoes, and because there was no windshield, the bugs splattered my face and filled my mouth. As I was coughing and spitting I saw in the rearview mirror Jerry running after me, but he was fast getting farther and farther away as I rocketed north on Vermilion Road on an out-of-control motorcycle.

The apple trees in Dodd's orchard were becoming a blur. Fear was bubbling up in my throat, and I started to shake, causing the motorcycle to veer from one side of the road to the other.

Ahead of me I suddenly saw the oncoming shape of a pickup truck driven by Leroy Emmerich, a local farmer. He swerved from one side of the road to the other, trying to get out of my way. Just when it appeared we would collide, he zigged and I zagged. We missed each other by inches.

Having somehow managed to straighten the motorcycle out, I was trying to think rationally how to stop it, when out of the corner of my eye I saw the blur of a large dog, barking and growling and dashing from Herman Portman's yard, which I was just passing. This dog had a long history of chasing cars and bicycles, and I guess the angry roar of the oncoming motorcycle was a real challenge to him.

He leaped as I went flashing by, and, growling, he sank his teeth into my flapping pant leg. This immediately whipped him off the ground and slammed him into the side of the speeding motorcycle—almost causing me to lose control again as he released his hold and bounced off, landing some twenty feet away. In my mirror I caught a glimpse of the dog scrambling out of the ditch and running with his tail between his legs for the safety of his home.

By this time I had reached a point where the road dipped down Meyer's Hill, a steep gully cut through the farmland eons ago by Chance Creek. It was the kind of hill we used to test-drive cars, to see if they could make it up the hill in high gear.

When I roared down the road to the bottom of the hill the speedometer was shakily registering 50 to 60 miles per hour. It was then I had an epiphany. I could stop the motorcycle by simply turning off the ignition! I turned the switch, the cycle emitted a loud, belching backfire, and the motor died. My ears were still ringing from its roar as I coasted to a stop on the crest of the other side of the hill.

As I stood there trembling and still trying to spit out bugs that splattered on my teeth and mouth, Jerry Leimbach and Dad came roaring up in Jerry's old truck. Right behind them was Leroy Emmerich in his truck.

Dad came out of the vehicle with amazing speed for a man with a crippled leg and a cane.

"What the hell did you think you were doing?" he shouted.

Still shaking, I could only point to the handlebars and croak, "Throttle—stuck! Throttle stuck!"

The motorcycle was loaded into the back of Jerry's truck, and I climbed into Leroy's pickup for the ride back to Henrietta Hill. As we passed Herman Portman's farm where the dog lived, we saw him cowering behind a tree.

"That's funny," mused Leroy. "That's the first time in years that that dog hasn't chased my truck."

I could do nothing but laugh hysterically.

I never rode the motorcycle again. It sat in our garage for a few weeks until a local man offered to buy it. I sold it on the spot.

SHOOTOUT AT HENRIETTA HILL

When I was a sophomore in high school, financial hard times prompted my father to keep our little gasoline station-grocery-truck stop open twenty-four hours a day. I would go to school, come home and do my homework (sometimes), then go to bed until 10 or 11 p.m., when I would go downstairs to the store to relieve my father, who had been there since 8 a.m. I would work the all-night shift, then go to school when he took over.

Henrietta was in an isolated area, and although crime was not high, it was a possibility. So I talked my father into allowing me to buy a gun to keep under the counter. It was a Colt .32-caliber semi-automatic pistol. (I already owned a .22-caliber revolver that I used for hunting on my grandfather's farm.)

One foggy spring night I was sitting at the lunch counter talking with my only customer, Mack, a driver for a uniform rental company in Lorain. He was having a leisurely predawn breakfast before his route of delivering clean rental uniforms to factories and businesses in the western part of the county.

It was about 4 a.m., and while we talked I heard a car drive up. A few minutes later, a man in his twenties wearing filthy clothes walked in and sat down at the counter. He ordered a cup of coffee and a hamburger. I served his coffee and went into the kitchen to make the burger.

He ate quickly and then pulled a handful of change from his pocket. He had just enough pennies, nickels, and dimes to pay his bill, with no tip. He walked out the door without saying anything more.

"That was a strange one," Mack said. "As soon as you went in the kitchen, he walked over and checked out behind the counters and looked at the cash register. I think if I hadn't been here he might have stolen something. He sure looked suspicious."

Before I could reply, we heard the car start up outside, and lights pulled under the portico over the gasoline pumps next to our front door. I went out and saw the same man.

"Fill 'er up," he said. (This was still the time when service stations had attendants pump the gas.)

I walked to the rear of the car, which was still running, and said, "You'll have to shut off the car. I'm not supposed to pump gas while the car is running."

"I can't shut it off. I have a bad battery and it won't start again," he shouted out the window.

I shrugged and started pumping gasoline into the car.

My eyes drifted to the license plate bracket on the rear of the car. The plate was missing. Just then I sensed a movement inside the car. Looking through the back window, I could see the man reach across the seat and open the glove compartment. The lights from the store illuminated the front seat enough that I could see him pull out a large black pistol.

I dropped the hose and said, "The telephone is ringing. I'll be right back." Before he could answer, I ran inside the store.

Mack was behind the counter getting himself a refill on his coffee. I looked over my shoulder and realized that the driver could not see what I was doing behind the counter. I rushed over to Mack and said, "The guy's got a gun. I think he plans to hold me up."

"Are you sure?" Mack said.

"Yes. Yes. I just saw him take a gun out of the glove compartment. He's holding it in his lap."

I reached under the counter and grabbed the two guns that were there. I handed Mack the .22 and stuffed the .32 semi-automatic in my belt, under the apron I was wearing.

"You take this gun and go out by your truck," I said. "You can back me up if he tries to put a gun in my face when I go to his car window to get paid for the gasoline."

Before Mack could argue, I whirled and ran back out the door and picked up the hose to continue fueling the would-be robber's car, all the while watching him through the rear window.

Mack came out of the store and walked alongside the stranger's car, pretending to examine a quart of oil in a rack next to the car window while trying to peek into the car. He put the oil can down and came back to where I was standing and nervously whispered to me, "You're right. He does have a gun in his right hand."

The stranger, now suspicious, was swiveling around looking for Mack, who had walked in front of his truck in plain view. With shaky hands, Mack pulled out the pistol I had given him and started to examine it to see if it was loaded. He accidentally pulled the cylinder release, and all the bullets fell out of the gun onto the ground. At this moment the man's tank was full. I hung up the hose and walked to the driver's window, my hand under my apron on my gun.

The man hesitated and said, "I need the oil checked." I didn't want to stand in front of his still-running car, so I said, "I can't check it unless you shut the motor off."

He thought for a second and said, "Do you have any flashlight batteries?"

I said, "Do you want me to get them for you along with your change?" Pointing out that I was still waiting to be paid for the gasoline.

All of a sudden he tromped on the accelerator. The car went screeching away from the pumps, almost knocking me down. Mack was still on his knees trying to find the bullets that had fallen out of his gun. I ran onto the state highway, chasing the car as it hit the pavement with tires screaming.

I yelled, "Stop! You didn't pay me!" And I pulled my gun and fired several shots in the air, which only made the car seem to go faster and start zigging and zagging down the road. The yelling and shooting brought lights on all over the neighborhood, and my father hobbled down the stairs from his bedroom above the store. Mack stood with a stunned look on his face, holding the still-empty revolver.

My father called the sheriff's office, and a deputy arrived to make a report. We were in the driveway, and I was pointing out which way the driver had gone, when the deputy asked where the gun was that I had fired in the air. I reached under my apron and started to hand it to him.

"Is it empty?" he asked as he began to reach for it.

"Oh, sure," I said, pointing it at the ground and pulling the trigger. The gun went off with a resounding "Bam!" and the bullet just missed the deputy's toe.

He confiscated my gun.

MY FIRST DINER

The first diner I recall eating in was in Birmingham, in Erie County, just across the county line from Henrietta. It was called the White Diner, and it was operated by a young news photographer named Walt Glendenning. (He would later become a dear friend and have a direct influence on my getting into television—but that's another story.) When I was a sophomore at Henrietta High School, the diner was our favorite hangout. It was an old trolley car that had rolled across northern Ohio in the 1920s. An earlier owner purchased the car when the trolleys stopped running and permanently parked it at the corner of State Route 113 and Route 60. You entered in the middle of the car, which was painted all white. To the right were four or five booths; to the left was an L-shaped counter that took up the rest of the car. The food was typical diner fare: hamburgers, milk shakes, fountain drinks, and a few blue-plate specials like meatloaf and spaghetti.

I was particularly fond of their milk shakes, which they made with Esmond Ice Cream out of Sandusky. They also used chocolate ice cream in the chocolate shakes. I don't remember much about the food beyond that because I was thrown out of the place on my third visit and was never allowed back in while Walter was around. It happened this way:

One night after basketball practice, one of the older members of the team, who had a driver's license, suggested we all go to the White Diner for a snack. We filled a couple of booths. Like most teenagers, we were a noisy, disruptive group. When someone at the next booth asked me to pass the catsup, I tossed it up in the air instead. It arced through the diner, barely missing the hanging lights, and landed safely in the hands of its intended receiver. Problem is, Walt Glendenning was watching. He gave me a stern warning that if I ever did that again, he would throw me out and not allow me back in.

Walt, at about six foot one, towered over me, and I believed him. But one of my friends, Joe Cucco, didn't hear the warning. When somebody at another booth yelled for the catsup, Joe launched it like a football. The intended receiver—I think it was Jack Dodd—wasn't ready. He missed the bottle, which shattered against the back of the booth, splattering catsup all over the booth and nearby counter. Walt, who had his back turned towards us and did not see the incident, wheeled around at the noise, put down his grease-covered spatula, and walked directly to me. He grabbed me by the back of my neck and, to the amusement of my classmates, propelled me out the door into the parking lot, informing me I was no longer welcome in his restaurant!

I tried to tell him I was not the guilty party, but he wasn't listening. So I sat on the fender of a car, watching my classmates laugh and point at me through the window as they finished their food. Even weeks later when I went to the White Diner, Walt ordered me out as soon as I walked in. It wasn't until years later, when both of us were working in television, that I convinced him I was not the person who had thrown the catsup.

Walter became a very dear friend and mentor. He went on to become a pioneer news photographer in Cleveland television and covered many major stories, including an exclusive story on Cleveland newspaperman Robert Manry during his history-making one-man sailing trip across the Atlantic Ocean.

The White Diner went through a series of owners in the '50s and '60s and, sadly, eventually was carted away to an uncertain end.

* * *

WHEN TELEVISION WAS NEW

When television was new and still a novelty, we had a wood encased set with a tiny seven-inch screen on our counter. My father had found some surplus school bus seats, and we lined them up in front of it. Farmers would crowd our little store in the evening to stare patiently at this box and watch a test pattern on WEWS in Cleveland. There was no activity, just the still shot of the test pattern and the sound of static over the speakers. The broadcasting day lasted only a few hours in the early evening. At about four in the afternoon, Bob Dale and Linn Sheldon would suddenly appear and talk about what would happen that evening. It might be a series of fifteen-minute programs of orchestra music on film, perhaps a puppet show, an old black-and-white movie, and then the national anthem and a prayer as the pictures disappeared and static filled the screen for the rest of the night.

Behind the counter, filling orders for ice cream cones and bottles of pop, I would listen to the farmers critique the performers and their shows. All of us marveled at the wonder of a person in Cleveland being seen and heard instantaneously here in tiny Henrietta. I began to fantasize about becoming a person who made his living on TV. But when I looked in a mirror, reality set in. People on TV were tall and handsome with booming voices, like Howard Hoffman on WXEL, Channel 9. I was short, stocky, had bad teeth, acne, and a high-pitched voice. No matter how hard I tried to imagine a future in the big city, I had real difficulty picturing myself on camera.

But dreams are hard to disown. Sometimes it takes very little to bring them back into sharp focus. A long, boring country evening once prompted me to entertain some of our truck-driving customers with a large empty cardboard box. I cut a window in one side, painted dials on the front, drew a speaker beneath the window, and put the box on the edge of the counter. I went behind it and crouched under the open bottom so that my head appeared in the window. With a little imagination, I was on television. I started reading headlines from the local newspaper and telling jokes. The truckers were appreciative, and one even left me a fifty-cent tip. It was the first time I had ever made money entertaining people.

Even then, in my wildest imagination, I would not have believed that I would go on to make my living and spend forty-two years of my life working in front of the camera in Cleveland television, or that I would also get to spend thirty years discovering what is at the end of those roads that led past Henrietta Hill.

THE FIRST MICROPHONE

I stood before my first microphone on a stage at Henrietta High School in March 1949. I was a freshman, and my class was sponsoring a talent show to raise money for a class project.

Because the show had been my idea, and because no one else in my class wanted to do it, I was master of ceremonies. Besides, I had a talent. I was fascinated by the new medium of television from watching it in our store, and I especially liked young ventriloquist Paul Winchell and his vent, or dummy, Jerry Mahoney. I would while away the hours trying to throw my voice in imitation, watching in the mirror over the soda fountain to see how much my lips moved as I tried to talk in a falsetto voice through closed teeth.

I had purchased a book through a mail-order company called Johnson-Smith that promised to teach me to be a ventriloquist. I had also saved my money to buy a Jerry Mahoney dummy, a smaller and much-less-expensive model of the one that Winchell used on TV. When you put your hand behind him, you could just pull a string that would make his jaw go up and down as you threw your voice. I practiced for hours and copied all of Winchell's material. Customers who tarried too long at the lunch counter became my captive audience as I rehearsed my act. But I rarely got any laughs or applause. Truth be told, I wasn't very good.

But that didn't stop me when the eight members of my high

school class debated ideas to make some money. We considered sponsoring a dance, but the junior class had that venue already booked. The PTA hosted the annual Halloween carnival as its fund-raiser. We had tried earlier to sponsor a sock hop with music played by a local radio disc jockey, but that soured when he failed to show up and we had to refund everyone's admission.

I raised my hand and suggested we sponsor a talent show— pointing out that more entrants would guarantee a bigger audience, since each performer's family would probably show up and buy tickets to see their kid compete. The class bought the idea, then debated over who would be the emcee. Some thought our class advisor, Mr. Gatts, should do the honors, but he declined. He said, "The guy who suggested this idea should be up there on the stage."

They all looked at me. A terrible student, I had low grades and probably low self-esteem. I participated in sports but usually sat on the bench. I wasn't very popular. I was the guy who came alone to school dances and stood on the sidelines watching. (I went alone to my senior prom, in fact. There was this girl I liked named June Parrish, from Elyria, whose family had a small grocery store. Weeks before the prom, I drove to Elyria almost daily trying to screw up my courage to ask her to the dance, but when I would see her my throat would constrict. I would buy a newspaper or jar of jelly as my excuse for being there, then leave. I ended up with a lot of newspapers and jelly but never the courage to ask her to the prom.) If they had had a ranking system in my class of eight, I would have been in ninth place. Probably for that reason, I suddenly very much wanted to be the master of ceremonies.

"I have a ventriloquist's dummy!" I blurted. My classmates just stared.

"I could do comedy routines in between the acts," I stumbled on, trying to convince them.

It finally boiled down to the fact that no one else really wanted to do it, but the only way they were going to let me on the stage was if I had help. I suggested my closest friend, Dennis Brill, whose academic career nearly paralleled mine, though he was better in sports. He thought it over for a minute and agreed to play Abbott to my Costello. Laurel to my Hardy. Martin to my Lewis. Well, you get the picture.

I would like to tell you that on the appointed night a new comedy team was born in the rural countryside of western Lorain County. Actually, we were beyond bad. We were terrible. It might have had something to do with our comedy writing.

I was on the stage about to introduce a brother and sister act from Wakeman, for example, when Dennis ran on stage interrupting me.

Dennis: "Neil! Neil! The squirrels are looking for you."

Me: "The squirrels are looking for me? Why?"

Dennis: "They think you're nuts." (Rim-shot)

There was very little laughter and lots of groaning from the audience.

My solo as a ventriloquist didn't fare much better. I was so nervous that I would pull the string making my dummy's mouth move when I was supposed to be talking, and not pull it when he was supposed to be answering me. When I concentrated on pulling the string at the right time, I would forget the punch lines to the jokes.

It was a very long evening. But Dennis and I somehow stumbled through it. There were nineteen acts, many of them from Henrietta, but also a handful from around the area. We had a paying audience of about fifty people, and when the night was over we had a profit of twenty dollars. The entire cast got a standing ovation as the curtain closed. Or maybe it was more like they were cheering the fact that the show was finally over.

My career as a ventriloquist ended that evening, but I did discover that, despite my nervousness, I enjoyed standing behind a microphone. I didn't realize that the evening was also a peek at my future.

* * *

THE MAHARAJAH OF MAGADOR

The talent show became our annual fund-raiser. Because no one else wanted the job and I liked it, I was the master of ceremonies. And I pushed the envelope a bit further when I was a junior by becoming one of the acts.

At that time the Vaughn Monroe Orchestra had a novelty hit record on the charts called "The Maharajah of Magador." It was sung by Monroe's sax player, who had the unlikely name of Ziggy Talent. I loved that song and would stand in front of a mirror for hours, lip-synching to the record player. I had so much fun that I decided to perform it on stage at the talent show.

I borrowed Grandfather Currier's old plaid bathrobe. For a turban, I wrapped my head in a large bath towel with a cardboard drawing of a huge gem pinned to the front. A long fake handlebar mustache completed my costume. I probably looked pretty silly—an overweight teenager in his grandfather's bathrobe, with a mustache, and a towel wrapped around my head, shaking and shimmying to a phonograph record I was pretending to sing. But I was amazed by the reception. I stopped the show.

All that applause went straight to my head. I suddenly thought of Hollywood, New York, Broadway. I had fantasies bigger than I was. The first person I wanted to contact was Gene Carroll.

Gene Carroll had been a big radio star in the 1930s. Radio in those days was like television today, and Cleveland was one of the centers of network broadcasts. Gene and his partner Glenn Rowell hosted a national variety show of music, comedy skits, and bad jokes called "The Gene and Glenn Show." Two featured characters, Jake and Lena, were both played by Gene.

The team split up in the waning days of network radio. Carroll moved to Hollywood and brought his Lena character to the hit radio show "Fibber McGee and Molly." By the late 1940s, however, apparently sensing the waning interest in radio comedy, he moved back to Cleveland to work at the city's first TV station, WEWS. He resurrected his Jake character to host the kids' show "Uncle Jake's House," and he brought his show-business experience to Cleveland television by hosting "The Gene Carroll Amateur Hour," giving young people in northern Ohio a chance to demonstrate their singing, dancing, and comedic skills. I was one of the young people who hoped to be "discovered" on the noontime Sunday show, showing all of northern Ohio my great talent for lip-synching.

My mother and father had been huge Gene Carroll fans since they were in high school. My mother had even kept a scrapbook of newspaper clippings about his career.

I called WEWS-TV and was told I would have to fill out an application explaining my act. Then, if Gene Carroll was interested, I would be summoned to an audition in Cleveland.

I met the mailman each day until the application arrived. I filled it out, mailed it in, and then sat by the telephone each evening awaiting the call from Gene Carroll. Weeks went by. I began to suspect that my application might have been lost when I finally got the call to come to Cleveland. But I wasn't going to WEWS. I was to go to Gene Carroll's own rehearsal studios at Playhouse Square.

On the day of the audition, I drove my rusted-out 1941 Chevy to Cleveland. I got lost a couple of times, driving for the first time in a big city, but finally found WEWS. I had a plan. My idea was to arrive at the studios about the time that Gene Carroll was coming off the air from his kiddie show. I would meet him before the audition and make such an impression that he would remember me when I tried out. I would use as my excuse the chance to present him with my mother's scrapbook of all things Gene Carroll. My thinking was that he would be touched by the gift and inquire about me, and I could casually mention I was on my way to his studios for an audition for his Sunday show.

It didn't quite happen that way.

I did run into Carroll in the lobby of WEWS. I nervously introduced myself and shoved the old scrapbook into his hands. He glanced through it, said, "Thanks, kid," and walked away with it under his arm.

In my mind I was screaming, *Hey! Come back! Aren't you go-*

ing to ask me who I am? What I do? But I just stood silently as he disappeared out the door.

I hurried over to Playhouse Square, telling myself I had still accomplished my mission and that he would surely recognize me when I stepped out on the stage for my audition.

It didn't happen that way, either. I never saw Gene Carroll, just some of his staff who hurried me into a room with a microphone and a window. I was asked what I was going to sing. I said I didn't sing, I was going to lip-synch, offering them the Ziggy Talent record. A phonograph was brought into the room, and the music started to play. I just stood there. A voice, not Gene Carroll's, came over a loudspeaker above the window: "This is an audition! Can you start singing . . . or whatever it is that you do?"

I stuttered an apology and dove for the paper bag I had my costume in. As I was donning my grandfather's bathrobe and trying to wrap the towel around my head, the disembodied voice over the loudspeaker impatiently said, "You don't have to put on the costume, just sing . . . or whatever it is that you do."

So, with the music cued again, I stood there, the fake mustache hanging down on one side of my mouth, wearing my grandfather's plaid bathrobe, and lip-synched my heart out to the "Maharajah of Magador." When I finished, there was a long minute's silence. Then the loudspeaker crackled, "Thank you. We'll let you know. Don't call us, we'll call you."

They never did.

BETTY

"Footfalls echo in the memory
Down the passage which we did not take
Towards the door we never opened."
—T. S. Eliot

Those words seem especially true when we remember first love. Everyone remembers the first time your love is returned

in kind. It is engraved forever on your heart. Mine was one that
flashed like spring lightning, then slowly cooled into memory, like
a golden autumn sunset you fondly recall from many years ago.

I never dreamed when we parted that a terrible tragedy awaited
one of us. Her name was Betty.

Betty Steinhour, from Castalia, Ohio. A mutual friend introduced us. My first impression was of a long-legged, teenage bru-
nette with sleepy eyes and pouting lips. I thought she was beautiful, and we felt an immediate connection. We liked the same
music and movies and had many common interests. A timid kiss
followed a first date, and in the days and weeks to come we saw
more and more of each other. She was soon wearing my high
school class ring, and we were "going steady."

I called her "Kitten." Her soft, throaty voice reminded me of
a cat purring. She had a quiet way of exclaiming "Hot dog!" in
an intimate moment that would make us both laugh. Betty was
sweet, kind, and loving. She truly cared for me. It seemed to be
the perfect relationship.

Memories tucked in the back of my mind like fading souvenirs
can be triggered by photos in an old album, places, a song, and
even seasons: Summer afternoons together on a sun-drenched
beach at East Harbor State Park on Lake Erie. Walking hand-in-
hand through a picnic grove not far from her home, feeding bits
of popcorn to fish in a nearby stream. Dancing cheek-to-cheek
to "Moments to Remember," sung by the Four Lads. The two of
us wrapped in each other's arms at the drive-in movie, not caring about the show. Saying little but expressing our feelings with
long sighs and embraces on her living room couch after her family had gone to bed. Stolen moments in my old Plymouth parked
in the moonlight on a back road. There were also the long phone
calls when we could not be together, and longer, passionate letters when a week would separate us.

But once she wore my silver ring and we had declared our affection for each other, Betty wanted to take our relationship to
the next level. Marriage.

Just the thought of it frightened me at that point in my life. I tried to analyze my feelings. Was I really in love? I always had been told that when you are in love you will know. I cared deeply for her; I really did, but was it love?

I was uncertain if I was ready to take on the responsibilities of a husband and family. Betty was still in high school. While I had just graduated, I still did not know where my life was headed. And Betty, while mature in many ways, seemed more concerned with the idea of marriage than she was with the many responsibilities that would come along with it.

I felt I was being rushed into a decision I wasn't ready to make. I decided, before anything happened, it would be best to break off the relationship.

I did it in an unfair way, offering her no explanation, just suddenly stopping my treks from Lorain County to Castalia. I did not return her phone calls and threw away her letters. It was the wrong way to end the romance.

Plus, now that we were apart, I was miserable. I really missed her. After a few agonizing weeks, I began to question my decision in ending the affair, and finally decided I had to see her again. I returned unexpectedly one evening and was told by her sister Jody that Betty was with friends at a local dance hall. I didn't know if she would want to see me, or even talk to me, but any questions in my mind were answered when she spotted me, ran across the floor, and leaped into my arms with tears streaming down her face. We walked outside into the night, clinging to each other.

It was a short-lived reunion. Within days I began to realize my old concerns about my feelings for Betty were still there. Nothing had really changed.

Our relationship finally came to an end. Not with a bang, but a whimper. We just slowly drifted apart. We saw each other less frequently, the phone calls and letters lessened, and one day they stopped. Some time later, I received a box in the mail containing the ring I had given her. I never saw Betty again.

Her sister, Jody Steinhour Wilson, recently told me, "You were her first love." Looking at a picture of her sister from those long-ago years, she sadly said, "All Betty really wanted in life was to have a husband and family. That's all she really wanted."

She got that wish. But it was a wish that turned to ashes.

Several years later, in 1966, I had just finished the 7 p.m. news on WEOL when the phone rang in the Lorain studio. I picked up the receiver and heard coins dropping into a payphone, then heard a voice I had not heard in years. It was Betty. Memories flooded back. It was a strained conversation. She wanted me to come to Huron late that evening to meet her at a night spot near the river. I explained I was now married and had two children, and I didn't think it was a good idea.

She told me that she, too, was married, but the man she had married was "a big mistake." She said she just wanted someone to talk with. She sounded upset. Considering our past history and the obviously vulnerable condition she was in, I didn't feel comfortable meeting her. I told her I was sorry, but I just couldn't do it. I tried to end the conversation by noting that I was at work and had another newscast in just a few minutes. There was a pause and then she said in a flat voice, "Okay, sorry I bothered you," and hung up. They were the last words she ever said to me.

Days later, on November 18, 1966, her estranged husband, David Sampsel, whom I later learned had been stalking and threatening her if she did not come back to him, went to the diner where she worked and shot her in front of nineteen stunned customers and coworkers.

I was doing the sign-on news at WEOL the next morning. Making my rounds for news items, I called the Erie County Sheriff's Office in Sandusky. They told me about the murder. At first I didn't make the connection. I didn't know Betty's married name. It was only later in the morning, trying to get more details about the killing, that I discovered the dead woman's next of kin was Marie Steinhour, Betty's mother.

I was shocked and saddened when I realized she probably had

been trying to tell me that she was afraid of her husband and believed he might harm her. It was an abusive marriage that now had ended in her death.

I searched my mind. If I had gone to meet her, would talking about her problem have helped? I probably would have encouraged her to call the police or to get a restraining order. But I learned that she had already taken those steps. In 1966, victims of spousal abuse were largely on their own. Police often did little to follow up domestic squabbles other than to try to separate the couple. I knew there was probably nothing I could have done, but still her death picked at my conscience and haunted me for years. I needed to know more.

I learned David Sampsel met Betty through her mother. Marie and Sampsel both worked at the Sandusky Ford Plant. Betty had just graduated from Margaretta High School in Castalia, and Sampsel could have seemed the answer to her dreams. He was a young man with a steady job, who appeared to care for her. It wasn't long before the two were getting serious about each other. They ran off one evening to Angola, Indiana, a town just across the Ohio border famous for "no-waiting" marriage licenses. They were married in a small wedding chapel and returned to Castalia the next morning as husband and wife.

Betty's wishes seemed to be coming true. Betty had a husband and her own home, and over the next six years she gave birth to three daughters. It looked like the perfect family she always wanted.

But all was not well. Sampsel had a mean streak, especially when he was drinking, and he began to abuse Betty. One evening, according to Betty's sister, Sampsel went into a rage and, in front of his three children, picked up a pot of hot chili that Betty had been making and threw it at her, the hot food splashing her and the walls of their home. His dark side showed in other ways, too. Betty's oldest daughter, Carol, told of her father using a lit cigarette to burn her as punishment when she was only five years old.

Betty finally had enough. She moved out and, on her mother's advice, called the police when Sampsel started to harass her.

Jody Wilson said the local police ordered Sampsel to stay away, but he kept trying to see Betty and convince her to come back to him. Betty called the police several times, Jody said, but Sampsel would leave before they arrived, leaving little they could or would do.

By now, Sampsel was living in the Eldorado Motel on the edge of Sandusky. He stopped at Jody Wilson's home and asked her then-husband for the loan of a shotgun, claiming he wanted to go squirrel hunting.

The situation between Sampsel and Betty had deteriorated. Jody suspected that David Sampsel was following her sister. He started to stop in at Sand's Diner on Milan Road, where Betty had taken a job as a waitress. He would get into arguments with her there.

According to other waitresses, Betty came to work very upset on the afternoon of November 18. She had apparently had another confrontation with Sampsel. Around 6 p.m., while she was waiting on customers, he came into the restaurant wearing a hooded sweatshirt and a heavy coat. He started arguing with her. He must have made threats that frightened her because after he left she called someone—witnesses thought it was her sister—and asked that person to pick up her young daughters at home and take them to stay with her mother. Betty was rattled by the confrontation, one waitress recalled years later, and "was so scared she broke out in hives, and we told her to go down in the basement and lie down for a while."

If she did, it was not for long, because Sampsel returned to the diner about 7:45 p.m., and the waitresses watched as he and Betty had another short but heated conversation. He suddenly turned and stormed out. Betty, obviously frightened, told one of the waitresses that she wanted to see what car he was driving and get the license plate number so she could call the police. She walked to the diner's door. She didn't realize Sampsel was standing just outside, waiting. There was a loud blast, glass broke, and pellets ricocheted around the diner. Betty collapsed onto the floor of the doorway with a massive shotgun wound to her chest and neck.

While pandemonium raged in the diner, Sampsel drove away. About five minutes later he walked into the Erie County sheriff's office in Sandusky and told Deputy Kenneth Dietrich, who was on duty at the desk, "You will be receiving a call of a shooting at the Sand's Diner. I just shot my wife."

In his car deputies found the murder weapon: an eighteen-inch-long, sawed-off .12-gauge shotgun. He refused to say anything else about the shooting, only that he wanted to speak to an attorney. He did tell deputies that he had left his room unlocked at the Eldorado Motel and asked if they would go and lock it. He also told them they would find the rest of the shotgun in his room. Erie County deputy sheriff Mike Clipson went to the motel and found a hacksaw and the cut-off portions of the barrel and stock of the shotgun.

A few days later, I walked up the steps of the Frey Funeral Home in Sandusky and found myself face-to-face with Betty's mother. She threw her arms around my neck and sobbed into my shoulder. Betty's casket was closed. A familiar photograph, the same one of her that I had once carried in my wallet, sat on top of the coffin surrounded by flowers.

I tried to tell Marie about my last conversation with Betty, but she was so grief-stricken that I don't think she heard what I was saying. Her only thoughts then were sadness for Betty and hatred for the man who had killed her, and probably the guilt she felt for bringing him into her daughter's life.

The seemingly iron-clad case against David Sampsel carried Marie and her family through the next few months. The Erie County prosecutor had charged him with first-degree murder. Deputies believed he had planned Betty's murder when he borrowed his brother-in-law's shotgun and then used a hacksaw to make it a weapon he could conceal. But as the trial neared, Sampsel's attorney filed a motion to throw out much of the evidence surrounding the shotgun, claiming deputies had searched both Sampsel's car and his motel room illegally, without a search warrant and without advising him of his rights to a lawyer. Although the prosecutor appeared to have a strong case, he offered Sampsel a plea deal. The first-degree murder charge would be dropped if Sampsel agreed to plead guilty to second-degree murder with a life sentence.

Judge James McCrystal accepted his guilty plea on June 4, 1967, and sentenced Sampsel to life in the Ohio State Penitentiary. Marie Steinhour and her family were not consulted about the plea agreement, but they grudgingly accepted it because they thought it would keep Sampsel behind bars for the rest of his life.

Several years ago, when I started to write this book, I decided it was time to tell Betty's story. Perhaps in some way it would help put my own mind to rest after years of feeling guilty for not responding to what had obviously been a cry for help from a frightened woman. I had lost touch with her family, and it took a couple of weeks to track down Betty's sisters, who were still in the Sandusky area.

What they said shocked me.

Life in prison for David Sampsel had lasted less than seven years. Then-governor John Gilligan had commuted the life sentence to time served on June 10, 1974. Jody Steinhour Wilson told me her family was never notified of the governor's action or the reason for Sampsel's early release.

"I just happened to be sitting with Mom listening to the local news on the radio, and heard that David and several other prisoners had their sentences commuted," she said. "We just couldn't believe it.

"Mom wanted to fight it," she said, "but it was already done. We didn't have a lot of money for attorneys. There just didn't seem to be anything we could do about it."

Nearly forty years had passed, but the wound still festered. Marie Steinhour had gone to her grave wondering why her daughter

had not received justice. Why her daughter's killer had avoided
life in prison by the stroke of a pen after serving less than seven
years, less time than some inmates served for minor nonviolent
crimes. I decided to see if I could find an answer to those questions for Betty's family.

I spent the next several weeks contacting officials of the Ohio
prison system, seeking someone who would dig into the old prison
records. I even traveled to Columbus and the Ohio Historical Society, where former governor Gilligan's official papers are stored.
I had hoped to find the original request to commute Sampsel's
sentence and the reasons behind it. I wondered if the Erie County
prosecutor had raised objections or if any attempt had been made
to contact Betty's family before a decision was made.

Sadly, because of budget constraints, the historical society has
not been able to catalogue and organize the Gilligan papers. They
are mostly in cardboard boxes. It appeared that the files were just
pulled out of filing cabinets and dumped into the boxes when Gilligan left office. Many were out of order and misfiled. I was given
access to the files, but it was like searching for a needle in a hay-
stack. After searching for hours, I concluded that it might take
months or years to find the right documents.

The Ohio Department of Rehabilitation and Correction does
have records about all the people who have been jailed in Ohio,
however. They told me that Inmate A125206, David Sampsel,
applied to the governor through the parole board on January 2,
1974. Upon a unanimous, 6-0 vote by the board, his sentence was
commuted from life to time served. The reason given:

"Inmate has maintained honor status, top work reports and
minimum rule infractions—one—during his incarceration for
this, his only conviction. In light of this and inmate's past produc-
tive work record, I believe justice is served by his commutation."

The report is not signed. There is no indication on the form
that the Erie County prosecutor or Betty's family was ever notified of the hearing. A month later Sampsel was put on parole. His
release became final on August 15, 1975.

I was told recently by a spokesperson for a battered women's shelter that the tragic events that led to Betty's murder in 1966 were fairly common. There was no law in Ohio against domestic violence until 1979, when it became illegal to threaten another household member. Even then police often handled a situation by ordering the person making threats to "walk around the block." Few arrests were made. If matters did come to an arrest, it was up to the threatened family member to file a complaint, usually adding more fuel to an already explosive situation.

The law was revised in 1994 and made Ohio a "preferred arrest" state, meaning that if there was probable cause that domestic violence had been committed, police were to make an arrest or write a report explaining why they did not. And probable cause in domestic violence is as little as the victim's word that it happened, without need for a witness or visible injury. Only the officer has to believe the victim. This "preferred arrest" was to lift the burden off the victim and allow the police to sign the charges. It came too late for Betty Sampsel.

On a beautiful Indian summer day in November 2006, forty years after she was murdered, I made my first visit to the cemetery on Bogart Road in Huron Township. Betty's sisters, Jody Wilson and Linda Beese, led me to a flat memorial marker nestled in the green clipped lawn. Golden and purple oak leaves were dancing across the gravestones, pushed along by a gentle wind. I had brought a small bouquet of roses that we placed on the headstone that read simply:

In Loving Memory
Betty J. Sampsel

The warm autumn sunshine washed over us as we stood with heads bowed, looking at the grave, each lost in our own thoughts and memories. I knew that it was time for me to finally say goodbye to a girl I once cared deeply for and to a woman whose tragic death had haunted me for forty years.

Scottish poet Thomas Campbell said it best in his poem "Hallowed Ground":

"To live in hearts we leave behind
Is not to die."

CHAPTER 2

The Early Years

As my high school years came to an end in the early '50s, my future seemed very uncertain. The superintendent of Henrietta High School had called me into his office during the last weeks of the school year and told me that, against his better judgment, I would be graduating with my class in a few weeks. He derided my attitude towards school, my lack of ambition, and predicted that in the coming years I would probably end up in the welfare system. He said he was recommending that I be graduated so I would no longer waste his time or that of the teachers.

In my heart I didn't agree with him. I did have hopes and dreams, but it was hard to dispute his reasoning when he displayed my near-failing grades in every subject. I left the school that day very despondent, wondering if I ever would amount to anything in life. I knew that college was not possible since my grades were so bad and my family just didn't have the finances to assist me even if I could get into a school. This was also a time of compulsory military training, and if I wasn't going to college, it meant I would probably be drafted into the army.

The Korean War was just ending that summer when I visited the Lorain County Fair in Wellington. While strolling the midway I paused at a display that featured the United States Marine Corps. I shook hands with the recruiter and a few days later I was taking an oath and becoming a member of the Marine Corps.

I never did anything heroic. I did mostly clerical jobs. I didn't serve overseas but my experience with the marines gave me motivation and a desire to learn. It also gave me friends that have lasted a lifetime and started me on a path that changed my life forever.

THE OBERLIN NEWS-TRIBUNE

In the last months of 1954 I was serving with the U.S. Marine Corps Reserve. I had volunteered to assist with the marines' annual "Toys for Tots" program to collect toys for needy children at Christmas. My commanding officer, Captain William Hewetson, and I went to Oberlin to try to get it some publicity in the local newspaper, the *Oberlin News-Tribune*.

Editor Brad Williams arranged for us to go to a local home with a photographer to pick up some donated toys. When we returned to the newspaper to be interviewed, the editor asked me what I was doing in the Marine Corps. I told him I had just completed a program at Camp Lejeune, North Carolina, in public affairs and news writing.

Williams said that he was thinking of adding a new reporter, and he was looking for someone with a local connection. Since my family still lived only a dozen miles from Oberlin in Henrietta, and since my obligations to the Marine Corps would end in a few weeks, would I be interested?

The pay was minimal, forty dollars a week. The hours were long and the duties were many. Besides being a full-time reporter, I would be expected to learn to use the giant 4 x 5 press camera and to take "useable" photographs. I would also have to help set type and put the weekly paper "to bed" each Wednesday evening, and also use my car to help deliver the paper to distribution points around southern Lorain County every Thursday morning. Since this was long before the era of cell phones, I was expected to be available to cover events that happened on weekends and even on my days off by leaving a phone number where I could be reached.

The *Oberlin News-Tribune* was owned by Charles Mosher, a Republican state senator and later a U.S. congressman. He usually was off in Columbus on legislative duties but would come into the paper weekly to write his column and an editorial as publisher. The day-to-day operation was left to Brad Williams. There were only two full-time reporters and a sports reporter. Bob Champion handled sports, and the other full-time journalist was a college student, Jim Fixx—an extremely bright young man who would go on to make cultural history in 1977 by kicking off the running craze in America with his best-selling book, *The Complete Book of Running*. (Ironically, Jim died of a heart attack in 1984 at the peak of his popularity while running along a country road in Vermont.)

My first assignments at the *News-Tribune* were the typical small-town stories. Pictures of social gatherings, a story on the opening of a new store. But this was also the Oberlin where many famous people were drawn by Oberlin College, whose campus intertwined with the town. One of the first celebrities I got to meet was the 1952 Democratic presidential nominee, Adlai Stevenson, who was in town to be the college commencement speaker. Watching Stevenson on the podium, waiting to speak, I was bemused by the fact that a candidate for the highest office in the land, the former governor of Illinois, obviously didn't care much about his clothing. As he sat with one leg crossed over another, I noticed a large hole in the sole of one of his shoes. He must have been wearing the same shoes a few days later, when a wire-service photographer took a picture and the hole became a nationwide story.

I was still learning to be a reporter. The influx of famous people visiting Oberlin gave me a chance to sharpen my skills, and in one case taught me a lesson in good journalism.

Famed war correspondent Marguerite Higgins, a Pulitzer Prize winner for her coverage of the Korean War, was speaking at Oberlin, and I was assigned to interview her. It had been a busy morning, and I had not had time to read up on her background. I had heard of her, of course, but didn't know much about her career. I thought I would just wing it at the interview.

Marguerite Higgins had a crusty, no-nonsense approach to the world, perhaps because she had been forced to fight for her place in journalism so many times because of her gender. I walked in, introduced myself, and started the interview with a rather innocuous question, "What brings you to Oberlin?"

She didn't answer, just sat and looked at me as though she was trying to decide something. Finally she said, "You don't have any idea why I am here or what I do, do you?"

Without waiting for my answer, she said, "Until you are better prepared and have some serious questions to ask, this interview is over." And with that, she got up and walked out of the room. At that moment, all I could think was, *What a bitch!*

But as days went by, I kept thinking about the incident, stung by her response. I began to realize that she was right. She had hit the nail right on the head. I had not been prepared. I had not done my research, and I was wasting her time. It was a lesson I never forgot, and I only wish I'd had the opportunity to meet her again and have the chance to apologize.

RADIO DAYS

I guess I could say that my broadcast career got started in 1961, when I had lunch one day with Howard Head, who operated a local collection agency. Howard and I had become friends when I worked for the Bear Furniture Company down the street. He listened to my stories of unhappiness with my job and finally said, "What would you really like to do for a living?"

Without thinking about it, I said, "I want to be in broadcasting. I want to be on the radio or television." I had neither the voice nor the looks for them, but that didn't stop me from dreaming.

"Funny you should mention that," Howard said. "I know Paul Nakel, who runs WEOL in Elyria, and he told me he is looking for a new newsman. Have you ever done any reporting?"

I told him that I had been a reporter for the *Oberlin News-Tribune,* and while serving with the Marine Corps had done a brief stint with the Marine Public Information Office and the

NBC Radio Show "Monitor." (I didn't mention that it was just once, the stint lasted just that day, and that I was picked because no one else was available.) True to his word, Howard arranged the interview with Nakel—who, much to my surprise, offered me the job as a full-time newsman at the radio station that had studios in Elyria and Lorain. The downside was that the job only paid eighty dollars a week, twenty percent less than I was already making.

I was married by that time, and my then-wife, Gay, and I had just had our first child, Melody. We had just moved into a new home we had built and had a sizeable mortgage. I had to convince Gay that taking the pay cut would get me into a career that offered far more financial rewards than the clerical job I had, and I would be doing something I had always wanted to do: be a broadcaster.

She reluctantly agreed, and I took the job. We struggled financially, but I loved it. I was covering boring things like council meetings and committee meetings, but the fires, accidents, robberies, and shootings that necessitated my being "on the scene" kept the job interesting. It also was giving me broad knowledge about the workings of local government and an inside look at police and fire departments.

The news director was Todd Burke, who did the early morning news. John Christman, the afternoon newsman, doubled on Sunday as host of the Latin music program since he spoke fluent Spanish. That left the night shift for me. For the next several years, I started work at 3:30 p.m. and worked until 1 a.m., six days a week. It was a nonunion job, and I quickly learned that you were expected to be available twenty-four hours a day, with no overtime.

WEOL was an unusual station. Because it identified itself as "WEOL, Elyria-Lorain" and wanted to keep advertisers in both cities happy, it had studios in both, so reporters had to split their time between towns about nine miles apart. The Elyria studios were on the fourth floor of the Elyria Savings and Trust Building on the corner of Broad and Court Streets. The Lorain studios were in an alcove off the lobby of the Antlers Hotel on West Erie and Washington. If you were unlucky enough to draw the midday shift, you spent the late morning in Elyria doing rounds at the county buildings, then would drive after the noon news to the Antlers in Lorain to do the hourly afternoon five-minute news shows.

The disc jockeys, Walt Harrell, Gary Short, or Bill Fenton in those days, were in Elyria at our master control room, and I worked in the remote studio in Lorain. We communicated by telephone.

The Lorain studio was tiny, just two rooms. The outer office served as a reception area and office for the sales manager and a secretary. The inner room was our studio with a console, a couple of file drawers, a small desk, a typewriter, and two police scanners, one tuned to Lorain police and the other to Lorain County police and fire frequencies. (Most police and fire agencies in suburban communities shared just two or three frequencies, which meant you had to listen carefully when you heard an emergency call to decipher the agency and location.) These police scanners were on twenty-four hours a day, silenced only when we did the news. Since the evening newsman was usually alone, following police and fire activities provided both news tips and some unintentional entertainment.

In those days, for example, the Vermilion Police Department was a rather small organization with only two police cars. Their radio calls sign were V-1 and V-2. V-1 was usually operated by the senior officer on duty. One evening I heard the following exchange:

"V-2 to V-1, I'm chasing a car that won't stop!"

"V-1 to V-2, where are you?"

"V-2 to V-1, heading east on the highway!!" responded the still-excited patrolman.

"V-1 to V-2, what highway? Where?"

"V-2 to V-1, we're going 90 miles an hour. Now we're going 100 miles an hour!"

"V-1 to V-2, WHERE ARE YOU???"

The obviously excited patrolman was now screaming:

"V-2 to V-1, ON THE ROAD, ON THE ROAD."

"V-1 to V-2, WHAT ROAD??"

"V-2 to V-1, HE'S JUST AHEAD OF ME!"

"V-1 to V-2, WHAT'S THE NAME OF THE ROAD YOU ARE ON?"

"V-2 to V-1, THE LAKE ROAD . . . Oops, never mind."

"V-1 to V-2, what do you mean 'Never mind'?"

"V-2 to V-1, I just ran out of gas. He's getting away."

* * *

I often felt claustrophobic in the tiny Lorain studio after the sales manager and his secretary went home at 5 p.m., so I would open the door to the lobby of the Antlers Hotel late in the evening. Guests sometimes wandered into the office, and I would wave to them through the big soundproof window in the news studio.

One night just as I started a ten-minute-long newscast, out of the corner of my eye I saw an obviously inebriated man stagger in and plop down in a chair directly in front of the studio window, just below my line of sight. I thought he might have come in to listen to the news. Other than hoping he didn't pass out in the chair, I gave it little thought until I got to my first commercial. I stood up to see what he was doing and was shocked to see him taking off his clothes. Having already disposed of his shoes and socks, he was now dropping his trousers and underwear. I started shouting at him to stop, but he could not hear me through the soundproof studio window. I couldn't leave the studio because they were about to put me on the air again from the control room in Elyria, where the commercial was just wrapping up.

The light came on signaling I was back on the air. I grabbed my headphones, jammed them over my ears, sat back down, and tried to pick up where I left off in the newscast, all the while trying to see what my drunken visitor was doing. All I could make out through the window was his head bobbing around as he apparently struggled removing his underwear.

The desk clerk in the lobby could not see into our office from his position. I was live on the air, alone in the studio, and couldn't call anyone for assistance.

When the next commercial started, I leaped out of my chair and pulled open the door to the office—where the obviously drunken man was sitting, naked from the waist down, happily urinating all over the floor and salesman "Buzz" Tyler's desk. I grabbed him by the back of his neck, yanked him out of the chair, and propelled him out the door into the lobby, doing my best to avoid the spray of urine he continued to produce. As I left the drunk standing outside, I saw the shocked look of a couple of women chatting in the lobby. I slammed the door and locked it. Then I raced back into the studio in time to finish the newscast.

I rarely left the studio door open or unlocked after that.

THE HEADLESS DRIVER . . . SORT OF

It was late at night. I was home in Henrietta when suddenly my police monitor, which I always kept turned on when I was off duty, crackled with a heart-stopping call.

"Better get somebody out here right away. I think I have a human head under a car."

It was the voice of a friend of mine, Oberlin police officer Walter Hopewell.

I ran to my car. On the radio monitor I heard other police responding to State Route 58 and U.S. Route 20 on the south edge of the city of Oberlin. I arrived in just a few minutes. Flashing police lights surrounded a dark blue car on the edge of the road.

As I walked up I heard Hopewell say, "I've called the coroner; he said not to disturb it until he gets here."

"Hi, Walt!" I said. "What's going on?"

"I saw this abandoned car on the edge of the road and I was checking it out. I looked underneath to see if there was a mechanical problem, and I came face-to-face with a human head!"

Corporal Paul Glansman of the Ohio State Highway Patrol had pulled up at about the same time I had arrived.

"Which side of the car is the head on?" he asked, walking toward the blue car.

"It's the right side, but don't touch it until the coroner gets here. It's freaky, man. I just looked under there, and all I could see was that head with all that long brown hair."

Glansman went to his knees and shined a flashlight under the car. He crouched there for several seconds, studying the head, and then looked up grinning at Hopewell.

"Call the coroner and tell them to disregard," Glansman said, reaching to pull the head from beneath the auto.

The "head" turned out to be a woman's wig that had been stretched on a metal coffee can. We later learned it had fallen out of the car and rolled underneath in the darkness when the driver ran out of gas and got out.

RIDING NIGHT PATROL

Contacts are important in the newsgathering business. It helps to be on friendly terms with a wide variety of people. In my years at WEOL, especially when I was working the night shift, I would often stop at the Lorain County Sheriff's Office in Elyria on my way home to chat with deputies in the small hours of the morning.

Frequently, especially if one of them was working alone in a patrol car, they would invite me to ride along. It was a great way to see their job from the inside as well as get to know the officers. I got to accompany them on many kinds of calls, from angry domestic disturbances to robberies-in-progress and even a few homicides. It was exciting and put me in a position to be the first reporter on the scene of many stories. But some calls were a bit hard to describe.

Deputy Dale Miller and I were patrolling near Wellington in southern Lorain County about 2 a.m. when we got a call from the dispatcher that a trucker had just reported two bodies in the middle of State Route 18 east of Wellington. With emergency lights and siren screaming, we sped to the location. Sure enough, a man and a woman were lying near the centerline of the busy highway. They were dead, all right—dead drunk.

They sat up as we blocked traffic with the cruiser and shined its spotlights on them. They appeared to be in their fifties, were highly intoxicated, and had apparently forgotten their car and walked from a rural bar about a mile away. Tired of walking, they decided to lie down and sleep in the middle of the road. Three trucks reportedly had just missed running over them. We put them in the backseat of the cruiser to take them to the county jail to sleep it off.

They were starting to sober up a bit by the time we got to Elyria. I asked the woman what her name was, and she replied, "Mary Magdalene."

The man interrupted her. "You think that you're the mother of God?"

"Yesh, I do," she slurred.

"Well, what does that make me?" he demanded. "What about me?"

There was a long silence. She had apparently lost interest in the conversation and was now trying to concentrate on walking as we entered the jail. She tripped going up the steps and muttered to herself, "Jesus Christ!"

"I knew it!" the man shouted. "That's who I am!"

On another early morning I shared a patrol car with Captain Charles MacDonald. Before becoming a deputy, he had served as police chief in the town of Grafton and had long experience in dealing with all kinds of people. I envied his patience and understanding in dealing with difficult situations.

We got a call about 1 a.m. that an elderly lady in Elyria Township had heard noises in her attic and thought she had an intruder. We responded and searched the small house, finding nothing disturbed and no one there except the elderly widow, who lived alone.

She said she was sure the intruder was just hiding from us

and that when we left he would start staring at her through the television set. Charley looked at me and then back at the lady and suggested she just turn off the TV. Then the intruder wouldn't be able to see her. She thought that was a grand idea. As we left, MacDonald told her to call the sheriff's office if she had any more problems.

We had not been gone for half an hour when we were again dispatched to the same house for the same intruder. Again we searched the house to satisfy the old lady that no one was hiding in her attic or basement. MacDonald suggested that he could use a cup of tea. She seemed happy to fix us all a cup, and we sat around her kitchen table drinking tea while he gently questioned her about how often she heard these noises in the attic.

"Oh, I know who is making the noise," she admitted. "It's those little men from outer space."

"What?!" I said, as MacDonald surreptitiously motioned me to keep quiet.

"You know," she said, "those little men in the flying saucer that hovers over my house. They keep talking to me over my TV—even when it is turned off."

"When do they do this?" MacDonald asked.

"Oh, it's every night about this time," she quickly answered. "And if I leave the room so they can't talk to me over the TV, they run up and down the attic stairs to get my attention."

"Wow!" said MacDonald, "I wish you would have told us this the first time we were here. You obviously don't have a space reflector in the house."

"A space reflector?" she asked.

"Yeah," said MacDonald. "Have you got any aluminum foil in the house? Go get it and I'll build you one."

A few minutes later, MacDonald had me place aluminum foil over the door to the attic. Then he fashioned a small hat of foil, bending the foil on top to form two antenna-like ears. He placed the hat on her head and told her, "The shield on your attic door will repel them so they won't dare run up and down the stairs.

When we leave, you put this special hat on and even wear it to bed tonight. As long as you have it on, they won't be able to broadcast or bother you."

Wearing her tinfoil hat, the elderly lady walked us to the door, thanking us repeatedly for helping her rid her house of intruders. That was the last call we had from her that night.

PRACTICAL JOKES

Being a radio newsman at night on a small, 1,000-watt station can often be boring. While Lorain County had its share of crime it wasn't always busy, especially weeknights late in the evening. But police and reporters will tell you it is a well-documented fact that a full moon brings all kinds of reports about strange happenings here on earth.

I was in the news studio in the Antlers one night when I got a phone call from our disc jockey, Bill Fenton, in the studio in Elyria. He was very excited.

"I just got a call from a guy who wants us to turn down our power," he said. "He claims he is hearing our radio station on his bedsprings."

We both laughed about the call, and I said something about there being a full moon. Almost immediately after we hung up, the phone rang again. Again it was Bill Fenton. "This is getting weird," he said. "Another guy just called and said he can hear our radio station on the barbed-wire fence out by his barn."

Moments later, a now very spooked Fenton called again. This time a caller from the nearby Sederis Hotel in Elyria wanted him to know that he was hearing the music Fenton was playing, but not on a radio. It was coming out of the bridgework in his mouth!

I suggested Fenton call the engineer on duty at our transmitter in Grafton to let him know and make sure that our signal was at proper strength. I also said if he got any more callers, to find out if they lived near the transmitter.

The engineer assured Fenton that the transmitter was operating normally and that there was no way the signal could be heard on a man's bridgework. And before he slammed down the phone, he intimated that perhaps Fenton had more than coffee keeping him awake.

By this time, Fenton was insisting we should call Hugh Coburn, the chief engineer, at home and alert him to an obvious transmitter malfunction. He also suggested that we call the general manager, Paul Nakel, and tell him about the bizarre happenings. I had to talk long and hard to convince him that it was just probably a quirk in the atmosphere and that it was best if we did not disturb the management.

Actually, it was just a practical joke. Deputy Ed Hale often worked the night shift at the Lorain County Sheriff's Office, and he, like me, loved practical jokes. It was a slow night, and all the calls to Fenton had been Deputy Hale using his talent for mimicry.

Practical jokes and broadcasters have a long history. After I later became WEOL news director, heading a four-man staff, the evening newscaster was a young man named Doug Doo, who had a warped sense of humor.

I worked the early morning, drive-time shift, and would arrive at the studio in Lorain between 3:30 and 4 a.m. to make my phone rounds and write the sign-on news. Doo would frequently pull pranks like taking the wheels off one side of the chair I used, so it would lurch to the side when I plunked down in it.

Another time he placed the microphone in a wastebasket. I didn't discover it until I threw the switch to put myself on the air and realized the microphone that usually sat on a stand on the desk in front of me was missing. I quickly looked around and saw wires leading into the tall wastebasket next to the desk. Grabbing my news copy, I got on my knees and did the first half of the newscast talking into the wastebasket.

It wasn't that Doo didn't like me. He just loved practical jokes. I tried at first to ignore it. Then I tried talking to him, explaining that I also liked humor, but that stunts like the hidden microphone could end up getting one or both of us fired. He was always apologetic—until the next time.

I discovered perhaps his most ambitious joke one morning when I came to work and was doing the 5 a.m. sign-on news. A movement in the control-room window caught my attention. I swore I saw a fish swimming across my vision!

I looked back down at my copy, thinking it was just a result of too little sleep and a fly or some kind of bug on the other side of the control room window. Then I paused to turn a page on my copy, looked up, and saw a large goldfish staring back at me.

When the newscast ended, I leaped to my feet and found that someone, probably Doo, had carefully taken one of the two glass panels out of the control room window and painstakingly caulked the insides of the seams where the plate glass was fastened. He had then used a glasscutter to cut about a two-inch strip of glass from the top of one window and replaced the glass. After that, he apparently hooked a long hose to the drinking fountain just outside the studio door, filled the space between the glass plates with water, and finally inserted two live goldfish into his newly made aquarium. In a nearby wastebasket I found the pieces of broken glass, an empty pet store fish container, and empty tubes of waterproof caulk. His explanation: He got bored looking into an empty office at night and decided to make the view more interesting.

CHAPTER 3

Breaking into TV

IN THE BEGINNING . . .

Walt Glendenning, my longtime friend from the White Diner, was working as a photographer for WEWS in Cleveland. In 1962, he made a suggestion that took my life in a brand new direction. His idea was that I should purchase a 16mm movie camera and learn to use it. With my contacts in Lorain County, he thought that WEWS might pay me for breaking stories that I reached first and filmed. I could make as much as thirty dollars for a story they used on the air.

Movie cameras were not cheap in those days, especially 16mm cameras, but I finally found a used, beat-up-but-workable Revere camera with one lens in a Lorain camera store for fifty dollars. That was more than half a week's pay, but we scraped up the money and made the purchase. Walt gave me some film to practice with and took me along on a couple of stories to teach me what had to be done for television news.

I had been feeding Glendenning tips of breaking events for a couple of years and had become acquainted with Joel Daly, who was the writer for the evening news on WEWS as well as one of the anchors. Coincidentally, as I was learning to shoot TV film, Daly was offered a job with WJW-TV, which wanted to try an experiment. They wanted to team two anchors on a single show that would deal exclusively with local news. This was new. Before that, the news was usually delivered by one person, and the weather and sports were separate programs. WJW, Channel 8, proposed a new concept—a half-hour show that had the anchors talking to each other, to the weatherman, and to the sports guy. To do this and concentrate on local events meant TV8's tiny news department would have to expand.

Daly called and asked if I would be interested in becoming a freelance reporter-photographer exclusively for TV8. They would pay me thirty-five dollars for a story they used and supply me with raw film. And since they were looking for local news, just about anything I sent them might get on the air, features as well as hard news. I talked to Walt Glendenning, who encouraged me to accept the offer as a better chance to make more money. In late 1962, I started an association with WJW-TV that would span forty-two years of my life.

THE GORY YEARS

Freelancing for WJW-TV while reporting full-time for WEOL, I joined Walt Glendenning and Ray Goll, another photographer friend who lived in Vermilion and was a freelance photographer for Channel 3, as unofficial photographers for the Lorain County Sheriff's Department, which did not, at the time, have an official police photographer.

All of us had police monitors in our homes, and the sheriff had our home phone numbers. We would be notified whenever there was a serious crime or accident where photos would be needed, and at least one of us would respond, no matter what day or time of night it might be. This gave us entry into some of the worst crimes and accident scenes in the county, and we could also take video and pictures for our respective TV stations while shooting official photos.

One of the first calls I responded to was a traffic accident near the state prison on Route 83 in Grafton. Two men and a woman had smashed their car into a tree across from the prison. The impact froze the speedometer at 104 miles per hour and decapitated the young woman, whose head flew from the front seat to the rear window ledge. They had not yet removed the bodies when I got there. When I turned on the big movie lights for our cameras, I found myself looking at the woman's head. The sheriff used the grisly film for months afterward in driver safety classes ordered by local courts.

I hated traffic accidents. Another night I heard the report of a bad accident less than a mile from my home in Henrietta. I ran out the door and reached the scene before any rescue workers or police. I left my camera in the car and ran to the wreckage to see if I could help any victims. A neighbor and I pulled the smashed door to the first car open and found that the violent impact had sheared off the backs of the front seats, leaving bodies piled one on top of another in the backseat. Climbing into the wreckage, we sadly discovered, one by one, that all four occupants, two men and two women, were dead. Since there was nothing we could do for them, I went back to my car, grabbed a still camera, and started taking pictures of the cars and bodies for the police before anything was disturbed. Several motorists who stopped to ogle the accident became irritated that I was taking pictures. Even when I explained that it was not for the news media but the sheriff's department, one man continued to berate and follow me around, trying to step in front of the camera each time I would try to take a photo. Luckily, a deputy arrived and ordered the man to stop bothering me, informing him that the pictures were for the investigation.

I did take pictures later for the TV station, but they were shots of the wrecked cars. The only shots of the bodies showed them covered by sheets and being loaded into an ambulance.

One of my stranger calls came at home late one afternoon from the sheriff's office. A man in South Amherst had reportedly just committed suicide by shooting himself, and the sheriff would probably need some pictures. I jumped in my car and beat the ambulance and police to the scene. A woman was crying on the front porch as I walked up to the house. I asked where the victim was, and she just pointed to the back of the home. I walked around the building to a back porch, where I saw a man lying on his back, a small pistol still gripped in his right hand. A pool of blood surrounded his head, and I could see what appeared to be a bullet entry wound between his eyes.

I ran to his side, knelt down, and felt for a pulse. Feeling none, I placed my hand on his throat, feeling for any sign that his heart was still beating. Nothing. I sighed, stood up, took my still camera from its bag, and began to shoot pictures. I heard sirens out in front, and two ambulance attendants and a deputy came around the side of the house.

"He's dead," I told the deputy as I moved to get another photo from a different angle.

The deputy motioned the ambulance attendants to hold up while I finished shooting.

Just then, the dead man gave a groan and moved.

I jumped. The ambulance personnel leaped onto the porch and started examining him.

"He's alive!" one of them shouted as they quickly scooped him onto a stretcher and hurried him to the ambulance. Moments later they went screaming off towards the hospital.

The deputy stood staring at me. All I could say was, "He looked dead. There was no pulse."

I got a call from the sheriff's office later that evening, telling me that, unbelievably, not only was the man still alive, but he had been treated at the hospital, released, and was now back home.

As it was explained by the doctors at the hospital, the man had purchased a small-caliber gun that day with the intention of shooting himself. But he pressed the barrel so hard against his head that when he pulled the trigger, the bullet couldn't exert its full force. It pierced the skin but not his skull. He cut the back of his head on the porch when he fell, a wound that was not serious but bled a great deal. The doctor said the bullet wound was about the equivalent of being punched in a fight, right between the eyes. It gave him nothing more than a bad headache. They put a bandage over the bullet wound and two stitches in the back of his head, gave him some painkillers, and sent him home.

Anytime I was called to a homicide or suicide scene after that, deputies would tease me by calling me "Dr. Death."

DEATH IN THE AFTERNOON

I was preparing a newscast in WEOL's Lorain studio at the Antlers Hotel when the police scanner squawked to life. I could hear the excited voice of a dispatcher announcing that an officer had been shot and that all cars should respond. I still remember the date—January 21, 1964, a Tuesday.

In seconds, the airwaves were filled with voices as police agencies from around the county tried to find out where the emergency was. I finally determined it was a Lorain County deputy sheriff who was involved, in a section of Sheffield Township called Campito, a mostly low-income area on the southern edge of Lorain. I grabbed a tape recorder and my 16mm movie camera and dashed to my car.

Police cars from cities all over the county were also screaming into the area as I pulled onto Clifton Boulevard in Sheffield Township. Officers with guns drawn were running towards a home. Some of the officers recognized me and quickly filled me in.

The "officer down" was Deputy Sheriff John Palermo. He had been shot by a man he was trying to pick up to transport to a mental hospital in Tiffin, on a warrant signed by the man's family in probate court. I learned later that Palermo and an unarmed auxiliary deputy, Eugene Kubuske, had been assigned to pick up thirty-five-year-old Elbert Rush, an unemployed steelworker.

When they arrived at the home and told Rush why they were there, he became agitated. He screamed that he was "not going back to Cuyahoga Falls" and a mental facility where he had been committed five times previously. Palermo tried to calm him down, but Rush ran into a bedroom and slammed the door. Palermo kicked it open and found himself staring at Rush, now armed with a .38-caliber pistol. Palermo tried to talk him into handing it over, but Rush suddenly fired, hitting Palermo, who fell against the door.

Kubuske, the unarmed auxiliary deputy, was standing by the front door. He dived off the porch behind a snowbank and heard several more shots. Critically wounded, Palermo stumbled through the front door and down the steps, collapsing next to his cruiser. He had been hit twice, once in the chest. Kubuske managed to crawl to him and heard him say, "Oh, my God. I don't want to die. Get some help." He died in Kubuske's arms seconds later.

Rush ran onto the porch and fired several shots at Kubuske, who was still holding Palermo's body, and at a growing crowd of onlookers, who immediately scattered. None of those shots hit anyone. Other police and I arrived on the scene about five minutes later.

Sheriff's deputy Charles MacDonald, crouching behind his cruiser, waved me to his side and told me that the man responsible for the shooting had run back inside the house and had fired more shots at approaching officers. He warned me to stay away from the front of the house and said they planned to fire tear gas into the home to force the man to surrender.

John Palermo, the murdered officer, was a part-time deputy sheriff and a friend of mine. I had ridden patrol with him several times on the late shift. He would often tell me about the work he was doing on a home he and his wife had recently purchased. John, a former army medic, was an easy-going person, the kind of officer who usually could defuse a tense situation by just talking. He rarely had to use force. This time something had gone terribly wrong.

I was edging my way towards the small house when I heard a shot. I ducked instinctively and ran towards the house next door.

I heard shouts of "He's coming out!" Officers yelled, "Drop the gun! Drop the gun!"

Rush had walked out the front door onto the porch with his

hands raised, but he still held the pistol in his right hand. When another gun suddenly fired, he dropped it and bolted back inside the house. It later turned out that a nervous police officer fired his gun accidentally, hitting no one. Not knowing if Rush had other weapons, police started to fire tear gas at the house.

I was on the porch of the house next door, only about ten or fifteen feet away, trying to shoot film for WJW-TV while covering the story for WEOL. I had just poked my head around the corner, looking through the camera lens, when I saw Rush looking back at me through a window. I jerked back just as a deputy fired a tear gas canister. The shot went high. The canister ricocheted off the overhang of Rush's roof, landed directly at my feet, and exploded, swallowing me in a cloud of tear gas.

I staggered off the porch, coughing and choking, my eyes filled with tears. I tripped and fell into a snowbank. Thinking quickly, I rubbed a handful of snow over my burning eyes. In a few minutes I was able to see well enough to wipe the snow off my camera and return my attention to what was happening a dozen yards away.

I had heard at least two more tear gas canisters fired, and the sound of breaking glass, so I was certain at least one penetrated the home. I was still coughing and gagging and blurry-eyed when deputies shouted, "He's coming out."

I raised my camera and saw Rush walking slowly with his hands raised out the front door of the besieged house. As police rushed the porch, Rush suddenly dropped his hands and launched his body at them. Two of them went down with him in a pile on the ground. He fought to punch, bite, and kick as several deputies, MacDonald, and Lieutenant James Mertz jumped into the fray to subdue him. All I could see in my lens was a pile of bodies with flailing arms and legs.

Then a noise behind me caught my attention. It sounded like a growl turning into a roar. A large crowd, later estimated at more than three hundred people from the neighborhood, many from a nearby bar, was moving down the street towards us. It was a mixed mob. Some were screaming for the police to kill Rush; others were shouting at police in the mistaken belief that they were beating him, not realizing he had shot an officer. Everything in me wanted to run for cover. But I kept shooting film, standing between the approaching mob and the brawl at the foot of Rush's porch, where officers were still trying to subdue him.

Suddenly State Highway patrolman Mike Michaels strode in front of me, blocking my view of the approaching mob.

"Everyone halt! Right where you are!" he said in a commanding voice. To back up his words, he raised the shotgun he was carrying and jacked a shell into the chamber.

The crowd slowed.

In a booming voice, Michaels shouted, "It's all over! Everyone go home!"

Several other deputies with shotguns joined the lone trooper, and the mob started wilting away. Rush had finally surrendered and was on his way to the county jail.

Still suffering the effects of the tear gas, I made some notes and then approached one of the private ambulances that had responded to the calls for help but were not needed. I hired one to drive my film to WJW in Cleveland. It was a common practice, in the days when most ambulances were operated privately by funeral homes, for reporters to hire an unneeded one at a major accident or disaster and taxi film to the station. We sometimes paid a little extra if they made the run with red light and siren.

I suddenly felt very tired as I crawled into my car to drive back to the radio station and file my story. Until then, like many of the police officers, I had been running on adrenalin. Now the full impact of the afternoon—the gunshots, the tear gas, and most of all the tragic loss of a friend—hit me all at once. I sat in my car staring at Elbert Rush's house. The front door still stood open, wisps of tear gas still floated in the air, and blood spattered the snowbank in front. I said a silent prayer for my friend, Deputy John Palermo.

* * *

THE BEATLES

I was looking for a brighter kind of news when the Beatles made their first Ohio visit in 1964. I decided to cover the new singing sensations for WEOL, and Walt Glendenning, who was covering their arrival for WEWS, invited me to ride with him to Cleveland Hopkins Airport. We met WEWS reporter and anchor Dave Buckel there, and we could hear the noise before we got inside the terminal. Thousands of teenage girls had invaded the place in hopes of getting a glimpse of their music heroes.

The plane had not arrived when we reached the observation concourse overlooking the terminal. Joyful hysteria might be the best way to describe the mood. Young girls and a scattering of teenage boys were everywhere. They were standing on benches; they were hanging from the railings along the edge of the observation deck; they had even climbed a drainpipe to the roof of an auxiliary building on the concourse. The few police on hand to control the crowd were so hopelessly outnumbered that they just shrugged their shoulders and walked away.

The problems increased each time a plane arrived. Screams reached ear-piercing levels as the aircraft taxied to the terminal. When the plane veered off to another dock, the shrieks faded to an excited babble.

Buckel, Glendenning, and I joined a handful of other journalists attempting to cover the story, and we shook our heads in bemusement at the teenagers' exuberance. I don't think any of us expected the evening to turn into a heart-stopping and possibly life-threatening situation.

The Beatles were arriving in a propeller-driven airliner, and airport officials feared some of the nearly-out-of-control crowd might get onto the field and in the way of the giant whirling propellers as the plane approached the terminal. So they radioed the American Airlines pilot and instructed him to take the plane all the way to the end of the airport instead of taxiing to the terminal and the waiting crowd. There, near the Cleveland Tank Plant that became the I-X Center, the Beatles were hustled off the plane and into a waiting limousine, which whisked them to their hotel.

The kids somehow got word of this change in plans, and a near-riot broke out on the observation deck. Realizing they were now in the wrong place to see their idols, the mob turned and stampeded for the exits. Within seconds, an amusing story on teenage hero worship turned into a life-and-death struggle.

We were caught in this flash flood of humanity, swept along like leaves in a mountain stream as we tried to brace each other against the flow. Glendenning was fighting to keep on his feet with his large camera on his shoulder, stumbling backwards as he tried to push away kids with one hand and keep shooting with the other. Buckel was pushed along like a log in a raging river, his head periodically bobbing up in the crowd. I lost sight of him as they roared through a door into another hallway. I was body-slammed into a wall by three teenage girls sobbing tears of frustration as mascara streamed down their cheeks. Their eyes reminded me of the walleyed look that cattle get in a movie stampede.

I no sooner pushed away from the wall than I was caught up again in the hysterical mass, finding myself wedged so tightly in a pack of people that I could not raise my arms. It suddenly dawned on me that if I lost my footing, I could be trampled before I could get out of the way of thousands of churning feet. The only sensible thing to do was to go with the crowd until it thinned.

I watched in horror as a still photographer was pushed into a glass wall by the crowd. I swear I could see the glass start to bend as the crowd piled up around him, trying to squeeze through a doorway in the wall. I feared it would shatter at any second.

When the mob I was in finally burst into the big airport lobby, I was able to work my way free and to the edge of the room, where I found both Glendenning and Buckel. Miraculously, when it was over and the concourse was cleared, we learned that no one was killed or even seriously injured. But it was a sobering lesson on how quickly a seemingly innocent situation can become dangerous.

The Beatles? We never saw them that evening. They managed to get away from their fans and were taken to their hotel. The only photo of the Beatles at the airport was taken by photographer George Shuba, who got a tip about the change in plans and got to the tank plant just as the Beatles were pulling away in their car.

THE WINDS OF APRIL

Palm Sunday 1965 fell on April 11 and bloomed as a muggy, warm, and windy spring day, the first in some time. My wife Gay and I took our daughters, four-year-old Melody and ten-month-old Melissa, out for an automobile ride. We stopped at a pleasant park at the intersection of Route 58 and 303 in Pittsfield, just south of Oberlin, where the statue of a Civil War soldier stood guard on a high granite pedestal. To the rear of the park was the congregational church and the township hall. Across the street was a small general store. I can't recall if we had a picnic lunch with us or just bought some pop or ice cream at the corner store. But we enjoyed a half-hour or so on a picnic bench, enjoying our first warm spring day.

That evening, back at our home in Henrietta, the telephone rang while we were watching a late movie on TV. A friend, Corporal Jim Dunn of the Elyria Post of the Ohio State Highway Patrol, wanted to alert me that a tornado had been reported in Seneca County, and the storm was headed towards Lorain County. At the time I was a newsman for radio station WEOL in Elyria as well as a part-time freelancer for WJW-TV, Channel 8 in Cleveland. I immediately called Don Leedy, the announcer-newsman on duty at WEOL, and asked if the weather bureau had issued any warnings. They hadn't, so I repeated what Dunn had said and urged him to keep an eye on the news teletypes.

I went back to my movie. The western sky was filled with lightning, and a few minutes later my telephone rang again. This time it was dispatcher Harvey Callahan at the Elyria Post of the Ohio

State Highway Patrol. He said he had just dispatched all available troopers to Pittsfield to check out a report that a tornado had just struck.

Within minutes I was in my car, racing down South Main Street in Oberlin in time to see the flashing lights of the Oberlin Fire Department heading south towards Pittsfield. I followed them across Route 20. As we got closer to the intersection of Routes 58 and 303, I saw pieces of twisted roofing tangled in treetops and wires draped across the highway. Suddenly we all came to a stop, our path blocked by huge trees that filled the roadway.

I had a two-way radio in the car that used what was known as a business band. It allowed me to contact my wife at our home as well as fellow journalists Walt Glendenning and Ray Goll. I called Gay and asked her to call Don Leedy at WEOL to get a bulletin on the air, and also to call WJW. Then I jumped out of the car, grabbed my 16mm movie camera, and started filming rescue workers as they struggled to clear the road. I walked around a downed tree to the center of the intersection and stood in awe at what I saw when I turned on my bright movie light.

Where my family had spent a quiet afternoon having a picnic was devastation. The Civil War statue lay broken. The pedestal was vacant, and its soldier lay face up under a snarl of wires and branches. Bits of insulation were wrapped in shredded tree trunks. An empty space with a pile of lumber was all that remained of the two churches on the corner and the little general store. I followed rescue workers into the rubble as they searched for bodies. Sadly, we began to find them.

Two friends, Metro Parks rangers Parker Miller and Bob Hartle, led me to a nearby barn and crawled into the rubble to see if any cattle had survived. In a nearby field, a car had rolled end over end. It was empty. In a nearby ditch we found the body of a woman, presumably the driver.

Lightning was still flashing and thunder rumbled in the distance. Rain spattered down on the rescuers, who were using flashlights and auto headlights to search through the darkness for other victims. Adding to the confusion, the county sheriff's radio frequency became jammed by atmospheric conditions, plus the many police and rescue organizations all trying to use the same band.

The county coroner, Dr. Paul Kopsch, saw me talking on my two-way radio and asked who I was able to reach. He commandeered the radio and had my wife call for more ambulances and emergency personnel. He told me he was setting up a temporary morgue at Allen Hospital in Oberlin.

Another WEOL staffer, Gerald Warner, arrived on the scene. I sent him to the hospital to start gathering names of the dead and injured while I continued to cover the spreading rescue operation, meanwhile using my two-way radio to hook into a telephone so I could do live reports on WEOL.

Throughout the long night I stayed anchored to the center of Pittsfield, where it appeared most of the deaths and the worst damage had occurred. I had used all the film I had with me and asked my wife to plead with WJW to send more film and a crew to assist me. I kept updating Don Leedy at WEOL and learned from him that damage reports were coming in from Grafton and Columbia Station, east of where I was.

As dawn finally broke, most of the trees were off the road. I was able to leave Pittsfield and follow the path of the storm east in my car. In Grafton I saw a Ford dealership that had collapsed on both new and used cars. A nearby home had its front wall ripped off, yet the furnishings inside looked undisturbed. But the tour was cut short when debris on the road flattened all four of my car's tires.

I left my car and hopped a ride in a sheriff's cruiser headed for Columbia Station. We found more homes destroyed there, and saw pieces of straw that had been driven through walls by the sheer force of the wind.

I made my way back to Pittsfield just in time to meet the WJW crew, photographer Peter Miller and Bob Wells, better known as Hoolihan the Weatherman on TV8. Bob, a pilot himself, was riding in a helicopter with Miller shooting footage of the devastation. Miller gave me all his unused film and took my exposed film with him as they flew back to Cleveland to get the story on the air. This was the era before satellite trucks and remote broadcasting technology.

When it was over, we learned the massive storm that had moved through our area on Palm Sunday spawned thirty-seven tornadoes and left 256 people dead in Indiana, Michigan, and Ohio. Most were in Ohio. The tornado in Pittsfield, a giant F4 with winds of more than 250 miles per hour, destroyed every building in the town's center and killed nine people. It killed another eight as it hammered across the countryside before lifting back into the sky near Strongsville. It had been the worst outbreak of tornadoes in more than thirty years, and a night never to be forgotten for the people who lived through it.

In the year following the tornado I was asked to help produce a documentary about the events that night as well as the rebuilding of Pittsfield in the weeks following the storm. The request came from Joe Stockstill, then director of the Lorain County Civil Defense Agency.

I agreed, and with the help of fellow photographers Walt Glendenning and Ray Goll, we managed to collect much of the 16mm black and white film that we had shot, as well as some follow-up material that had been filmed by the three Cleveland TV stations, WJW, WEWS, and TV3.

I wrote the script with the help of Stockstill while Glendenning did the editing at WEWS. The end result was a film, approximately forty minutes long, that told the story of the tornado from the start shortly after 11 p.m. and followed the cleanup and slow rebuilding process that took months.

The following summer the film was unveiled at the Lorain County Fair where it was shown almost hourly in a special tent theater. It drew huge crowds and requests for showings at organizations throughout the county. Over the next few years the film was often used by private groups as well as police agencies and rescue groups like the American Red Cross.

As the years went by I lost track of the film. It wasn't until 2007, when I was asked to speak at a meeting of the Lorain County Historical Society about the tornado, that I recalled the movie and tried to track it down. However, a check of Lorain County Civil Defense officials turned up the fact that no one had seen the film in years. Similar checks with other police agencies around the county also failed to turn up the missing tornado movie.

Possibly the old film may have been thrown away, but it also could still be out there, a record of a historical event, forgotten in the bottom of a box, stashed in an old cupboard or closet in some organization or agency.

I MOVE TO TV FULL-TIME

Persistence paid in 1967, when I ended my freelance career at WJW-TV and became a full-time staffer.

I had been nagging TV8 news director Norm Wagy for a full-time job for months. He kept putting me off, saying, "Soon. But not right now."

I developed a plan. I contacted Norm's secretary, Kathy Hruby, and asked for a list of all his personal appearances and speeches. I figured I would show up at as many as I could to keep reminding him, as subtly as possible, that I wanted to work for him full-time.

To Wagy, it might have looked like I was stalking him. Whenever he gave a speech in western Cuyahoga County or Lorain County, I would turn up in the audience and make a point of telling him how much I enjoyed his speech afterward. I thought I had gone too far one evening in Lorain, when he spotted me in the crowd and stopped his talk to tell me that I must not have anything important to do if I could be there listening to him. I wasn't sure if he was joking or getting tired of my following him around. A week later, however, I got the call I had been hoping for: Wagy told me he had full-time openings on the staff for an investigative reporter and an editorial writer.

I passed on the editorial writing job but told him I would like to apply for the investigative job. We set up an appointment, and I drove a few days later to TV8's old studios at 1630 Euclid Avenue.

It was a short interview. Wagy said this was the first time TV8 was hiring someone as a reporter, not an anchor person. Until then, they had to press the booth announcers into service when they needed a reporter to accompany a photographer. Now Wagy hoped to add a trained reporter to his staff. The catch was that the primary duty was to be an *investigative* reporter, developing a story behind the scenes and appearing on air only when it was complete and ready for broadcast. Was I interested? Absolutely.

He took me upstairs to meet with Ken Bagwell, the station vice-president and general manager, and program director Bob Huber. I was directed back to Wagy's office after that, but he was busy. He said, "I'm waiting for Ken's approval on your hiring. Why don't you go out in the lobby and wait?"

I wandered back to the front lobby and sat down on a couch. It was 10:45 in the morning. I had skipped breakfast because I was too nervous about the job interview. Now it seemed almost in my grasp, and I was hungry. But I didn't want to leave the building to eat because I was waiting for Wagy.

I waited. And I waited. Noon came, and then 1 p.m., with no sign of Wagy. I asked the receptionist if he was still in the building. She assured me that he was.

By 5 p.m. my stomach was growling, and I began to fear that there was a problem. But I couldn't figure out why, if they didn't want to hire me, they didn't they just come out and tell me. Why leave me here waiting in the lobby?

As the clock edged towards 6 p.m., I convinced myself that I was not going to be working for WJW-TV and that I had spent a fruitless day in Cleveland. I was angry at Wagy for not at least telling me that he couldn't hire me. I was angry at Bagwell for torpedoing my hopes and dreams. I decided that at 6 p.m. I would leave an angry note for Wagy and go home.

Just as I was mentally constructing what I would say in the

note, Wagy, wearing his topcoat and carrying a briefcase, came out of the newsroom and into the lobby, stopping with a surprised look on his face when he saw me.

"Neil. Why are you still here?" he said.

"You told me to wait here while you got final approval of hiring me from Ken Bagwell," I replied in an icy tone.

"Oh," he said. "Sorry. I didn't realize you were still here. Yeah. You're hired. You start tomorrow. Good to have you aboard."

He shook my hand and walked out of the building, leaving me standing there dazed at the sudden turn of events. I had to ask the receptionist to confirm what he had just told me. I didn't even think to ask how much money I was going to be making.

And that is how I started full-time in television.

That investigative job, by the way, lasted about two weeks. Since I was the only reporter on the staff who didn't have anchor duties, I was constantly in demand for breaking news, sometimes as many as six or seven stories in one day, and just did not have time to do any deep investigative work. I didn't complain because I enjoyed breaking news and being where the action was. It would be a dozen years, in fact, before Carl Monday was hired as the station's first real investigative reporter.

Norm Wagy became a friend and one of my favorite news directors. He apologized several times for forgetting and leaving me in the lobby for nearly seven hours.

THE VIETNAM WAR PROTESTS

The late 1960s and early '70s were filled with growing antiwar sentiment, fueled by college students who were being asked to leave campus and fight the war in southeast Asia. I ran into my first antiwar demonstration at Oberlin College in 1967. I was assigned by TV8 to cover the demonstration planned against air force recruiters coming to the campus.

It was fairly peaceful. Seventy-five student protesters surrounded the three recruiters who walked into Wilder Hall, sitting on the floor around their table in the lobby. The problem started when the recruiters left the table to go to the snack bar in the building for lunch. While they were eating, several interested students walked over to chat with them, causing the demonstrators to kick it up a notch. Moving to the snack bar, they formed human barricades, linking arms around each recruiter and virtually imprisoning them where they sat, making it impossible for potential recruits to approach.

Not all the students backed the protesters. Several scuffles broke out between the two factions, with the recruiters caught in the middle. I saw one student grab a protester around the neck and hurl him to the floor. That started a real brawl.

I suddenly found myself knocked to the floor as tables overturned and fists flew. I crawled from beneath a table and started filming the violence just as Oberlin Police, called by college security for backup, entered the room. Oberlin officer Walter Hopewell, trying to break up a fight between two students, was bowled over by two other fighting students and found himself staring from the floor into my camera. The melee lasted perhaps fifteen minutes before calm was restored and the recruiters were escorted off campus.

But that wasn't the end of protests at the school. When classes resumed in the fall, protest meetings started again. The most violent confrontation started on the morning of October 26. Student organizers had word that a U. S. Navy recruiter was coming to the college that day. Protesters on motorcycles were posted at various roads leading to Oberlin, and they alerted about fifty protestors waiting on Tappan Square when they spotted the navy car.

As the car headed north on North Main Street and stopped for the light in front of the Allen Memorial Art Museum, protesters swarmed into Lorain Street and surrounded it, stopping traffic and making a hostage of the recruiter. WJW's newsroom had been alerted that there might be trouble, so photographer Ralph Tarsitano was sent to Oberlin to be on hand.

It was my day off, and Gay and our two daughters had come

with me to Oberlin that morning to do some grocery shopping. I spotted Tarsitano in the WJW news cruiser and waved him down while Gay and the girls went on their errands.

We were standing on North Main Street next to the cruiser as the navy recruiter was surrounded almost in front of us. Ralph grabbed a camera and ran to start filming, while I jumped into the cruiser for the two-way radio to advise the station what was happening and to suggest sending another camera crew. Assignment editor Mickey Flanagan told me there was no other crew available right then and asked me to assist Tarsitano.

Captain Norm Schmidt of the Oberlin Police arrived. Using the loudspeaker on his patrol car, he ordered the protesters to get away from the car and disperse. They ignored him. Despite pleas from Schmidt and people I believed to be college officials, the car was still surrounded, and the number of protesters continued to grow as curious students arrived to see what was happening. Schmidt finally drove away while we waited to see what would happen next. We later learned that he had called the sheriff's office and surrounding towns for more officers to assist.

At one point, when the crowd around the back of the car suddenly thinned, the recruiter attempted to back up and get away. He ended up hitting another stopped car and was quickly surrounded again.

It finally came to a head about noon. The recruiter had been sitting in his car most of the morning and was pleading with the students surrounding the car to allow him to go to a nearby service station to use the restroom. The protesters decided to vote on the sailor's request, the result of which allowed the recruiter to get out of the car while they continued to block the road.

The navy man headed for the restroom, finally free, while his car was surrounded. We heard a banging noise a few minutes later. From the other direction, a line of policemen in riot gear marched twelve abreast towards the demonstrators, banging their nightsticks on their plastic riot shields. They were accompanied by a fire truck.

They stopped about fifty feet from the surrounded car, and Captain Schmidt again ordered demonstrators to disperse or be arrested. In fact, the police had decided that since the recruiter was out of the car and unhurt, they only wanted to disperse the crowd and open the road, not arrest anyone. The protesters jeered. Schmidt gave a command, and a water cannon on top of the fire truck spewed water at them. But it seemed to have little effect on the determined students. Then police fired smoke and tear gas grenades, which protesters snatched off the ground and hurled back.

Tarsitano and I were between the police and the protesters, and at that crucial moment Ralph discovered his camera had run out of film. We dashed for the WJW news cruiser, and I rolled down a window, grabbed a box of film from the back seat and hopped in the front with Ralph as he tore the camera cover off. At that moment, police fired another barrage of tear gas. A student picked up a still-smoking grenade and tossed it through our cruiser's back window. It landed on the front seat between Tarsitano and me. I was sitting with my door open and one leg out of the car, and Ralph was behind the wheel. When I saw the sputtering gas grenade, I instinctively threw myself out the door and onto the ground. The grenade went off, filling the inside of the cruiser with the noxious fumes and temporarily blinding Tarsitano.

I led him out of the car and urged him to open his eyes and face what little breeze there was since we had no way to wash out his eyes. The demonstration was scattering as clouds of tear gas floated over the scene, and students were coughing and choking and running.

Ralph still had trouble seeing, so I got him into the car, rolled all the windows down to blow out any remaining fumes, and started for Allen Memorial Hospital just up the street. When we arrived at the emergency room, it already had a handful of students also suffering from the effects of tear gas.

Ralph's vision was still blurry but improving after a nurse washed out his eyes, so we headed back to the scene. The students had regrouped and were now planning to march on the police station, where they said they would turn themselves in. They hoped to draw more attention to their cause by bogging down the police department with the sheer number of arrests and the accompanying paperwork. When they arrived at the police department, however, officers told them they were not interested in arresting them and suggested they just go home. There were no incidents and the crowd just drifted away.

It was a strangely quiet way for the day to end.

THE 1968 OHIO PEN RIOT

The heat was partly to blame for a vicious riot that broke out in the historic old Ohio State Penitentiary in Columbus on August 20, 1968. As the temperature approached 90 degrees that day, inmates in cellblocks C and D took nine guards hostage. But the situation had been ready to erupt for months. The problem started in June when inmates rioted and set fire to several buildings before guards took control. Tension simmered all through July and August.

After taking hostages, inmates immediately delivered demands to the warden. They wanted several guards fired, amnesty for the rioters and hostage-takers, and that a reporting of their demands appear in the media. Officials tried to negotiate, but the riot involved several different groups of inmates who had no clear agenda and argued among themselves. That evening officers discovered inmates had broken into the prison hospital to steal drugs and into the prison commissary for sugar and other items that could be used to make low-tech firebombs.

Then arguments broke out among inmates during a news conference they requested, and the hostage-takers threatened to behead a hostage if their demands were not met. The warden ended the news conference and started making plans to rescue the hostages. Tension grew the next day when one inmate stabbed another.

I had been dispatched to Columbus before dawn on August 21 with TV8 cameramen Bob Kasarda and Michael Wagner. We arrived as a new contingent of Ohio National Guardsmen rolled up to the prison in their army trucks.

Martin Janis, in charge of prisons as director of the Ohio Department of Mental Hygiene and Correction, told me and other reporters that the National Guard was only there to spell the exhausted prison guards and Ohio Highway Patrol Troopers surrounding the prison, especially near the entrance on Spring Street. But we shortly saw troops that I recognized as members of a combat engineer unit on both the roof of the cell blocks and in a ground-level area near the prison entrance.

While much of the prison was surrounded by a tall wall with guards perched in glassed-in booths, the front of the old building with its offices was open to Spring Street, where reporters and many guards gathered. Mixing in with us were several men in khaki uniforms. I was surprised to learn they were inmates— trustees on honor status who usually were allowed outside the prison walls during the day. Several attached themselves to reporters, making themselves useful by fetching us cold sodas from vending machines inside and identifying various officials. I was shocked to learn that several of these trustees were serving life terms for murder.

About 2:30 p.m., we noticed activity among the National Guardsmen on the roof and near us on the ground. A Columbus police officer with a bullhorn suddenly ordered everyone not part of the security force to move off the prison grounds to a parking lot across the street.

A column of Ohio State Troopers wearing riot helmets and carrying shotguns appeared from around the corner of the prison. I recognized the officer in charge, Lieutenant Floyd M. Smith, who was a longtime friend from his days stationed at the Elyria Patrol Post. Then commander of the Mansfield Patrol Post, he had volunteered to lead the assault on the prison with twelve troopers.

As Columbus police herded the other reporters and photographers across the street, Smith motioned to me and said, "Stay here with us. We're gonna go in and get those guards."

I stepped in close to the assault force where the Columbus police could not see me, and we all moved up against the wall of the administration building. My photographers, Kasarda and Wagner, had already moved their equipment to the parking lot across Spring Street.

Lieutenant Smith told us there would be two explosions. Demolitions people would first set off a charge on the roof of the cellblocks as a diversion, and a second charge would be detonated seconds later against the side of the same cellblock, around the corner and about a hundred feet from where we stood. That blast, it was hoped, would make a hole big enough in the sandstone and concrete walls to allow Lieutenant Smith and his troopers to dash into the captured cell block.

He had no sooner told us this when a tremendous blast went off on the penitentiary's roof. Debris rained down on us. My ears were still ringing when a second, louder explosion literally pushed us back against the wall as the side of the prison exploded in a cloud of dust, stone, and smoke. I couldn't hear anything. I could see Lieutenant Smith's mouth working as he turned and started running towards the massive hole in the side of the building. His troopers followed, leaping over the rocks and other debris and disappearing into the smoke-filled hole.

I ran after them. I was just starting to hear faint sounds again as my ears started to work. I reached the shattered rocks in the side of the wall, climbed through the hole, and the world turned reddish brown as dust enveloped me. I could hear shouts and faint pops that were gunfire, but I was disoriented and had no idea where the troopers had gone. Someone suddenly grabbed me and propelled me back outside the hole. It was a Columbus policeman leading another armed contingent inside, and he ordered me at gunpoint to get away from the rubble-filled cell block.

I got out of the way of the advancing police and guards and checked my audio recorder. The case, like me, was covered with red dust from the explosion. I wiped off the controls and discovered that the batteries were just about dead.

Lieutenant Smith is now retired and living in Missouri. Years after the incident he recalled for me the moments he led force men into the prison under siege.

"It was dust or smoke everywhere," he said. "It was very difficult to see. I had told my twelve men there were six levels, and we were going to go up those stairs fast. As we cleared each range, the last two officers would drop off to secure that area, until we had found all the guards."

He said they first found only prisoners, who quickly surrendered. It was when Smith and two troopers reached the top floor that they found the nine guard-hostages locked in a cell with a large, padlocked chain holding the door shut. Smith fired twice at the lock with his shotgun, and they were able to release the guards. One inmate guarding the hostages hid behind a mattress, refusing to surrender, and Smith shot him in the shoulder.

"We got all the guards out alive," Smith said. "They were crying and trying to hug us while we were still trying to round up all the prisoners."

The troopers also found that the inmates had stockpiled bags of sugar and cans of lighter fluid on the sixth level. They apparently planned to make a low-grade napalm out of the ingredients to ignite and pour down the stairway on their attackers. Smith's attack with his twelve officers was so fast that the stunned prisoners never had a chance to put their plan into action.

Back out in front of the prison, Kasarda and Wagner filmed the freed guards as they were led, dirty and shaken, from the prison. Some were on stretchers, but most were able to walk to waiting ambulances. I walked alongside to interview those who wanted to talk about their ordeal. We were allowed later into the ballpark area of the prison, where grim-faced state troopers marched the rioting prisoners and began a systematic search of each one. Tension was still high, but the authorities were back in control of the prison.

Five prison inmates were dead, and five inmates and seven officers were injured. But thanks to the bravery and quick action of Lieutenant F. M. Smith and his State Highway patrolmen, the nine guard-hostages walked out alive.

We drove to Columbus airport and put our film on a plane to Cleveland for the 6 p.m. news, and I fed the rest of my story to our newsroom. News director Bill Feest got on the phone to congratulate us on a good job, and suggested we stop and get a meal before coming back to the station for my live report on the 11 p.m. news.

It was 5 p.m. by the time we started the three-hour trek up I-71. All of us were filthy from the debris of the explosions, our clothes were soaked with sweat from the 90-degree weather, and we discovered that all of us had left home that morning without much cash. We had $2.40 among the three of us. Other than that, all we had—in those days before Visa and MasterCard—was a WJW company credit card that was only good for gas at Sohio gas stations. We whipped into the nearest station, filled up the car, and were trying to figure out how to buy dinner for three for $2.40 when Mike Wagner suddenly looked at the credit card and lit up with a big smile.

"We are going to have steak with all the trimmings for dinner," he announced.

He pointed down to the symbols on the card. They identified the various businesses operated by Standard Oil that would accept the credit card in payment. One was a luxury chain of motor inns, and one of them, coincidentally, was just across the street.

Bob Kasarda wrinkled his nose as we pulled into its parking lot and said, "You know, all of us could really use a shower and a chance to clean up."

We marched to the registration desk and explained our plight. We wanted to rent a room for an hour to take showers and pick up some fresh shirts from the hotel gift shop. And we would charge it, along with three dinners, on our station credit card.

The clerk looked disdainfully at our dust-covered, sweat-streaked faces and said, "Certainly, gentlemen. Do you have a reservation?"

I said no, and explained that was why we had just told him our story of a busy day at the penitentiary and . . .

"I'm sorry, sir," he interrupted, "but there is an event at the state fairgrounds this week, and all rooms are taken."

"You have nothing?" Wagner nearly shouted.

"The only thing not rented is the Governor's Suite," he smugly replied.

"We'll take it!" Wagner snapped back at him.

"That's $250 a night," the clerk replied.

"Is this credit card good for it?" Wagner asked.

The clerk reluctantly looked it over, then handed us the key to the suite. We almost ran to the room. The shower felt so good that the three of us ended up wandering around the suite's several rooms in various states of undress. Wagner was nude when he called our attention to a closed floor-to-ceiling drapery.

"That must be the best view in the house," Mike said as he pushed the remote control to open it.

The drapes moved swiftly and silently apart like the curtain on a stage. There Mike stood, naked to everyone in the family-packed hotel swimming pool just outside.

That's how our day of covering a prison riot ended. A little embarrassment but a wonderful cooling shower, with large, thick, fluffy towels in an expensive suite, followed by a steak dinner with all the trimmings.

THE GREAT CHASE

It was a quiet early spring afternoon on March 27, 1970. I was checking the newswire machines when I heard the Cleveland police monitor above the assignment desk at TV8 suddenly come to life.

"All cars in the third district, we've got a hostage situation going on at the county jail!"

Reporter Bob Franken and I both ran to the back door of the station. I jumped into a news cruiser with photographer Ralph Tarsitano, and Franken grabbed photographer Bob Begany and soundman Dale McLinn. We all sped to the Cuyahoga County Jail on East 21st Street in downtown Cleveland.

While Franken tried to get inside the jail to see what was happening, I headed to a large gathering of Cleveland police near a ramp to a rear entrance to the building. Two women, seventy-one-year-old Louise Honour and sixty-two-year-old Norina Dellaria, both Christian Scientists, had been in the jail holding religious services, something they had been doing weekly for a half-dozen years. On this day, however, three inmates—James Snyder and Thomas E. Thomas, who were being held on federal charges for escaping from a Mississippi prison, and Clevelander David E. Carpenter, who was being held for forging an auto title—decided to use the religious service as their means to break out of jail.

They somehow obtained some knives and a fake gun carved out of soap. They grabbed the two elderly women and threatened to harm them if guards did not let them out of the cell block. They then made their way to the basement, where they ran into Sheriff Ralph Kreiger, who tried to convince them to release the women and surrender. When they refused, he offered himself as a hostage to replace the women.

They said no and demanded a shotgun and a police car to escape in. A Warrensville Heights police car had just arrived in the basement garage, carrying a prisoner for booking. Unable to negotiate with the prisoners and fearing for the women's safety, Kreiger gave in and allowed the inmates and their hostages get into the police car. When they demanded a gun, he ordered a deputy to hand over a shotgun with just one shell inside.

Kreiger tried to stall, claiming that he had to notify police outside that the hostages were in the stolen police car, and not to shoot at it as it left the jail. But the trio of escapees was getting nervous. They put the women in the car, placed the shotgun against Mrs. Dellaria's head, and demanded that Kreiger open the garage door. He did. With tires squealing, they shot out the door and up the ramp onto East 22nd Street.

As the car whooshed by where I stood with reporters and policemen, no one moved for maybe ten seconds, but chaos erupted as the Warrensville police car turned the corner onto Payne Avenue. Policemen and reporters ran and scrambled for cars. Sirens went off, emergency lights flashed, police shouted commands at each other.

I spotted Begany and McLinn near their news cruiser, and ran to them. We jumped into the car and took off in pursuit of the fleeing police car.

By this time dozens of police cars, sheriff's cruisers, and cars of U.S. Marshals had taken up the chase, which now was circling Public Square in downtown Cleveland. The escapees apparently didn't know how to find the freeways and were caught in rush-hour traffic.

If the situation hadn't been so serious, it would have been funny, reminding one spectator of a Mack Sennett comedy. The stolen police car went round and round Public Square with a gaggle of other police cars and news cruisers following like some giant kite tail. Puzzled citizens who were just trying to get home found themselves in the middle of a mad chase that filled the air with dozens of flashing red lights and the wail of a score or more of sirens.

The carousel-like chase was suddenly broken as the stolen car carrying the prisoners and their hostages shot south on Ontario Street and onto the ramp to Interstate 71. It went from bad to worse as the chase reached speeds of 80 and 90 miles per hour. The escapees wove in and out of the homeward-bound traffic, heading south.

Brake lights started flashing on the cruisers ahead of us as we approached the Cuyahoga–Medina County line, and the parade came to a sudden stop. Begany swung our news cruiser onto the berm, and we joined other news cars trying to get to the front of the line to see what was happening.

A lone police car from Brunswick was sitting crossways on the two lanes of I-71, blocking the Warrensville Heights car. It appeared that Sheriff Kreiger and others were trying to negotiate with the escapees. After a very tense few moments, threats to harm the two women led the sheriff to order the Brunswick car off the road. The stolen police car shot away at high speed to the south. Police and reporters scrambled back into their cars and again gave chase.

We later learned that U.S. Marshals had convinced the three escapees that they needed to gas up the stolen car and arranged for them to get off I-71 at a service station on Route 18, hoping for another chance to talk them into surrendering. A marshal paid for the gasoline but was unable to convince the escapees to surrender or to release the two women. Once the tank was full, they sped away, southbound on I-71 again. The marshal was so frustrated that he threw his credit card at the station attendant and raced off in pursuit without it.

For more than two hours the parade of police cars and news vehicles headed south on I-71, with news agencies trying to jockey closer to the fleeing prisoners and their hostages. More police vehicles and news cars joined the chase at each community we passed. The trail of police and news vehicles now stretched literally for miles along the freeway. More confusion ensued when we finally reached Columbus, as the escapees drove around aimlessly, first on I-70 headed west, then east, and finally south again on I-71.

By now it was dark. As we rolled along I-71 near Washington Courthouse, the escapees, who had been holding a constant speed of about 60 miles per hour, suddenly sped up. Speeds again approached 100 miles per hour, and the danger increased.

Just then, we saw clouds of dust and headlights spinning out of control in the median strip ahead of us. It turned out to be Sheriff Kreiger. His unmarked police car had blown a front tire and spun off the highway. Fortunately, it didn't roll over, and he and his deputies were able to quickly change the tire and rejoin the chase. They didn't need to hurry. Using their police radio, the escapees announced they were running low on fuel again and planned to stop at the next service station.

They weren't alone. Most of the police cars and news vehicles were also getting low on gas.

We could see a service station in the distance as the parade reached an exit at Ohio Route 38. Most of the assemblage was kept on the highway while the sheriff and other negotiators drove to the service station, made arrangements, and waved the escapees to the gas pumps.

It looked like the great chase was about to come to an end. Reporters were fuming because we were being held too far back to see what was happening. We learned later that while an attendant pumped gas into the stolen car, officers approached and tried to talk with the prisoners. They didn't want to talk but demanded some candy bars and soft drinks, which were brought to the car. As the attendant finished fueling, the escapees peeled out with tires squealing, back onto Interstate 71.

While some police cars continued the chase, the rest of us queued up at the pumps and urged the attendant to hurry refueling our cars. The poor man, still reeling from dozens of policemen and guns descending on his service station, demanded to know who was going to pay for the gasoline that he just pumped into the Warrensville Heights car. While Begany filled our car, I ran inside the station, grabbed a handful of candy bars for the three of us, and hurled some cash at the lady behind the cash register. Moments later we were back on the chase, which was now far in the distance.

Fortunately, TV8 photographer Cory Lash, alone in his news cruiser, had also joined the chase in Cleveland and kept going. His tank was also getting low, but he stayed with the chase as it left the service station. I was able to communicate with him via our two-way radio and discovered that the escapees had slowed down after the rapid take-off, almost as if they were waiting for everyone to catch up. Sure enough, a few minutes later we saw flashing lights ahead of us. We were able to overtake Lash and squeeze into his place in the procession while he pulled off at the next exit to refuel.

It was getting late when the gaggle of cars pulled into downtown Cincinnati, and again the escapees apparently became lost, darting up and down the one-way streets. At this point, we lost them. We tried several main thoroughfares without luck, stopped at a traffic light and tried to decide what to do next, when suddenly from behind us came the Warrensville Heights police car, followed by the flashing lights of police agencies from all over Ohio. It was like being in the middle of a silent movie chase. Cars raced up and down narrow streets. A Cincinnati police cruiser and a Cincinnati TV news car collided as both tried to take a corner at the same time. They shouted at each other but kept on going, wrinkled fenders and all.

Then there was a call over the police radio from the escapees. They were going to stop at a service station to allow the two women to go to the restroom. They had been held hostage in the car for well over six hours. The escapees warned police to stay back and not approach them while they escorted the women to the restroom.

I spotted Paul Sciria of WKYC-TV in Cleveland. Sciria was a Cleveland legend because of his close sources in law enforcement agencies. He always seemed to know what was going on, and police would tell him things that they would not tell other reporters. As I approached, I heard officers telling Sciria that when the women were out of the car and in the restroom, out of danger, police snipers were preparing to shoot the three escapees, to stop the chase before innocent bystanders were hurt.

But as we watched, expecting shots to ring out, the women got out of the car and stood between the police and the escapees, blocking any possible shot by snipers. The prisoners, armed with a shotgun, stayed behind the women all the way into the building. They emerged the same way a few minutes later. It was revealed later that the women, sensing the danger of the moment, had purposely put themselves between the police and the men to protect them.

Within moments the chase was resumed as the stolen police car, with its escapees and hostages, careened over the Ohio River across the I-71/75 bridge into Covington, Kentucky—where Kentucky State Police joined the caravan of cars. We could hear some of the police chatting over our monitors and making bets the chase would go all the way to Florida. With the pursuit now in its seventh or eighth hour, it seemed like a real possibility. But while Ohio authorities had been reluctant to attempt to stop the fleeing car while it was in motion, Kentucky State Police had other ideas.

Just as we reached a very rural area of the interstate, near Dry Ridge, Kentucky, four Kentucky State Police cars boxed in the prisoners' car. Using shotguns, the troopers blew out the tires of the Warrensville Heights car and forced it into a median strip. Kentucky troopers surrounded the car before it came to a halt and quickly were dragging out the escapees.

No one was hurt, and the women were safe. And most of the news media missed the actual apprehension. The Kentucky State Police had blocked us off along with most of the pursuing police cars when they boxed in the escapees. We arrived with our cameras and microphones just as they were hustling the prisoners into a cruiser and driving them away. The women had already left the scene. One of the longest and wildest police chases in Ohio history was over.

Several hours later, on our way home, we stopped just before dawn at an all-night restaurant south of Columbus. While we were eating, Sheriff Kreiger, his deputies, and the two women who had been hostages also came in for breakfast.

We joined them at their table. The two women told us they were tired but physically okay. Norina Dellaria said the three convicts had acted like "true gentlemen" during their ordeal.

"I don't think they meant to hurt us. They just wanted to get away," she said.

Louise Honour said, "During the chase, we spent most of the time in prayer."

As for the three escapees, they were taken to Lexington, Kentucky, and tried for kidnapping and transporting a stolen vehicle across a state line. All three were found guilty and sentenced to twenty years in jail.

A WORD ABOUT NEWSCRUISERS

They usually aren't used for multistate chases, but a look behind the scenes at television's news cruisers might be interesting.

In the first years of television street reporting, it was common to put at least the name of the station on the side of a station wagon or sedan that might have been used by engineers or the sales staff as well as the folks in news. That changed in the early 1960s when "City Camera" was born at WJW-TV. The new newscast was built on the idea of taking pictures of just about anything in the city and getting them on the air that evening.

It seemed like a natural idea to use the sides and top of the big station wagons as traveling billboards to advertise "City Camera" and to help photographers and reporters get into the scenes of accidents and major events. The cars had the TV8 logo and "City Camera" name emblazoned on their sides, and yellow emergency "gumball" lights on top.

The idea worked. Cleveland had only three TV stations on the air in the early 1960s, so their audiences were huge, and TV was still a novelty. People would get excited to see a big white station wagon cruising the street with "City Camera" painted on both sides. They would wave and peer inside to see if Doug Adair, Joel Daly, or Dick Goddard might be aboard.

But all those showy times ended in 1968 during the Glenville Riot. The cruisers were equipped with two-way radios and police monitors as well as being stocked with extra clothes, film, camera accessories, and maps to find our way around the city. Several news cruisers from WJW and other stations became targets of angry mobs. One cruiser was attacked and set on fire. A piece of pipe was hurled through the windshield of a City Camera vehicle. Some photographers started driving their unmarked personal vehicles when they had to enter the riot zone. Others left the marked cruisers parked, and even rented unmarked sedans from Hertz to use while the riots continued.

When new cruisers were ordered after that, the billboard logos and lettering were left off. Even the flashing yellow gumball on the roof was removed, replaced by a portable light with magnets on the bottom that was carried inside the car for stories where extra warning lights were needed. Even the ubiquitous station wagons were replaced by simple four-door sedans, in whatever color was available at the dealer.

It would be nearly a decade, with the advent of minicam live trucks and news helicopters, before stations again started advertising on their vehicles. Besides, it is pretty hard to disguise an ENG, or Electronic News-Gathering, truck with a microwave tower and satellite dish on the top.

MORE MOB SCENES

In television, you are not only responsible for your own safety, but for your photographer's as well. When videotape was first used in the field, the cameras were heavy and bulky, and the photographer often was weighed down by a heavy tape deck hanging from his or her shoulder. Not only bulky, a camera on the shoulder made photographers blind on one side. In a tense situation, I posted myself as close to the photographer as possible so that we could watch each other's backs.

This happened one day in the '90s, when photographer Bill West and I were doing a story near Jacobs Field in downtown Cleveland. A street person with some obvious mental problems started harassing West, screaming at him to shut off his camera and leave. When he started to approach West's blind side, I got between them and tried to distract the man. He then turned his anger on me, and the noise had attracted a small crowd of street people. They surrounded us, and the situation looked like it was going from bad to worse. I grew even more concerned as the man got closer to me, screaming so loud that spittle was spraying me. He suddenly reached into his pocket, and I feared he was about to pull a weapon.

Fortunately, West spotted a passing police cruiser and signaled them. The officers, seeing what was going on, jumped out of their car, and grabbed and handcuffed the man. It turned out he was unarmed, just a man with some anger issues.

On another occasion, photographer Cook Goodwin, a new sound technician, and I were dispatched to a strike by a local union in the Flats. On the way to the picket line, where trouble was expected, the new sound technician entertained Cook and me with stories of his last job working with an auto thrill show. He said that after crashing and smashing cars, he would leap from the vehicle and smile and wave at the applauding audience. Dangerous stunts, he said, held no fear for him.

We arrived at the strike scene just as a nonunion group of workers had tried to cross the picket line in their cars. Cook grabbed his camera and bailed out of the car. I joined him, and we started running for the confrontation. Rocks, bottles, and sticks flew through the air, and the nonunion workers were stalled in their attempts to enter the plant.

Cook and I stopped to make some pictures as the strikers rocked the cars of the nonstrikers, trying to turn one of them over. Cook looked around and saw no sign of the new sound technician. I urged him to continue filming anyway. Then the nonunion cars started peeling away from the scene. The strikers saw us filming the violence and started to throw stones and bottles. We kept shooting film, without sound, and then backed away to our car in case any angry pickets decided to follow. As we reached the car, we saw the new technician huddling on the floor. He had become frightened when he saw the first violence and locked himself in.

He resigned a week later.

You never knew what might happen, especially with a large angry crowd.

Photographer Ted Pikturna and technician Hap Halas were dispatched with me and a WJW live truck to a changing East Side neighborhood one hot summer's night. There had recently been considerable friction over an influx of African Americans into what had been a mostly white ethnic neighborhood. On this night, police had been called to an intersection near a bar several times when fights broke out in the street. When we arrived, several hundred people were milling around the intersection. It was a mixed crowd, and while various factions exchanged some sharp words, so far there didn't seem to be any violence. I jumped out of the truck and walked into the crowd to see if I could identify some spokespersons that we might interview.

As I walked into the mob, people started shoving and pushing, and I was suddenly surrounded and pushed into the center of the street. Ted told me later that all he could see was me entering the crowd and then disappearing. He thought I might have been knocked down, so he jumped out of the truck and came crashing through the crowd to help me.

I was in the middle of the mob, surrounded. But I was surrounded by friendly faces. Someone had recognized me as I left the TV truck, and people crowded around asking if I had any free "One Tank Trips" pamphlets to hand out.

The station had recently started offering booklets describing some of my trips, free of charge, with a self-addressed, stamped envelope. Some of the photographers had discovered the free booklets were good icebreakers in tense situations, so most carried a box of them to give out.

So on this hot summer's evening, when the police responded to reports of another mob at the intersection, they found Ted and me handing out "One Tank Trip" booklets, while I signed autographs.

CHAPTER 4

Getting Started
(and Getting Lost)

R. F. D.

I discovered I really enjoyed doing feature material in my first
years at WJW-TV, especially when it related to traveling around
Ohio. I would volunteer story ideas about people who made their
living going door-to-door with a singing telegram business; a
hundred-year-old man who lived in a nursing home but who still
carved wooden flutes; a man who had spent years building a concrete boat in which he and his family planned to sail around the
world. I discovered it was fun to tell people's stories.

Coincidentally, shortly after I began my sporadic travels, CBS
News in New York allowed Charles Kuralt to begin wandering
America in a camper for his wonderful series "On The Road." He
was doing the same thing I was, except his was a full-time as-
signment, and he had all of America to choose from. I thought: If
Kuralt can do it, why not me?

But having the idea was one thing. Selling it to management
proved a bit more difficult.

We had a small staff, and no one could be spared to take off for
weeks at a time and just roam around Ohio looking for interesting people and stories. Nor did the station have a camper, and
they told me they didn't plan to buy one. So back to the drawing
board.

If I couldn't do this kind of story on a regular basis, I suggested a half-hour or hour-long documentary we would call "R.F.D.," the term for rural mail delivery, as an umbrella title for the interesting people I found in rural areas of Ohio. As for a camper, I would borrow one from somebody.

News director Bill Feest agreed to the idea after much thought and with a couple of stipulations. We had to shoot the entire documentary in just one week, and we could not travel out of northeast Ohio. He didn't care whether I used a camper or not, as long as the station didn't have to pay for it.

I went through my stories from the past year and found several that fit the "On the Road" format and for which we still had outtakes—the film edited out of the original story. There was usually quite a bit, which gave me the opportunity to re-edit and use parts of the interview that had not been on the air. Then I started looking for new ideas around the Cleveland area. Once I had several stories lined up, I set up a schedule for shooting. All that was left was coming up with a camper like Kuralt used.

I found something even better.

My good friend David Harper had left the Ohio State Highway Patrol and was now working as personal assistant and driver to John Morse of Hudson. Morse, the CEO of the Morse Instrument Company, hated to fly, so he bought a new bus like the ones Greyhound used and had it refitted into a traveling home and office for him and his wife, Helen. They had even taken the bus all the way to Alaska so John could enjoy his hobby of making wildlife movies.

I was explaining to Harper my documentary idea and the need to come up with an RV when he suggested that John and Helen might enjoy a day watching us make a television documentary. And that is how I came to do my first documentary on TV, driving around northern Ohio in a bus that would put many rock stars' custom coaches to shame.

Chuck Schodowski was the director, and Bob Begany and Roger Powell worked as the film crew. We started the show with me standing in front of WJW at 1630 Euclid Avenue, talking about where we would go and what we would do. While I talked,

Dave Harper pulled up the bus with John and Helen Morse aboard and stopped right in front of me. It was a great opening and even drew a crowd of onlookers trying to figure out which rock star had just offered me a ride.

John and Helen Morse were an absolute delight to work with. They turned their bus over to us as we followed the backroads of Ohio to visit with painter Richard Treaster, syndicated cartoonist James Brannigan and schoolteacher/bus driver/farmer Betty Leimbach.

While taking a lunch break aboard the luxury bus, we filmed a quick tour. John and Helen showed the interior that included a fully equipped kitchen, bedroom, living room, and even a small movie theater. At the end of the interview I turned to the camera and said, "Charles Kuralt, eat your heart out."

"ONE TANK TRIPS" IS BORN

"One Tank Trips" was born in 1979 during the oil crisis that followed the Iranian revolution.

Panicked motorists rushed to fill their tanks with increasingly expensive fuel, creating long lines at gasoline stations. The inflation rate hit double digits.

Virgil Dominic, then the news director of TV8, decided to do a multireporter series called "Consumer Watch" to help viewers get more for their money. I was assigned to the unit to do a weeklong series on places folks could go on vacation that would take only one tank of gasoline to reach and return home.

To be frank, I was not excited about the assignment. For the previous year or so I had been doing a weekly segment called "The Ohio Reporter," similar to Kuralt's "On the Road" series, which took me around Ohio for stories on interesting places, things, and people. I believe Virgil selected me for the travel segment because I was familiar with the state. But I couldn't believe that telling people about tourist attractions in Ohio would be all that interesting or informative.

I didn't really put much effort into the series. I went to Marietta to do a story on a cruise boat; visited Cedar Point amusement park; took a look at a couple of state parks, and ended with a cruise on the *Goodtime* cruise boat in Cleveland Harbor.

None of us could believe the response that the travel segment received. Folks phoned asking for more ideas. Letters poured in seeking additional destinations. Not only did Virgil Dominic decide to make the series weekly, but he decided to keep it on TV8's prime 6 p.m. news show.

Despite my original lack of enthusiasm, I had discovered the fun of exploring our state and started some serious research on where I could go each week. What made the assignment even better was that Virgil, and most of the news directors who followed over the next quarter century, let me decide where to go. While this gave me the responsibility to keep coming up with fresh and original ideas, it also cut down on planning time because I did not have to seek someone else's approval on a destination.

I started looking for ideas by subscribing to newspapers all over the state. I got on the phone and called chambers of commerce in every corner of the state, asking for tourist pamphlets and suggestions about destinations. And I talked with the photographers at TV8, who were constantly traveling around northeast Ohio and to other locales. I asked them if there were places they spotted in their journeys that they would have enjoyed visiting.

Over the next six months we traveled to just about every major tourist attraction in Ohio. And I realized I had a problem. Using Virgil's original dictum that "One Tank Trips" should be just that, to destinations that took one tank of gasoline for a round trip, I was quickly running out of places to visit. I needed to go farther.

I spent a weekend pondering my maps and material trying to pinpoint new attractions. I couldn't help but notice that if I slightly enlarged the area to which I was restricted, there were many new towns, lakes, rivers, and interesting points to visit.

I went to Virgil's office on Monday and made my case to consider it a "One Tank Trip" if we used one tank just getting to a destination instead of out and back on the same tank. If we did this, I pointed out, I could reasonably travel from Cleveland to seven other surrounding states and even into Canada, giving us an almost inexhaustible supply of interesting destinations. Virgil thought it over and agreed. From that point on we visited places like Saginaw Bay, Michigan; Cumberland, Maryland; Pigeon Forge, Tennessee; South Bend, Indiana; and Georgian Bay, Canada.

We tried each year to make at least 70 percent of our trips within the borders of Ohio. The other 30 percent would be to any town, city, or state where I found something interesting, as long as I could reach it on one tank of gasoline.

THE FIRST ONE TANK TRIP

I gained an advantage over other journalists simply by my longevity in the area of trips and travel. Public relations and marketing people and the operators of tourist attractions might deal with some reporters for a few years, but I had been around for more than thirty years. I came to know not only the attractions of the state, but also the people who ran them and their families. Several became personal friends. My very first "One Tank Trip" resulted in a friendship that now spans two generations. When we began the series in 1980, I really had no idea how to do it or whom to call. No similar localized travel features were on the air. We decided just to travel to a town and see for ourselves what there was to see and do. Our first destination was Marietta, Ohio.

The reception was less than spectacular when photographer Bill West and I pulled into the famous river town at the confluence of the Ohio and Muskingum Rivers. Seeing a sign for the local chamber of commerce, we walked in and announced to the elderly woman—as well as the only person there—that we were from Cleveland and had come to do a "One Tank Trip."

She looked up from her desk and said, "We don't have any

tanks here. Are you sure you're not looking for Fort Knox, Kentucky?"

I explained that we were from a television station and were trying to do a story using one tank of gas. But she had fixated on the word *tank* and was convinced we were looking for the army.

"My husband served in a tank at Fort Knox," she said.

By this time I was choking back laughter. We finally gave up, left, and wandered over to the waterfront and the Lafayette Hotel. I asked to speak to the manager, but he wasn't in. I then told the clerk that we wanted to take some pictures of the riverboat décor inside the hotel to go with our story. She said she wasn't authorized to permit me to take pictures in the hotel and suggested we come back another day.

Bill and I were discussing our failure to communicate and the time we had wasted as we drove along Muskingum when I heard a strange noise. Through the trees we saw a giant paddlewheel churning up the brown river water, pushing a gaily painted red and white riverboat. Through the willow trees it looked like a scene from a Mark Twain novel. We followed the boat to its dock under the Washington Street Bridge, where we first met Captain Jim Sands of the *Valley Gem* Sternwheeler.

Captain Jim and a partner had built the boat with their own hands. After starting a tour boat operation, Sands bought out his partner and now ran hourly tours up and down the Ohio River. He gave us the first warm welcome we had received in Marietta and invited us to join him on a tour getting ready to depart.

As we sailed down the Muskingum and made the turn into the Ohio, I stood in the pilot house telling Sands of the problems we had since arriving. Sands was a true riverman, tough and ready to say exactly what was on his mind. He picked up his ship-to-shore phone and called both the chamber of commerce and the local hotel. I don't recall his exact words, but when he was finished we were invited to dinner at the hotel, and chamber officials would be ready to guide us around town to any place we wanted to visit. We later learned that Sands was a member of the local tourist and convention bureau. He even arranged for a small speedboat so

West could get some pictures of the *Valley Gem* from the river as we passed downtown Marietta.

We spent a delightful afternoon with Sands on the boat, listening to his tales of the river and the river town that had been home most of his adult life. He made more calls and arranged for us to visit a pasta factory and an artist across the river in West Virginia. When we got to the hotel that evening, Captain Jim and his wife, Peg, were there to greet us and host dinner in the Gun Room.

This turned out to be the first of many trips I would make over the next three decades to Marietta, and they often featured the *Valley Gem* and its many different tours. I came to know Jim and Peg and their sons, Jim Junior ("Jimmy") and Jason ("JJ").

The family decided to build a new *Valley Gem* in the mid-1980s. They completed it in 1989, just in time to host President George H. W. Bush for a cruise down the Ohio River.

Sadly, son Jimmy, long ill with leukemia, passed away at the young age of thirty-two in 1990. Although grieving heavily, Jim and Peg carried on the business. And JJ gave them a proud moment in 1992, when at the age of eighteen he became one of the youngest persons to receive his river pilot's license. As Jim liked to brag, "Mark Twain was an old man of twenty-four when he got his license."

I lost my good friend Jim Sands to diabetes in 1998. But his legacy survives, and a new generation—Jason and his wife, Katie, with life-long friend Captain Don Sandford—now runs the *Valley Gem*.

A HISTORY-MAKING FLIGHT OVER LAKE ERIE

One of my more unusual trips happened in the 1970s when a young Brecksville man announced that he planned to be the first person to fly a hang glider from one country to another. Chuck Slusarczyk said he would fly his glider from Cleveland's Edgewater Beach across Lake Erie to Rondeau Bay, Canada, a distance of about fifty-four miles.

The huge kite that he'd dangle beneath had no motor, so in

order to make the crossing he arranged to be towed by a large speedboat that could reach nearly 50 miles per hour.

"I expect to be in Canada in an hour and a half," Slusarczyk told me and other reporters who gathered around him on the beach on a hot, humid August day.

Photographers Ralph Tarsitano and John Hamilton were with me. Since TV8 did not have a boat, we had scrambled to find a speedy craft to keep up with Slusarczyk as he glided above the lake. We were unsuccessful until deputies from the office of then-sheriff Ralph Kreiger arrived on the scene. They had a sleek cabin cruiser, adorned with the sheriff's star and black-and-white stripes, and equipped with flashing red lights and a crew of three. The deputy sheriff in charge told me that if we didn't mind sharing space with WEWS's Lee Bailey and cameraman Tom Polk, we were welcome to come along on the official escort boat.

At 7 a.m., Slusarczyk gave the signal that he was ready to go. His giant Sea Ray boat started north, picking up speed. The cable, about a thousand feet long and coiled on the beach, started snaking into the water. Slusarczyk hoisted his hang glider above him, and as the cable became taut, he took a couple of running steps and it lifted him gently into the air. He soared above the speedboat that was now picking up more speed.

I was aboard the sheriff's boat just offshore, where we had filmed the takeoff. Now we urged the sheriff's crew to catch up with Slusarczyk and crew as they disappeared into the morning haze over the lake.

What none of us had considered was that the sheriff's boat had only half the horsepower of Slusarczyk's boat. The added weight of eight people cut our craft's speed even more. We slogged along, straining to catch a glimpse of Slusarczyk or his boat.

An hour and a half later, we sighted land. As we got closer to the Canadian shore, we could see Slusarczyk's glider resting in the sand. He had made it, but we had missed the entire flight, other than the takeoff.

Wading ashore, we were greeted by a large number of vacationing Canadians who had heard about the flight on the morning news and had come down to the beach to see Slusarczyk's arrival. Many had brought coolers of beer, soft drinks, and sandwiches, and an impromptu welcoming party was already in progress.

"What happened to you guys?" Slusarczyk asked as he offered us each a beer. "I thought you were going to escort me over here."

We explained that we couldn't keep up with his faster boat and had just blown our chance to cover his history-making flight. Slusarczyk, always conscious of public relations, said he was considering making another landing, since many of the Canadians had also reached the beach too late to catch his arrival.

With our encouragement, he hooked his cable to his boat and took to the sky again, this time heading south. A few minutes later, with our cameras trained on the sky, we saw him turn and head back for us, the glider floating through the sky like a giant bird with a human in its talons. As he closed in on the shore, his boat suddenly made a right-angle turn and raced down the shoreline while Slusarczyk maneuvered his glider down to just a foot above the water. He glided past the cameras and back to the sky as the boat circled. At the top of the circle, Slusarczyk cut loose from the cable, banked his glider, and made a graceful descent onto the beach in front of the cameras. The Canadians and the reporters broke out in spontaneous applause. Chuck Slusarczyk had just—officially now—made history.

After interviews and reaction from our Canadian hosts, we settled down for a beach-party lunch. Around one o'clock, our sheriff's crew advised us that we had to leave for home if we planned to make our 6 p.m. newscast. They had obtained a compass bearing from some Canadian fishermen that would take us right to the mouth of the Cuyahoga River.

Our trip home was under way for about thirty minutes when the deputy operating the boat motioned Ralph Tarsitano to join him at the wheel. Tarsitano had mentioned that he had spent several years in the Coast Guard and was stationed at the Port of

Cleveland. Wanting to be spelled at the wheel, the deputy asked Tarsitano to take over and told him just to follow the compass bearing. What Tarsitano had neglected to tell him was that he had little experience piloting a boat, and most of his Coast Guard service was as a photographer.

The lake was still as glass, and Tarsitano kept the boat pointed south as it droned on toward Cleveland. Many of us fell asleep. Tarsitano, however, was having difficulty reading the compass, which was on a ledge above the wheel. He picked it up and placed it on the floor between his feet so he could just glance down and make sure he was on course. What he didn't realize was that the compass was now sitting only inches above the motor, and its vibration apparently caused it to swing to another reading.

He had been at the wheel nearly an hour when the deputy in charge picked up his field glasses and peered at the horizon, expecting to see land. To his surprise, there was no land, only water. Then he saw that the compass, now on the floor, was swinging from heading to heading.

He took over the wheel and tried to determine our heading by dead reckoning. But it had grown cloudy, there was no sun to be seen, and the waves were starting to build. He got on the radio, only to find that it had stopped functioning.

"Not to worry," he announced. "Lake Erie is surrounded by land. If we just keep heading in a straight line, we'll find land, identify where we are, and follow the shoreline home."

For the next thirty minutes we all strained our eyes, looking in every direction for a sign of land—any land. Wondering what we would do when we ran out of gasoline.

"Land, I see land!" shouted Lee Bailey.

Sure enough, dead ahead, was a long beach with a few pine trees reaching to the sky. But where were we?

We were soon close enough to identify more features—just sandy coastline and more pine trees. Could it be an area west of Vermilion? Maybe we were near Mentor Headlands?

The deputy, looking through his binoculars, spotted a man

walking on the beach. We drew as close to the shore as we dared, and whistled and shouted at the man, who had his back to us. The crashing waves apparently drowned us out. The quick-thinking deputy hit the siren on the boat and shouted through the loud-speaker, "Ahoy!"

The elderly man, startled, literally jumped into the air as he turned around. He finally came down to the shore and shouted, "What do you want?"

The deputy called back, "Can you tell us which way it is to Cleveland?"

The man replied, "Eh??"

The deputy shouted through the loudspeaker, "Which way to Cleveland? We're lost!"

"Whatja say?!" the old man shouted.

"WE'RE LOST, DAMMIT! WHERE THE HELL ARE WE?!" shouted the deputy.

"Oh," answered the old man, "you're at Point Pelee Park."

We were back in Canada, having gone in a circle.

After determining which way was south, the deputy checked our gas and some charts and calculated we had enough gas to reach Kelleys Island, where he could refuel before heading for Cleveland. Bailey and I started talking about renting an airplane at Kelleys Island to take us back to Cleveland in time for the 6 p.m. news.

The weather was getting worse. The waves were now one to three feet, and it was difficult to keep a steady southern course. It wasn't long before we were lost again. We saw fishing boats in the distance and aimed toward one. We pulled alongside. It was a commercial fishing boat with a crew that didn't speak English.

Tarsitano pushed to the rail. "Let me talk to them," he said. "I think they're Italian, and I understand some Italian."

It turned out the crew was Portuguese and didn't speak Italian. But with pidgin English and lots of hand waving, we finally communicated that we needed directions to Kelleys Island, and they pointed south.

Twenty minutes after five o'clock, we pulled into the dock at the island. Bailey, his photographer Tom Polk, and I leaped off the boat and ran to the nearest telephone to see if we could rent a plane to fly us to Cleveland. The only one available was a four-seater. That meant that Tarsitano and John Hamilton, my photographers, would have to remain with the boat. Grudgingly, they waved me on, agreeing they would return to Cleveland with the deputies after the boat was refueled, while I flew back to try to get the story ready for our 11 p.m. news.

An island taxi carried Bailey, Polk, and me to the airport, where we climbed into the small plane. Moments later we were airborne when the pilot pulled out a map and started searching for Cleveland.

"I just moved here from Alabama," he said. "This is my first day flying this area, and I've never been to Cleveland."

The three of us almost shouted as we told him to forget the map, keep the plane low enough to see the shoreline, and head east until he found the Terminal Tower.

A half hour later, we touched down at Burke Lakefront Airport. I dashed through the terminal, hailed a taxi, and told the driver to rush me to our studios on South Marginal Road. I literally ran into the newsroom with my film in hand, thinking of how I was going to write about our adventure, when assistant news director Dan Hrvatin met me and said, "Don't bother to write anything; we don't have room in the show." It was August 8, 1974, and President Nixon had just announced that he would become the first U.S. president in history to resign.

As Chuck Slusarczyk later said of his history-making flight that was virtually ignored, "Timing is everything."

A postscript: As I was unwinding in the newsroom, finally having my first food and drink since noon, the telephone rang. The operator said it was a collect call from Ralph Tarsitano. I accepted.

"Zurcher," Tarsitano rasped over the phone, "the boat started taking on water when we hit seven-foot waves just off Cedar

Point. So we docked here and we don't have any way home. What should we do?"

I suggested that he and Hamilton call a cab and have themselves taken, with their equipment, to Griffing Flying Service near the entrance to Cedar Point and charter a plane, as I did, to complete their journey. I didn't have the heart to tell him the story we had been working on all day wasn't going to run.

Another hour went by. I was still trying to write some kind of a story that might be used within the next day or two when the phone rang again. It was Tarsitano.

"Zurcher!" he screamed in my ear. "There weren't any cabs! We carried most of our equipment all the way over here and the airport is closed. Do you hear me!? Closed for repairs. They're repaving the friggin' runway! You got any other bright ideas?"

I confessed I didn't. It was already 9:30 at night.

"I'll handle this myself!" he screamed at me as he slammed down the phone.

I found out later that, using a company credit card, he had enticed a local Buick dealer to rent them a new station wagon in which he, Hamilton, and the deputies finally made it back to Cleveland.

I don't think any of us will ever forget the day that Nixon resigned.

GOING OFF ROAD

Videographer Ron Strah and I were headed into the forest region of western New York. Bill Castle, who owned a unique bed and breakfast called Pollywog Hollër, had given me directions to his place over the phone. As you leave the Allegany Indian Reservation on New York Route 17, the towns become smaller and the homes farther apart.

"He said to watch for a barn at the bottom of this hill, on the left-hand side," I told Ron as we started down a long incline with forest on both sides. At the bottom of the hill was a weathered barn with a gravel road beside it, which led off to the left. So far, the directions were perfect.

We traveled the gravel road for several miles, noticing it was getting narrower and rougher. Suddenly, at the crest of a small rise in the road, the gravel ended. Stretching out before us was a dirt road that looked as though it had just been freshly carved out of the earth.

"Are you sure this is the right way?" Strah asked. "This road doesn't look too good, and if it's muddy, we may not get out of here."

"Oh, I'm sure if the road was impassable he would have told us," I replied.

We continued on. The road was passable, despite the periodic need to avoid some huge holes or boulders that had been unearthed by the road scraper.

We were crawling now, at about 10 miles per hour, hoping to see the road resume as a paved highway, or at least one covered with gravel.

Looking out at the deep forest that surrounded us, I recalled reading a newspaper report just that morning about bears being spotted in this area of New York, and wildlife officials warning residents to avoid confrontations with them.

As we crested a hill, the dirt road ended. Ahead was freshly turned earth that looked like a newly plowed field. Going farther would be impossible.

We got out to look around. Walking through the soft dirt confirmed our fears. Had we gone any farther, we would have sunk up to our hubs. Problem was, the dirt road was only as wide as our car, making it impossible to turn around. Backing mile after mile would be laborious.

I reached for our cell phone to call Bill Castle to see if he could figure out where we were and offer us some way out. But we were too far out of a service area to get a signal. We were stuck.

Ron and I sat in the car in silence, each of us trying to figure out what to do next. I suspect Ron was also thinking dark thoughts about the directions I received. Suddenly he said, "Here comes the cavalry!"

Behind us, I could see a dot on the road getting larger. It finally turned into a large four-wheel-drive truck. But instead of stopping as it approached, it pulled off the edge of the road and prepared to go around us.

We jumped out of the car and flagged the driver down.

"Is Pollywog Hollër around here?" I asked the driver.

"Yup. Just about a mile up the road here," he gestured.

"What about the road?" Ron asked.

"Oh, that," the truck driver answered. "It washed out durin' a big storm about a year ago, and since it's not used much, the county has been kinda slow rebuildin' it."

"Well, how do we get out of here?" Ron asked.

"Oh," said the truck driver, as though he just realized we were stuck. "If you want to wait about an hour, I'll get the grader goin' up ahead and come back and cut you a path."

Mumbling to ourselves that we didn't have any choice, we agreed and watched him pull away. About forty-five minutes later, true to his word, he came grinding back up the hill in a road grader, pushing aside small boulders and dirt, making a narrow path for us down the hill to where the highway resumed.

Finally on our way again, we had only traveled about a mile when we saw a rusting sign reading "Pollywog Hollër." We had arrived, but no one was at the road to meet us. I had explained to Bill Castle that we had a lot of equipment and would need to park as close to his home as possible. He pointed out that his home was a former hunting lodge and was not near the road. It was, in fact, a quarter of a mile from the highway on the other side of a woods and stream. The only way to get there was to walk. His last words to me had been "I'll try to work something out."

His solution stood next to the driveway. Two large construction wheelbarrows. We decided to carry the equipment in by hand. As Ron unloaded the car, I looked at the field in front of us. It contained a series of strange sculptures. Some looked like deranged windmills, others like giant, long-abandoned tricycles. Near the edge of the field was an opening in the woods and a path.

"I don't know where Bill is, but I'll bet that's the path to the cabin," I said as Ron finished putting his equipment in canvas bags for us to carry.

We entered the woods, staggering under our load of cameras, tripods, lights, and other equipment. We had not gone a hundred feet when, rounding a curve, we found a door in the middle of the trail. It was an ornate door, standing in a doorway, but on either side was nothing. You could just walk around it. To the side of the trail we saw what appeared to be mutant mushrooms, made of concrete and painted purple. Ahead of us, throughout the woods, were dozens of giant, rusting sculptures, some nearly as big as the trees that sheltered them. Others were tiny objects nearly hidden in the fallen leaves. It was like walking through some strange fantasy land.

It took about fifteen minutes to reach the other side of the woods, where we heard the gurgle of a small waterfall. As we approached a wooden bridge, on the other side of the stream and nearly hidden in the limbs of surrounding trees, we saw a huge log cabin and a smiling, bearded man waving a welcome from the porch. We had finally reached Pollywog Hollër.

Bill Castle had once been a businessman, but a heart attack led him to change his lifestyle. He went back to school, took art classes, and became interested in sculpture. He offered the property around his hunting lodge to colleagues who were also artists as a place to store their projects, hence the variety of work we had seen on the way in from the highway. He also decided to move out of his modern home and turn his hunting lodge into a non-electric bed and breakfast, where he could share his art and his new, healthier lifestyle.

A stress-free life was what he was seeking. Sitting on the huge front porch overlooking a bubbling stream, serenaded by thousands of frogs, it seemed to us he had found it. Pollywog Hollër, he noted, lived up to its name.

WRONG WAY ZURCHER

Many of the photographers who worked with me at TV8 would marvel at a strange skill I seemed to have.

We could be traveling in a relatively strange area of the state, and while the photographer drove, I would nod off. But some instinct would wake me when we reached a crucial change of route or a turn. They would think I was asleep when I would suddenly say, "Turn left at the next corner." And usually I was right. They would even brag of my uncanny ability to sleep and navigate at the same time. This was before GPS systems and Mapquest, back in the time when people still had to read maps.

This is not to say that we did not occasionally get lost. More than once, while seeking our hotel or a looking for a restaurant in a strange town, we found ourselves taking a wrong turn and ending up in a part of town where even the local police refused to go.

Photographer Greg Lockhart will never let me forget a One Tank Trip that he and I took from Cleveland to Frankenmuth, Michigan, and then into Canada and across the northern side of Lake Erie to Niagara Falls.

It was a busy, two-day trip, and I offered to take a turn driving as we entered Canada north of Windsor. Greg handed over the keys and climbed into the passenger seat.

The north side of Lake Erie, unlike the Ohio side, is sparsely populated. There aren't many towns, and it is a boring drive once you are on the QEW highway. Greg was sleeping and I was thinking about the things we would do in Niagara Falls that evening and at nearby Niagara-on-the-Lake before we started home.

The hours went by, as did the miles, and I continued to daydream as we headed east, only once in a while reminding myself to look for the turnoff north of Hamilton, Ontario, to take us to the falls. I don't know how I missed it, but I suddenly saw on the horizon the CN Tower in downtown Toronto. I had overshot my turn by nearly sixty miles.

I looked over at the passenger seat and saw that Greg was still sleeping soundly. Very carefully, so not to wake him, I took an exit at the Toronto city limits, crossed the ramp, and started back west to our Hamilton turnoff. Greg suddenly awakened and stretched. He looked around and asked, "Where are we?"

"Oh, maybe an hour or so out of Niagara Falls," I replied.

"That's funny," he said, looking at his watch. "I thought we'd be there by now."

I could feel the flush creeping up my neck, but I ignored his comment and kept driving.

"Say," he said, "shouldn't the sun be setting behind us?" Just then he saw an exit sign to Mississauga, a suburb of Toronto. His head snapped around in realization and a smile lit up his face.

"Is the One-Tank-Trip man lost?"

"Not anymore," I grumbled in reply as I kept staring straight ahead.

We got into Niagara Falls an hour later, and the next day I let Greg drive home.

PLACES AND NAMES

Have you ever wondered about the name of the place where you live? It's usually a simple matter. A town near the water might be called Bay Village. A small community where farmers live might be christened Farmerstown. How about a place of great charm? Charm would be a nice name. All those places are here in Ohio.

When I was a youngster in Lorain County, the intersection of State Routes 113 and 58 in Amherst Township was known as Whiskeyville. At that time it had nothing but a couple of service stations and an old bar, named the Timbers because it was made of logs. While I was perusing a book on local history at the library one day, the name "Whiskeyville" jumped out at me. I read on and learned that the crossroads were given that name by locals because there once were no fewer than five taverns grouped around the intersection. Inspired by the serendipitous find, I armed myself with a modern atlas of Ohio and set out on a cross-state trip to discover the origin of several other intriguing place names.

The first one was Knockemstiff in Ross County. A stop at the county sheriff's office in Chillicothe assured me that there was such a place, but that little was left of it—no signs, only a general store and a church. Armed with directions, we set out over the hills and down some gravel roads into the back country of Ross County. Videographer Mark Saksa and I were about an hour into our mission when we realized we were lost. One gravel road looked pretty much like the next. Either the county was saving money on road signs or vandals were stealing them. After finding ourselves at the same corner we had passed minutes earlier, we both confessed our confusion and started looking for someone to show us the way.

That proved a difficult task.

In sparsely populated Ross County you can drive for miles down a country lane and never see a house, barn, or person. Eventually, at the crest of a small hill, we spotted a decrepit mobile home clinging at a tilt to its hillside location. At the edge of the property was an old apple tree, and under the tree two men, their arms covered with tattoos, were working on the rusted hulk of an old pickup truck. I should point out that Mark and I were traveling that day in one of our large Ford news cruisers, which had many antennas and, at a glance, resembled police cars. As we whipped into the driveway, the two men looked up, spotted our car, dropped their tools, and ran pell-mell for the mobile home.

Puzzled, we sat in the car, wondering whether we should get out. We had heard reports that some of the people back in the hills of southern Ohio can be unfriendly to strangers.

A head popped out of the trailer home. "What 'joo want?" it shouted.

"We're lost!" I shouted back.

The head materialized into a short, heavy woman with stringy hair, wearing a threadbare dirty black dress. Barefoot, she marched resolutely towards our car. Reaching Mark's window, she looked at him and said, again, "What 'joo want?"

As she opened her mouth, we could see that she only had one

tooth, right in the front of her mouth. I don't know why, but I couldn't take my eyes off it.

"To tell you the tooth . . . I mean truth," I spluttered, "we're looking for Knockemstiff, Ohio."

Mark was trying to lean away from the woman, who now had her head almost in the window.

"Why you wanna know?" she demanded, spraying spittle over Mark and giving both of us a whiff of something she must have eaten a few days before.

I quickly told her that we were from a television station and explained our mission. It must have satisfied her because she pulled back out of the car and pointed down the road.

"Hit's right at the bottom of the holler," she said, "but ain't nothin' worth seein' there."

We thanked her and quickly backed out of the driveway. As we peeled off down the road, I looked back and saw the two men we had apparently frightened still standing in the shadows inside the mobile home.

At the bottom of the hill we found a crossroads, and the woman was right, there *wasn't* much there. A church, a couple of modest homes, and a cement-block convenience store. But then we saw it. The sign in front of the store, though badly faded and in need of paint, read "Knockemstiff Store."

We whipped into the parking lot. Mark grabbed his camera and started videotaping the sign and the buildings around the intersection while I walked into the store.

Only a fly-specked fluorescent light illuminated the interior. Some sad-looking apples and limp oranges sat on a counter that also offered bread and a few canned goods. A youngish woman behind the counter looked at me as I walked in, but said nothing. I walked up, introduced myself, and explained our mission. I asked if she could do a short interview and perhaps explain the community's strange name.

"I don't like newspaper people," she grumbled.

"I'm on television," I said.

"Don't like them either," she added. "Now git outta my store."

Outside again, I was standing with Mark by the store sign, trying to decide what to do next, when a rusty pickup truck pulled in and parked next to the building. One of the largest humans I have seen unfolded from the front seat in camouflage clothing. Behind his head I could see a gun rack with two rifles in it.

"My wife tells me you don't know the meaning of the word *git!*" he said.

I hastily assured him that we were just leaving but decided to take one more shot at completing our mission. I explained what we were trying to find and appealed to him to point us to someone who could help. I don't know if he just wanted to get rid of us or was amused by what we were trying to do, but the next thing I knew he invited me inside the store, where he went to a telephone and made a call. A few minutes later, I was sitting on a lawn chair in front of another crumbling mobile home, as a longtime resident of the community told me this story:

"Long about a hunderd years ago there was three, four taverns at the intersection, real mean places, and two of them taverns, they was each run by a lady. Well, one night a gambler from down in Portsmouth, Ohio, got into a poker game at one of the ladies' taverns and, wouldn't ya know it, he was cheatin' and the lady caught him at it. She tried to throw him outta her place, but he put up a fight and they rolled out into the middle of the road. Well, the lady across the way who run the other tavern, she saw what was happenin' and she come runnin' and jumped into the fight. All three of 'em was rollin' around on the ground, and the crowd of men was gathered 'round, cheerin' 'em on, when one of 'em shouted, 'Knockemstiff, ladies, knockemstiff!' And you know, everbody started to laugh, and from then on, the name of the town was Knockemstiff."

THE FANS

One thing that was difficult to get used to when I worked in television was the reaction of fans.

Strangers would walk up and say, "Hi, Neil!" and I wouldn't

have the slightest idea who they were. But I would probably spend the next hour trying to recall where I had met them. Usually it was just a case of them seeing me on TV so many times that they felt they knew me.

I always tried to be polite and grateful for the recognition. Without their support, I wouldn't have a job. I developed a habit of saying, "Hi there! Gosh, it's good to see you," when a stranger would walk up and greet me. I felt this generic greeting covered me in case I had met the person before or, as was usually the case, it was a fan just meeting me.

I could be embarrassed, however, such as the time I was working in the TV8 booth at the I-X Center during the Sports and Travel Show. Thousands of people poured down the aisles each day. I was handing out booklets promoting "One Tank Trips," and the sea of passing faces became just a blur punctuated by fleeting greetings from attendees who recognized me. An elderly woman walked up to our booth and said, "Hello, Neil."

I responded with my rote, "Hi there! Gosh, it's good to see you." As I shoved a booklet in her hands and started to turn away.

"You have no idea who I am, do you?" she asked.

I looked back at her, another face in the countless faces I had seen in the past two days. Nothing registered. I decided honesty was the best policy.

"No, I really don't. Help me out. Where did we meet?" I asked

"I'm your aunt Olga O'Hair," she pointedly answered.

And she was. She was my father's sister and my favorite aunt, one I visited frequently. But the recognition receptors in my brain had been numbed by the sheer number of people I greeted. I had no idea Aunt Olga enjoyed events like this show, nor did I expect to see her.

A more numbing experience happened during the era of men's leisure suits. Remember them? Polyester suits that were worn with an open-collar shirt that showed off a man's hairy or hairless chest? I had a white leisure suit that I particularly liked and was wearing it one evening at the Bit of Budapest Hungarian restaurant in Parma Heights. As I was leaving, I passed a group of women diners who were members of a bowling team celebrating the end of their season. One woman who'd had a bit too much to drink recognized me and leaped to her feet, calling my name and blocking my passage.

"Hey! You're Neil Zurschurrr from TV8!" she slurred as she suddenly stumbled and lurched towards me. Her hand shot out to catch herself, and she grabbed the front of my shirt and a handful of chest hair. Hanging on with a death-grip, she tumbled to the floor and yanked out the handful of chest hair.

I let out a bellow as the flash of pain hit me. She looked up from the floor, raised the hand still clutching strands of my chest hair, and asked, "Can I keep these as a souvenir?"

The only time I remember being impolite to a well-meaning fan was in Massillon at their annual Father's Day Antique Car Show. I had spent the morning at a TV8 tent with my 1959 Metropolitan and badly needed a bathroom break. I walked to a McDonald's just up the street.

I was in the men's room at a urinal when I noticed the man standing at the next urinal was staring at me. "You're Neil Zurcher from 'One Tank Trips,' aren't you?" he said.

I said I was. He dropped what he was holding and stuck out his hand out, saying, "I've always wanted to shake hands with someone on TV."

As far as I know, he still hasn't shaken hands with anyone on TV.

CHAPTER 5

Family

I am often asked if my wife got to go with me on One Tank Trips. Even if WJW had approved, it would have been difficult for her because Bonnie had her own career as a registered nurse. She worked full-time, first at St. John's Hospital and later at Fairview Hospital.

I traveled for the most part with the station's talented photojournalists. Almost all of them were my companions at some point on the trips we took over the twenty-five years. Some of them, especially Bill Wolfe, Bob Begany, Bill West, Jim Holloway, and Jim Pijor, seemed to really enjoy getting the One Tank Trip assignment. Not every photographer did. Some only liked doing "hard news" assignments, like murders, disasters, and scandals. They wanted to be where the action was. But they were professionals, and they all worked very hard to get the shots I needed for the travel stories.

Most One Tank Trips were enjoyable, family-friendly experiences. I did occasionally get to share them with a member of my family. I was slated to make a trip one day when my son, Craig, was about four years old. My wife had left for work, and our babysitter called to say she was sick. This was an emergency. What would I do with my four-year-old son?

I took him with me. I called videographer Ralph Tarsitano, whom we call "Tarts," explained my problem, and asked if he objected to Craig riding with us. (I didn't bother to clear it with WJW-TV.) Everything went fine on the shoot, a pretty piece about

Christmas coming to Chagrin Falls. Craig seemed to enjoy the attention he got by being the youngest member of a TV crew. He was fascinated by the holiday lights, the decorated store windows, and all the excitement.

A department store Santa Claus was sitting in a window talking to youngsters. Tarts had seen several kids press their noses against the window to watch, but by the time he got the camera in position they had wandered off. He pointed to Craig.

"Put him over by the window and let me get a shot of him watching Santa," he said.

I wasn't too sure about that.

"Uh, Tarts," I began, "I forgot to get clearance to bring Craig along."

"Nobody's gonna recognize him back at the station," Tarsitano replied as he motioned Craig into position. "Don't worry."

When Craig looked through the window, his four-year-old eyes got as wide as pie plates as he beheld Santa Claus talking to the other youngsters. I used the shot, which was one of many. A day later I was summoned to the office of then-news director Phyllis Quail.

"Was that your son Craig on that Christmas piece last night?" she asked.

I admitted that it was, but before I could begin my assurances that it was an emergency and would not happen again, she interrupted me.

"That was cute," she said. "You ought to take him with you more often. Our viewers like to see that we have families just like them."

I hastily agreed and said that, when possible, I would consider doing just that. At the same time I was mentally calculating how much I could also save in babysitting fees on days I traveled.

So, off and on, for the next ten years, especially during school holidays and the summer, Craig was my partner on One Tank Trips. He got to steer a real paddle-wheel boat down the Ohio River and sat in the fireman's seat of a steam-powered locomotive. He rode a jetboat up the Niagara gorge, took elephant rides, and petted baby tigers. The first lady of Ohio took him on a tour of the Governor's Mansion and even let him raid the governor's private garden. He watched the sun rise and set in different states. He got to do things that many youngsters could only fantasize about.

But Craig never caught a fish.

I must confess I am not a fisherman, and I took Craig fishing probably fewer than a half-dozen times. When we visited the new Geneva State Park in Geneva-on-the-Lake some years ago and a charter captain offered to take us where the really big fish were biting, we jumped at the chance.

The boat was only about nineteen feet long, and some four- to six-foot waves were beginning to roll as we headed out. We bobbed around like a cork in a barrel as we pushed a mile or more out to the fishing grounds. When we reached the spot, Craig had to hang onto the rail with one hand as he cast his line with another.

Almost immediately he had a bite, a big one. It almost bent his fishing rod in half. Then the fish began to run and the charter captain and crew began to shout advice to Craig:

"Snug up your line!" shouted one.

"Let him run a bit! Don't let him break the line!" called another.

For the next twenty minutes, as the boat tossed and turned, Craig did his best to follow the instructions, the fish getting closer and closer. Then I noticed Craig's face turning a light shade of green.

"Are you getting seasick?" I asked.

He gave me a miserable look and nodded as he continued the battle to land the fish.

The captain and crew continued to call out advice until Craig suddenly handed them the rod and leaned over the rail, very sick. Even with experienced fisherman on the line, it took several more minutes to bring the near-record-sized walleye on board.

Craig, now pale and shaking, was sitting and looking into space as the captain held the fish by a gill and pushed it in front of his face.

"Look at that," declared the captain. "It's just a half-inch short of a record."

Craig looked at the glassy-eyed, smelly fish a couple of inches from his nose and turned to hang over the rail again.

He stayed there most of the way into port. When we reached the dock, the captain held up the fish again and asked if Craig wanted to clean it on shore or pack it in ice to take home. Craig, still a bit green around his own gills, said he didn't even want to look at that fish, or any other fish, as long as he lived.

The fish went home with the captain and crew.

MORE TRAVELS WITH CRAIG

When Craig was about eighteen months old I took him with me one evening to the local service station. I had turned off the ignition but left the keys in the lock while I pumped gas. Craig was at an age where he liked to stand behind the steering wheel and go "Vmmmm! Vmmmm!" I could see his head shaking excitedly as I filled the tank. But when I stepped back to hang up the hose, I saw him turn and grab the sill of the car window, pushing down the door lock at the same time. I desperately grabbed the door handle, trying to open the door before it locked, but too late. I ran to the other side of the car and tried that door, but knew I always locked it when Craig was riding with me.

Craig thought it was a game. He laughed watching me run back and forth. When I returned to the driver's side, he pressed his hands and mouth against the inside of the window, slobbering all over the glass.

"Craig!" I called to him. "Grab the silver thing there and pull it up." I pointed to the pressed-down lock with no success. Craig continued to grin at me and slobber on the inside of the window.

By this time the service station attendant had come to the pump island to see what was going on.

"I think we have a door jimmy someplace," the attendant offered.

A minute later, he tried to slide the slim piece of steel down the channel beside the window. The appearance of a stranger so close to the car frightened Craig. He began to cry. I could only watch helplessly as his crying got louder and louder.

"I don't think these things work on Fords," the attendant told me.

"What do I do now?" I asked, as Craig's cries rose to a new level.

"Well," the attendant said, shrugging his shoulders, "we can either break a window and reach in, or call the police."

The thought of breaking a window and showering broken glass over my already hysterical son wasn't appealing, but neither was the embarrassment of calling the law.

A small crowd had gathered. One well-meaning man tapped on the windshield, trying to calm Craig. A woman shouted at him through the side window, "Don't worry, baby! We'll get you out!"

All this confusion and noise frightened Craig all the more, and his crying turned to red-faced screaming. A passing Westlake policeman, seeing the crowd around my car, pulled into the station and joined the throng.

He offered to use a tire iron to crack the window, but I convinced him to try his door jimmy. He slipped it into the channel by the window and fished around for a minute or two. There was a click, and the lock popped up. Craig was rescued.

As he grew older we learned that Craig was less than impressed by some of the things we showed him. Traveling with a tour group to Alaska, for example, we got up at 3 a.m. to ride sixty miles through mountain passes in an old school bus for one of the truly magnificent sights in the Western world, Mount McKinley in Denali National Park. Guides told us that almost three-quarters of the people who make the trek never get to see the whole mountain; because it is so high, it makes its own weather and is often sheathed in clouds. But this morning was special. The sun was shining, and, as we rounded a bend, we could see the mountain thirty miles ahead, bathed in sunshine, not a cloud in sight.

Even our guide, who drove the bus along this route daily, was bubbling over with excitement and whipped out a camera to join us roadside as we clicked pictures of each other with the mountain at our back. Since we were taping for WJW, I got some reactions of folks aboard the bus. When I approached Craig with a microphone and asked what he thought, he looked at the mountains surrounding us and at the towering peaks of Mount McKinley, and said into the camera, with the disinterest that only a teenager can display, "You see one mountain, you've seen them all."

BREAKFAST WITH THE GOVERNOR

Bonnie was able to travel with me occasionally, although our schedules did not often mesh, and we were honored over the years to be invited on several of the Ohio familiarization tours, as they were called. On several of them, the Voinoviches mentioned that Bonnie and I should visit the governor's historic official residence when we were in Columbus.

We had always thought that they were being gracious and that the invitation wasn't really serious. I mean, Neil and Bonnie Zurcher just drop in at the Governor's Mansion because we're in the neighborhood? Yeah, right.

We had an attitude adjustment in December 1996, when I had an appointment to do a story on the governor's newly renovated statehouse office. Someone from his staff called shortly before Christmas and asked if I could do the story that Friday. I started to tell her I was on vacation when she said that the governor would personally lead the tour if I could do the story then. I decided I could spare a day of vacation. The next day the governor's office called again. Since I was coming to Columbus, could my wife join me? And could both of us join Governor and Mrs. Voinovich for breakfast at their residence before he went to the statehouse?

I guess they really meant those invitations. I said yes.

When I got home that night, I casually mentioned to Bonnie that we were invited to have breakfast with the governor and his wife on the Friday before Christmas.

"What am I supposed to wear?" she asked.

"I don't know," I replied. "Clothes, I guess."

"You didn't even ask what we're supposed to wear?" she demanded.

I don't think much about clothes. People who know me well know that I consider "dressed up" to be a pressed set of faded denims and maybe a sweater over a faded favorite shirt. Actually, come to think of it, that's usually what I wear when I'm not dressed up, too. My wife, however, takes such matters much more seriously.

"Would you please call them back and just ask if it's a 'dress-up' breakfast?" she asked. "Also find out if there will be a lot of people there, and maybe we can find out what they are wearing."

So I called the woman at the governor's office and was told it would be informal, probably with just the Voinoviches, the two of us, and a mutual friend. I reported back to Bonnie, who asked me what an "informal breakfast" meant.

"It probably means they'll have robes on over their pajamas," I joked. She didn't see the humor.

"You have got to find out what we are supposed to wear," she insisted.

So I called the governor's office again. "What should we wear to the breakfast with the governor?" I asked. I suspect the woman there was getting a little tired of my daily calls about the breakfast. "Oh," she said, "just wear whatever you normally wear."

I interpreted that to be my daily attire of faded jeans, old shirt, sweater, and my favorite mustard-yellow jacket. I told Bonnie that the governor's office had said just wear whatever, that it was very informal. Furthermore, because we would be driving to Dayton to visit my daughter's family after breakfast, I suggested that traveling clothes would be just fine. With misgivings, Bonnie finally agreed.

On the morning of the breakfast, Bonnie put on a comfortable pair of slacks, some low shoes, and a sweatshirt that proclaimed "Ohio Is for the Birds," picturing some cardinals frolicking in the snow. We walked to the front door of the mansion and rang the doorbell.

The housekeeper opened the door and invited us in, just as a perfectly coiffed Janet Voinovich came down the stairs to meet us, wearing a smartly styled suit. My wife's eyes shot daggers at me. Janet seemed to take no notice. She gave each of us a hug and took us on a brief tour of the residence while we waited for the governor. Moments later, Bonnie dug her fingernails into my hand as the governor joined us, dressed in a suit and tie. As we went into the dining room to sit down for breakfast, my wife whispered in my ear, "You're dead meat!"

Actually, it was a very enjoyable breakfast. George and Janet Voinovich treated us like old friends, and as we traded stories I think Bonnie forgot to be uncomfortable about our casual attire. If we ever get invited to the White House, however, my wife assures me that *she* will decide what we wear.

TOURING WITH THE GOVERNOR

I've had many memorable trips over the years, but one that particularly sticks in my mind was a dinner by candlelight in a century-old log cabin, tucked away in the hills of southern Ohio. Our hosts were the governor and first lady of Ohio.

Then-governor George Voinovich invited Bonnie and me to join him and his wife, Janet, on a bus tour of tourist attractions in southern Ohio with a group of travel writers from around the country. The trip aimed to boost Ohio tourism and to underline tourism's importance to Ohio by having its chief executive lead the tour.

One out-of-state writer, in fact, later told me she accepted the invitation just to see if the governor would really show up to take part. She expected him to drop in sometime over the weekend, give a talk to the writers and leave, leaving underlings to lead the tour. She joined the tour just as the bus was leaving. When we arrived at our first destination, she asked when the governor was going to arrive and was shocked to learn that the nice couple chatting with her on the bus—the ones wearing sweatshirts and walking shoes who had just introduced themselves as George and

Janet—were the governor and first lady. They didn't even lead the tour, really. They just joined the rest of us in wandering in and out of attractions, asking as many questions as the writers did of the people at each destination.

The first evening ended at the Inn at Cedar Falls, a hundred-plus-year-old log cabin and complex located in the heart of the Hocking Hills State Park. It was a beautiful autumn night, and candles glowed in each of the cabin's windows. Inside, innkeeper Ellen Grinsfelder and her staff had been working to prepare a gourmet feast for the writers and the governor and his staff. During dinner, the governor and Mrs. Voinovich table-hopped, talking with all of the writers and reminiscing about their affection for the Hocking Hills. George said he first discovered the area when he was a student at nearby Ohio University. Janet Voinovich remembered when their children were small and the whole family would rent a cabin for a vacation there.

Our accommodations for the night were in a converted barn behind the cabin. Each room, while rustic, had a bathroom and electricity—but no TV, no radio, and no clock! As dinner ended, we wandered up the path to our rooms, the path illuminated only by moonlight. In the morning we were fed a wonderful gourmet breakfast and had time to wander the gardens around the cabin, where many of the dining room's herbs and vegetables are grown.

The inn sits in the middle of the 10,000-acre Hocking Hills State Park. It is only minutes away from some of Ohio's most famous attractions, like Old Man's Cave and Ash Cave, with miles of trails to hike and wonderful rock formations to see. While autumn is spectacular, each season lends a special beauty to the park system.

THE STAND

Not all of our adventures were on the road. In 1990, Bonnie and I decided to explore the world of self-employment as the trial run of something we might like to do when I finally tired of One Tank Trips and retired. We had long thought about operating "The Stand," a soda fountain and restaurant at Linwood Park in Vermilion. When the operator did not renew his lease, we suddenly had the opportunity to take over the business. Little did we know what we were getting ourselves into.

Our first lesson arrived in April when we surveyed the stand after signing the lease. Not only was the building sixty years old, but all the equipment with it was old, worn out, and often not working. I frantically called companies that lease industrial refrigerators, coolers, and restaurant equipment. My first lesson: Most would lease to us only by the year. Because we only planned to open during June, July, and August, they weren't interested.

My second lesson: Even used equipment like coolers and commercial refrigerators can cost thousands of dollars—thousands more than we projected we would make that summer. Since we weren't sure we would want to run it for more than one year, we were reluctant to invest in the new equipment. The park, which owned "The Stand," was sympathetic to us and offered to pay for a new stove, on which Bonnie hoped to duplicate recipes from a long-gone hotel that once graced the park's lakefront. But they balked at replacing coolers and refrigerators. That was our responsibility.

I finally solved that dilemma through a friend, Kevin Ruic, who had just closed a racetrack he operated and put several coolers and refrigerators in storage. Toft Dairy in Sandusky, whose ice cream we planned to carry, felt sorry for us and rented us a used ice-cream dipping cooler for the summer. We were finally ready to open.

That was when we discovered the wonderful world of teenage help. We could only afford to pay minimum wage—although the local burger chains were paying a dollar to a dollar and a half above it. Once when we found teenagers willing to work for us, we learned about band camp, cheerleader camp, football practice, and a host of other activities that teenagers are expected to attend during the summer. It left less than a month when we were not desperately trying to fill a shift left vacant by a teen going off to cheerleader camp.

By pressing my sister-in-law, Susan Nager, into double duty as bookkeeper and soda fountain clerk, and hiring a young woman just out of high school, we staggered through the summer of 1990—when, you may remember, it rained on eleven of the fourteen weekends.

Did I say staggered? We lurched from one crisis to another. The night before the Fourth of July—the biggest single weekend of the summer—someone forgot to close the upright freezer in the back room where our ice cream and meat products were stored. Did I mention the building was not air conditioned? We had gallons and gallons of ice-cream soup in the morning, and pounds and pounds of rotting hamburgers and hot dogs.

Then there was the evening the park board of directors held an ice-cream social just across the lawn from our store, effectively killing our ice-cream business for the night. To add insult to injury, they bought their ice cream from a store outside the park.

The whole summer was like that. Tragedy was added to the mix when my father suddenly passed away. Our experiment had become the worst of times. I vividly remember working alone in the store late one night after spending the entire day on the road on a One Tank Trip. The temperature was still in the upper 80s at 11 p.m. that night when I closed the stand and started to mop the floors. When I counted the day's receipts, I discovered that we had made $14.25 in eleven hours. I decided I wasn't meant for the restaurant business and would be better off traveling and writing about people who were.

A VACATION FROM HELL

I am constantly asked, "Where do you go on your personal vacations?" I usually respond with a grimace and a shudder as I recall my own Vacation from Hell.

We had decided to take a family trip to Wyoming to visit my stepbrother, Jim Birrell, and his family. Because my father and stepmother were coming with us, we decided to drive, rather than fly, and see a bit of the country.

The trip started nicely. I packed our four-door Cadillac with Bonnie, Craig (who was about seven years old), my father Oscar, and my stepmother Edna. The drive went smoothly until the third day. I was behind the wheel as we entered Nebraska.

A series of billboards proclaiming North Platte as the home of Scout's Rest, Buffalo Bill Cody's ranch, piqued our interest. It was a blazing hot day in the Nebraska flatlands, and the local radio station said the temperature was approaching 100 degrees as we pulled into the ranch's parking lot. With the sun high in the sky, I grabbed my prescription sunglasses from the sun visor and tossed my regular glasses onto the dash of the car as we climbed out to start our tour.

We spent a pleasant two hours touring the home and barns of the famous Wild West star. As we returned to the parking lot, I winced as I grabbed the sun-baked door handle to open the car. We all climbed in, and I reached for my regular eyeglasses on the dash. As I put them on, the world seemed to turn a milky blue. I ripped off the glasses. What had been two optically ground plastic lenses were now two oblong globs of plastic. My glasses had melted in the Nebraska heat!

This was before one-hour eyeglass stores in malls and shopping centers. Besides, there were no malls or shopping centers near North Platte. I had no choice but to put on my prescription sunglasses and wear them for the rest of the trip. It caused some curious glances, especially at night when we would walk into a dimly lit restaurant and Bonnie would have to guide me across the room to my seat.

On our fourth day, after we dropped Dad and Edna at stepbrother Jim's home in Cheyenne, Bonnie, Craig, and I continued to Cody, Wyoming, planning to see the famous Cody Rodeo.

Clouds were building as we drove to the outdoor arena that afternoon to buy tickets for the evening performance. The place was nearly sold out, and the only tickets still available were the most expensive. I handed over eighty dollars for three passes, and we went back to our motel to cool off and check out the pool. But by the time we got there, the sky had darkened and lightning was painting the horizon. Instead of swimming, we spent the afternoon huddled in our tiny motel room, listening to the grandmother of all western storms crash and bang around us.

It was hours before the storm subsided and the power, which failed early in the storm, came back on. Now the wind began to howl. I stepped outside to find the temperature had plummeted and the sun was hidden behind low, fast-moving gray clouds that gave a look of November to the July afternoon.

We drove to the arena, our car rocking back and forth in winds that the local radio station said was "gusting at speeds of up to 70 miles per hour." Dodging the rolling sagebrush and wind-borne debris, I turned to Bonnie and said, "Surely they will cancel the rodeo." But the parking lot was filled.

We clung to each other as we leaned into the wind, trying to make it to the entrance. A lady with a beehive hairdo sat in a small booth taking tickets at the gate.

"It's a bit windy tonight," she offered, as she snatched my tickets and punched them, handing the stubs back to me.

"You mean the rodeo is still on?" I asked incredulously.

"Oh, it's just a bit breezy, darlin'," she replied. "You should have been here last week when it was really windy."

"I think I would like a refund, or tickets for tomorrow night, when it's less windy," I said.

"Sorry, darlin'," she answered. "There is no refunds if the rodeo goes on. We've never missed a show, except durin' World War II."

We staggered into the stadium. My eyes, behind dark glasses, were stinging from the flying sand, and we were choking on clouds of dust. We finally found our seats—in open bleachers facing the full fury of the storm that lashed the dusty field serving as the arena.

We caught glimpses of bucking horses and cowboys flying through the air when the wind momentarily abated. Most of the time, we were covering our faces to keep from swallowing the dust. The howl of the wind covered much of the sound of cowboys, cattle, and horses. It was especially fun, when we could see, to watch the steer-roping competition. When the cowboys tried to lasso the steers, their ropes blew back, encircling them and their horses, while the steers merrily chased dust clouds around the arena. The wind began to die just as the evening mercifully came to an end.

But our problems were not over.

We returned to Cheyenne a few days later to pick up my father and stepmother for the trip home. We had decided to take the northern route through South Dakota for some sightseeing. Our first stop was at Mount Rushmore in the Black Hills.

Dad had an artificial leg, so he usually rode with me in the front seat for extra room. After we parked at Mount Rushmore, all of us got out of the car except him. "What's Oscar waiting for?" Edna asked.

"He must be listening to some music he likes," I replied, noting that I could see his head bobbing back and forth through the rear window.

I decided to hurry him along because the golf cart and guide we had arranged to take him and Edna to the viewing area had arrived. I walked to the passenger door and saw that instead of bobbing in the time of the music, Dad seemed to be thrashing around all over his side of the car.

I opened the car door and was greeted with a fusillade of obscenities. He shouted something about his hand. Then I saw he had apparently grabbed the post between the front and back doors when Edna got out of the car, preparing to use it as a lever to swing himself out. Not noticing, she slammed the door, trapping his hand. Fortunately for him, the car had large rubber gaskets around each door that cushioned the blow. We took him to a first-aid station, where it appeared that the fingers were badly bruised but not broken.

More trouble followed.

Late that afternoon, as we continued our eastward journey along Interstate 90, clouds to the north grew darker and darker. It looked like a real prairie storm was brewing. Edna suggested several times that we should stop for the day and wait it out. My father and I agreed that the storm appeared to be far to the north and that we could probably drive around it. But the sky grew more ominous. I had to turn on my headlights. Sagebrush rolled across the prairie on both sides of the road. Clouds of dust at times obliterated the sky. Ahead I could see an overpass, sheltering several motorcyclists parked there. One of them suddenly ran to the edge of the road, pointed at my oncoming car, and waved his hands in a frantic way. The world turned liquid just then as a cloudburst smashed down on us. I wrestled with the wheel, trying to see. When the wind lifted the rain from the car for a moment, I saw an off-ramp and took it.

At that second, the rear of the car lifted off the road and then slammed back down, as if a giant hand had picked us up and then dropped us. I slammed on the brakes and skidded to a stop just short of a brick building. I yelled at everyone to put on their seat belts. The car was rocking back and forth in the wind, and I feared it might roll over. It didn't, but the rear window was unable to withstand the wind's assault. Broken glass and the storm's roar exploded into the car.

Then, just as suddenly as it had started, it was over. The storm abated, and we climbed shakily out of the car to assess damage. Craig was bleeding from a finger, but Bonnie quickly determined it was only a superficial cut. The building in front of us turned out to be a combination gasoline station and restaurant, so she took Craig inside to find a bandage. Looking at our car, we saw paint was sandblasted down to bare metal. Where it wasn't, pieces of grit and straw were embedded in the paint. Inside, where there had been trim painted to look like wood, there was now bright silver. Some hubcaps were gone, as was the rear window.

We were in Kimball, South Dakota, population 150. A tornado had just struck, leaving some cars and vans turned over on the interstate highway. As we drove through the tiny town looking for a Cadillac dealer to replace our windows, we could see the tops of trees gone, chimneys toppled, roofs missing. Power was out, and I-90 to the east was blocked. We decided to head back to the last town we had passed for assistance.

The local Cadillac-Chevrolet-Buick-Pontiac-John Deere tractor dealer assured us he could fix our window—as long as we could wait three or four days while parts were shipped by bus from Sioux City.

We decided it was time to end this vacation. Window or no window, it was time to head home. The local dealer gave us directions to a hardware store, where we bought some heavy clear plastic sheeting and duct tape. We limped home looking like the Okies of the Great Depression: plastic flapping in the wind, our mud-spattered car without hubcaps. We drew crowds wherever we stopped and had to tell and retell the story about "Vacation from Hell."

A SAD TRIP

Through the wool of my sleep-clogged brain I could hear knocking.

"Mr. Zurcher!"

I thought it was just a weird dream. Then I heard it again—a loud knock followed by someone's muffled shout.

"Mr. Zurcher! Park rangers!"

Craig and I were sharing a room in a remote cabin at Salt Fork State Park. I woke with a start as the pounding on the cabin door continued. I stumbled to the door and found two rangers standing under a nightlight over the doorway.

"Mr. Zurcher?" one of the rangers asked. "You have an emergency phone call from your wife. She asks that you call immediately."

I looked at my watch. It was about 1:30 in the morning. "Is she all right?" I asked. "Did she say what the emergency was?"

The rangers said their dispatcher had only told them that Bonnie had asked me to call home immediately, and it was an emergency.

They suggested I might want to go to the Salt Fork Lodge to use a phone since the cabins had none and cell phones worked only sporadically in the rural area.

I went to the second bedroom and awakened Bob Begany, the photographer on this One Tank Trip, and asked him to keep an eye on nine-year-old Craig, who was still sleeping, while I drove our news cruiser to the lodge about a mile away.

It was a beautiful night in early summer, and a predawn ground fog drifting through the trees gave the scenery an otherworldly appearance in my headlights.

Herds of deer wandered freely among the trees, seemingly unconcerned. I had to drive very slowly to avoid striking the animals that seemed to have only disdain for my presence on the roadway.

There was a bridge to the front door of the lodge, and three deer were standing on it as though watching the comings and goings of the night crew inside the lobby. They seemed reluctant to move. Inside, a clerk pointed me to a pay phone. I dialed home with shaking hands, and Bonnie answered almost immediately.

Once she heard my voice she said without preamble, "Honey, your Dad passed away this evening."

I slumped down beside the telephone.

Bonnie said he had died while preparing for bed after watching the Cleveland Indians' game on television. They thought it was probably a heart attack. He was eighty-three years old. My daughters, Melody and Melissa, had already been informed.

After talking a few more moments, I hung up and stumbled out the door to head back to the cabin. Ten or twelve deer grouped around my car. My vision was blurred by tears, but it seemed that the deer dropped their heads in a look of sadness that matched mine.

As I made the slow drive through the fog-laced park back to

the cabin, I recalled phoning my father at home last evening. Bob, Craig, and I had been in nearby Cambridge to eat dinner at a local restaurant, and I used its pay phone to call Dad to tell him about our day. It had been a pleasant afternoon, doing a series about houseboat rentals. We cruised the man-made lake at Salt Fork State Park in a houseboat, cooked lunch in the galley, and ate on the deck. We fished, shot video, and then checked into a cabin for the night. Now my father, Oscar Zurcher, was gone. Dad had been a friend as well as my father. When I reached the cabin, I wiped my eyes, took a deep breath, and went inside. Bob was dressed and sitting in the kitchen drinking coffee. I told him what had happened and asked him to give me a few minutes to awaken Craig and tell him the news. Bob started to pack our gear. Craig throughout his life has had trouble showing emotion. You only know how deeply he is hurting by his actions.

As gently as I could, I told him his beloved grandpa had died. He said very little, just asking if we would go home. I said we would, and he rolled over and appeared to go back to sleep while Bob and I packed the car and contacted rangers to leave the keys.

I awoke Craig and led him to the car. He climbed into the backseat. I asked him if he had any questions or needed anything. He said no, and stared into the night in silence.

Because I was familiar with the park roads and the hazard of deer, I drove the first five miles to get us onto the interstate highway, where Bob took over so I could call relatives and my assistant, Patti Braskie, and ask her to cancel the week's planned activities and interviews. We reached WJW a couple of hours later, dropped off Bob and the station wagon, and picked up our car to drive home. Bonnie came out to meet us. We stood silently in the driveway, holding each other.

1. Summer of 1942 at Linwood Park in Vermilion. I'm wearing the helmet my step-uncle, Hubie Hahn, used to wear while barnstorming in his airplane. I aspired to be a daredevil after watching a motorcyclist perform with Lucky Lott and his Hell Drivers at the county fairgrounds.

2. Zurcher's Henrietta Service on Henrietta Hill, as it looked when my family took it over in 1945. Farmers and their families stopped in for a little food and gossip, and to watch our television (wood-cased, with a seven-inch screen). As I pumped gas out front, I watched travelers speed past on the state highway and longed to go with them.

3. Working in our store at Henrietta Hill in 1950. I'm wearing my father's shirt. Around this time I talked my father into letting me drive, even though I didn't yet have a driver's license. The first time was a disaster.

4. My first red convertible, which I bought at the junkyard for $40. In the back seat are my cousin Marge O'Hair, my brother, Noel, and my grandfather John Zurcher. In the front are my little sister, Caroline, and another cousin, Hollie Fairfield.

5. Betty Steinhour as I remember her, about 1959. Neither of us could have dreamed the tragedy that awaited her. *(Courtesy of Joan Steinhour Wilson)*

6. Collecting toys for the Marine Corps Toys for Tots drive in Oberlin in 1954 (with Captain William Hewetson). Little did I know that this news photo would lead to my start in journalism. *(Oberlin News-Tribune)*

7. An early shot of me at the microphone in the Elyria Studios of WEOL. I would spend the first part of the day in Elyria, then drive about nine miles to Lorain to broadcast later in the day from the radio station's other studio, located in the Antlers Hotel.

8. Shooting film for WJW-TV at a jailbreak in Elyria. With me is Walter Glendenning (center) who talked me into buying my first 16mm camera, and Ray Goll, who also freelanced for Cleveland TV stations. *(Claire Glendenning Boose)*

9. Images of Pittsfield, Ohio on the morning of April 12, 1965, the day after the community was destroyed by a tornado, which killed nine people. Just hours before the tornado hit, my family and I enjoyed a quiet lunch in a small park in the center of town. That night I returned to find only wreckage. I spent nearly two days covering the disaster.

10. When I started working for WJW-TV full-time in 1967, I was a general assignment reporter. For many years I covered news stories such as the Civil Rights battle, and I interviewed the Reverend Dr. Martin Luther King, Jr., many times when he came to Cleveland. This photo was taken on his last trip to Cleveland, shortly before he was assassinated.

11. There were two blasts at the Ohio Penitentiary on August 21, 1968: one on the roof, and the other in the side of the cell block where guards were being held hostage. This is a scene as the Ohio State Troopers charged into the hole left by the blast. I was right behind them.

12. National Guard troops arriving at the old state penitentiary in Columbus on August 20, 1968, after prisoners rioted and took nine guards hostage.

13. I got involved in a lot of on-camera stunts for WJW-TV. This was at Cleveland Public Auditorium. A trapeze artist invited me to ride to the top of the auditorium on her trapeze. I did it, but what she suggested when we got to the top of the auditorium really shocked me.

14. I didn't know the rope was slowly disintegrating as I climbed down the front of the WJW-TV studios at Playhouse Square. Photographer Ralph Tarsitano was leading a crowd chanting "Jump, jump!"

15. On the back of an elephant just as the race was about to start. A few seconds later the elephant bolted and gave me the scare of my life.

16. Here I am standing in front of a five-foot-tall frog in Valley City, home of the Jumping Frog Festival. This event gave Dick Goddard the idea for the Woollybear Festival.

17. Most of the news staff of WJW-TV, in 1969, in an alley behind our Playhouse Square studios. Left to right (back row): Truman Foster, film editor; Hal Morgan, WJW radio; David Williams, TV photographer; Roger Powell, TV photographer; Pete Cary, reporter; Bill Feest, news director; Dick Goddard, weatherman; Neil Zurcher, reporter; Cory Lash, TV photographer; Peter Miller, TV photographer; Chuck Sanders, TV photographer. Left to right (front row): Cook Goodwin, chief photographer; Bob Kasarda, TV photographer, Ralph Tarsitano, TV photographer; Bob Begany, TV photographer. *(WJW-TV)*

18. On assignment in Washington, D.C. in the 1970s with former news director Norm Wagy, who was then Washington bureau chief for Storer Broadcasting.

19. At the Circus Vargas I rode on a trapeze beneath a motorcycle, which balanced on a steel cable and took me over a cage filled with tigers and lions. I didn't dare look down. As we prepared to start the ride on the cable over the lion's cage, they tied my hands to the side of the trapeze to make sure I didn't fall off. I suspect they were afraid I would change my mind.

20. The presiding bishop of the Free Spirit Association Church, Inc. This formal portrait was taken as a gag by one of the church members, George West, who owned a photo studio in Parma Heights. I actually presided over a couple of weddings. (George West)

21. This Greyhound bus was converted into a luxury RV by Hudson industrialist John Morse and his wife, Helen. They lent it to Lorain County police officers to carry some orphaned youngsters to one of the first Operation Open Heart outings. In the picture are former Ohio State patrolman David Harper, Helen Morse, TV8 photographers Bob Begany and Roger Powell, me, and Chuck Schodowski.

22. A summer picnic of members of the board of the Free Spirit Association Church in the summer of 1974. From left to right: Julie Ann Cashel, "Vicar" Dick Goddard, "Bishop" Lisa Tarr, "Presiding Bishop" Neil Zurcher, "Bishop" John Tarr, "Bishop" John Gullo, "Bishop" Jeff Maynor, "Bishop" Gary Carruthers, "Bishop" Jim Hale. *(Jim Hale)*

23. My good friend Johnny Tarr surprising me with a birthday cake at the Bit of Budapest Restaurant in Parma Heights. John was certainly one of the most unforgettable people I met in my years of travel.

24. Photographer Bob Begany covering an early morning fire in Ravenna when the temperature was minus 5 degrees. This shot proves we weren't always on "One Tank Trips."

25. My very first "One Tank Trips" car. It was my fifth birthday. Check out the license plate. It was an old plate from my father's company car.

26. Getting ready to shoot an opening scene with one of the first cars we used for "One Tank Trips," borrowed from Bill and Bonnie Cutcher of Brownhelm. It was an American Bantam made in Butler, Pennsylvania.

27. As "One Tank Trips" grew in popularity, I needed a publicity photo because people started writing the station asking for pictures . . . of the car. The little 1959 Nash Metropolitan was the car we used the most during twenty-five years of "One Tank Trips." *(WJW-TV)*

28. My diminutive BMW Isetta looked like a refrigerator on wheels. It was the most cantankerous car I ever owned. It was used on "One Tank Trips" for just fifteen months.

29. In the early 2000s I purchased this fiberglass replica of a 1929 Ford Model A. We used it on the air for only a short time because it failed to catch on with our viewers, who wanted the little Nash Metropolitan back.

30. A publicity shot for a "One Tank Trips" newspaper ad, taken at the Western Reserve Historical Society's Crawford Auto Museum. *(WJW-TV/ Chet Roberts)*

31. Getting ready for another season of "One Tank Trips" on TV8. Photographer Chet Roberts gets prepared to do a roadside "standup" with me.

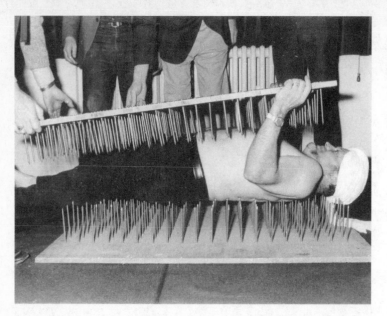

32. Vernon "Komar" Craig demonstrating his ability to lie sandwiched between two beds of nails while bystanders climbed on top. I first met him when he was managing a cheese and gift shop in Amish country and had no idea about his secret identity.

33. With Komar at the IX Center at the TV8 booth handing out "One Tank Trips" booklets. He broke his ankle on the way to meet me but ignored the pain.

34. The infamous T-shirt decals for the Neil Zurcher Fan Club. There were stacks of these in closets at TV8 for years after.

35. Getting ready to parasail over Sandusky Bay. I took a camera along and thought I was pretty brave to snap several pictures two hundred feet in the air. The captain set me straight when I landed.

36. One of my strangest stunts ever, skydiving inside a building. It's called "Flyaway." An airplane propeller in the basement sends up a column of air strong enough to make a human float.
(John Paustain)

37. The day we invaded Milan. This shot happened as I was driving my tiny BMW Isetta into the gravel pit area and suddenly found myself nose-to-nose with an M60 tank. The picture was taken by longtime friend Marvin Barr. *(Marvin Barr)*

38. Yep, that's me surrounded by a bevy of the high-kicking New York Radio City Music Hall Rockettes. I didn't manage to kick so high.

39. For this *Cleveland Magazine* cover I traded in my usual blue jeans for a tux and stood in front of the city skyline to help make the headline more convincing. At least *Cleveland Magazine* let me keep my cap. My formal outfit and the Nash attracted a surprising proposition on the drive home from the photo shoot.

40. My wife Bonnie helped design this Cupid costume for a weird publicity shot to promote a series of "One Tank Trips" we did for Valentine's Day. *(Bonnie Zurcher)*

41. Governor George and First Lady Janet Voinovich with Bonnie and me on one of the several "Fam" tours the governor led promoting Ohio tourism for the national travel media.

42 My son Craig, TV8 photographer Bill Wolfe, and me on board the *Crown Princess* on our longest One Tank Trip ever—to Alaska. For this trip, we had to make an exception to our one-tank-of-gas rule.

43. Returning from the last televised "One Tank Trip" in July 2004. To my right are producer Lisa March and photographer Ali Ghanbari. The car was a 1993 Geo Convertible, the last car I purchased to use on the series. It matched the others in size but had air conditioning and a working heater as well as an automatic transmission.

44. With my father, Oscar Zurcher, in the mid-1980s He gave me my love for travel in Ohio.

45. The whole family gathers for my induction into the National Academy of Television Arts and Sciences Silver Circle in 1999. From left to right: my son-in-law Peter Luttmann, my daughter Melissa Luttmann, Bonnie, me, my son Craig, my son-in-law Dr. Ernest McCallister, my daughter Melody McCallister.

46. The next generation: my grandkids, Allison McCallister, Bryan McCallister, Ryan Luttmann and Jason Luttmann. *(Melissa Luttmann)*

47. Bonnie and I donated the BMW Isetta to the Canton Classic Car Museum, and after my retirement from TV made a long-term loan of the Nash Metropolitan to the museum. You can see both cars there today.

48. The former Zurcher's Henrietta Service sits vacant today. Going back to look at the old building brought back a flood of memories for me.

CHAPTER 6

Hotels and Motels

THE ADVENTURE OF FINDING A MOTEL

On one of our first trips, to the National Museum of the United States Air Force in Dayton, videographer Bill West and I decided to stay overnight and do more taping the next day.

We had no reservations anywhere. It was almost dark when we finished for the day and started our search for a motel. Not far from the museum, a sign said, "OTEL."

The door to the office was locked. A clerk motioned us to the side of the building, where a small window was equipped with an intercom and guarded by bulletproof glass.

A tinny voice asked if we had reservations. I said that we didn't but were looking for two single rooms for the night.

A metal drawer, like those in all-night gas stations, popped out of the wall and hit me in the stomach. Inside were two registration forms.

"That'll be forty dollars per room, each!" announced the tinny voice from the intercom.

Bill, who was studying the spray-painted graffiti on the motel's walls and had noted an abandoned car in its parking lot, suggested we look at the rooms before handing over our money.

The clerk looked slightly offended but agreed to meet us at the front door.

The three of us walked to a row of rooms next to a large, smelly dumpster at the rear of the complex. The doors to the rooms had three dead-bolt locks each. The clerk pulled a ring of keys from his belt and started searching. After opening all the locks to the first room, he turned the handle and pushed. Nothing happened. He finally put his shoulder against the door, gave a hard shove, and the door swung open.

Inside were a metal-framed bed, a small table, two mismatched chairs, and a television set that looked as though it belonged in a museum. I walked to the bed and sat down to check the mattress. My chin nearly hit my knees as the bed sagged to the floor under my weight.

"I don't think we want this room," Bill said as he helped me up.

"No problem," the clerk replied. "I show you another one. Much better."

He led us around the corner to a side of the motel hidden from the highway, where two large, surly guard dogs paced back and forth in a fenced-in area, growling.

"Uh, what are the guard dogs for?" I asked.

"Oh, we keep them in the office at night to discourage hold-ups," the clerk replied with a smile.

He led us to another room that also had three locks. This time the door sprung open as soon as the locks were released. The room was decorated as plainly as the other one. I walked to the bed but did not sit down. I just leaned over and pushed on the mattress.

It was like pushing on the floor, as hard as a rock. As I straightened up, I noticed several dead bugs, feet up on the windowsill, while a few others, looking suspiciously like cockroaches, scurried for cover.

Bill saw them, too, and headed for the door. I followed. The clerk pursued us down the driveway.

"How 'bout I give you a better price?" the clerk said.

"No!" we both answered.

"I give you both rooms for twenty dollars a night," he said.

"No!" we answered.

"I make it fifteen dollars a night," he said.

We kept walking.

"Hokay," the clerk shouted after us, "I give you my best deal—ten dollars a night!"

We drove off, leaving the clerk standing in the middle of the driveway.

Hours later, at a point where we were considering sleeping in the car, we finally located rooms in a large chain motel. But our adventure in lodging was not over yet.

About three in the morning, a roar that sounded like an explosion or a tornado brought me out of a sound sleep and to my feet. With heart racing, I stumbled to the door and peeked out. There in the hall were about a dozen bikers who apparently were having a convention. After a bit of overindulging, one of them had just won a bet that he could ride his motorcycle up the stairs and down the hall.

After that, we always asked the desk clerk if any conventions were going on, and we always asked to see the room before we registered.

BACK ROADS OF OHIO'S AMISH LAND

It was a foggy spring morning. It had rained almost all night, but the mist was burning away as the sun teased us with the promise of a balmy day.

Bill West and I had driven to this gravel road in the Doughty Valley, east of Millersburg, to do a report on what I called an "Amish motel," a collection of log cabins operated as a campground by an Amish family. The cabins had just been completed only weeks earlier, and we had convinced the publicity-shy owners that it would be good for business if we showed their new enterprise. We had also promised not to take any pictures of the owners.

The cabins were scattered down a hillside that overlooked the Doughty Creek, which flows through the valley. Across the valley, emerging from the morning fog, you could make out the stainless-steel storage tanks of the Guggisberg Cheese Company.

I stepped out of our car and immediately noticed a strong odor of horse manure. But being in Amish Country, where horses are the main means of transportation, I gave it little thought. Bill was setting up his camera as I walked to the edge of the hillside for a good look at the cabins. The wet ground was covered with straw. I stepped onto the steep path heading towards the cabins and felt my feet start to slip. I threw up my arms to regain my balance, but both feet went out from under me. I landed on my back and started to slide down the hill, through the mud and straw. When I finally came to a stop about thirty feet down, I knew where the smell of horse manure had come from. They had just seeded the hillside and spread fresh manure for fertilizer. I was now coated from my head to my heels with a mixture of horse dung, straw, and wet mud.

Bill and an Amish woman came skidding down the hill to help. They helped me to my feet, both trying—not too successfully—to smother their laughter as I stood up, mud and dung dripping from my hair, my back, and my legs.

"Where's the bathroom?" I asked the Amish lady.

She covered her mouth with one hand to disguise a smile and used the other to point to a small wooden building at the bottom of the hill.

"There it is," she said, "but there's no running water here."

"Where's the nearest place I can clean myself up?" I asked.

She pointed across the valley towards the Guggisberg Cheese Company's store.

I started walking up the hill to our news cruiser. As I approached the door, Bill jumped in front of me and said, "Where are you going?"

I was going to get in the car and have him drive me to the cheese company to use their modern bathroom, I said.

"You're not going to get in my news cruiser like that!" he said, refusing to budge.

"Well, how am I supposed to get over there, then?" I snapped. He pointed to the hood of the car.

A few minutes later, clinging to the hood of the news cruiser, spread-eagle across it like some large animal bagged in a hunt, I was driven down the hill and across the valley, past startled Amish families in buggies, and to the cheese factory where I was finally able to wash up.

SMOKE AND FIRE NORTH OF THE BORDER

Videographer John "JP" Paustian and I had traveled to Canada to do a series on places to stay north of the border. An old gristmill converted into a comfortable inn in the tiny town of Elora, Ontario, was one of the more delightful stops. The town had been built more a century earlier by Scottish immigrants, and it did look like a Scottish village. Low stone walls enclosed some of the homes; cobblestone streets and sidewalks meandered up and down the rolling terrain, and at the foot of one street stood the Elora Inn, once the Elora gristmill, built over a small stream. Water rushed in one side of the building, turned a wheel, and continued downstream on the other side. The old mill wheel had been converted to an electric generator that supplied power for the inn and a good part of the town.

The inn's attractions were a kitchen, whose gourmet dishes drew customers from a hundred miles away, and its rooms. My room, with exposed beams and a rustic look, had walls two feet thick. The builders of the structure had meant for it to last a long time. JP wanted some way to visually impart the beauty of the room and its spartan furnishings.

"Why don't you climb into bed," he said, "and I'll turn off the lights. We'll illuminate the room as though moonlight is coming in the window, and we'll hear the sound of the river and see you sleeping."

I agreed, put on pajamas, and climbed into bed beneath a window with a two-foot-wide sill. JP put a stand holding the large television lights in the window well. Then, using a series of shutters, he directed a small beam of light through a filter onto my face. The effect was just what he hoped for. The rest of the light lit the room softly, showing the bare walls and creating a feeling of warmth and great age.

While he set up his camera, I lay in bed idly looking around. On the ceiling above me was the nozzle of a sprinkler system for fire protection. Next to it was a round box, apparently a smoke detector, with a small flashing red light. My eyes drifted to the window well, where the light stand was situated. The shutters on the light were brand new, and the heat of the big television bulbs was starting to cook the paint. A thin wisp of smoke drifted up towards the top of the window well and into the room.

"JP," I said, "there's some smoke coming from the 'barn doors' on your light, and there's a smoke detector right above your head. I wonder if . . ."

Beeeeeeeeeeep! A shrill scream suddenly came from the smoke detector. We both jumped.

"The sprinklers!" I shouted. "We've got to shut off the damn alarm before the sprinklers go off!"

JP leaped into the air and grabbed the shrieking smoke detector with both hands, trying to twist off the cover to reach the battery. Unfortunately, the detector was not battery-powered. It was wired into the ceiling. As JP crashed back to the floor with the cover in his hands, he brought with him a piece of the ceiling and the wiring. Pieces of plaster showered down on me in the bed, and we could hear other alarms going off in the hallway.

I grabbed the phone in an attempt to reach the front desk to advise them there was no fire. The operator cut in, asked me to hang up because the hotel had an emergency, and hung up before I could tell him that we were the cause.

"Oh, my God, listen to that," JP said. "They must have called the local fire department."

We could hear the low wail of fire engines and other emergency vehicles getting louder and louder.

JP had managed to yank the wires off what was left of the smoke alarm, and the shrill alarm was finally stilled. But we could hear other alarms in the hall and the voices of people coming out of their rooms to see what the commotion was about.

I ran to the window and looked down into the courtyard. Fire trucks were coming across the bridge, and people were running towards the inn. I dashed back to the phone and again tried the front desk. This time I convinced the operator to not hang up and to listen as I explained what had happened.

Within seconds, the other alarms were stilled. There was a loud knock at the door. JP answered it to find a gaggle of firemen with axes and a fire hose crowding the hallway.

The fire chief checked the smoke alarm and told inn officials, who had now joined the crowd, that the alarm would have to be checked before the room could be rented again. Then he gave JP and me a lecture about checking such things as the location of smoke alarms before creating conditions that could cause a panic.

When the firemen left, we turned to the inn manager, fully expecting he'd tell us to pack our bags and get out. He said, "We'll have maintenance come up and clean things up a bit, eh? Do give us a call first if you decide to set off any more alarms tonight, all right?"

Even the next morning, when we checked out and offered to pay for the damage to the room, the manager displayed real Canadian hospitality and waved off our offer, saying "You boys gave this town the most excitement we've had in the last six months."

Three days later, JP and I had another encounter with fire alarms, but this one wasn't very funny.

We had pulled into Toronto and checked into the giant Delta Chelsea Hotel. We had looked at small bed and breakfasts and quaint inns during the week, and now we wanted to see what the big metropolitan hotels had to offer. We had a two-bedroom suite with a common entrance on the twenty-second floor.

We had just completed an interview with a hotel official in my bedroom, regaling him with the story of our experience at the Elora Inn, and had been assured that the Delta Chelsea was fireproof, with a good central alarm system. He had been gone only two or three minutes when a klaxon horn went off in the hallway outside our door.

"Well, there goes the fire alarm," JP said, joking.

Then a speaker in the room crackled to life. A man with a heavy accent said something about an emergency. We could not understand anything else he said.

"You know," JP said, "I think I smell smoke."

I sniffed the air. An acrid odor came from the direction of the door.

The public address system blared to life again with the same man in his heavy accent. This time we understood the words "fire" and "tenth and eleventh floors," and a plea to stay off elevators and remain in our rooms.

We both bolted for the door. The hallway outside was filled with heavy black smoke, making it almost impossible to see more than a few feet. An exit sign glowed through the smoke to our left.

"I don't know about you," JP said, "but I'm for getting out of here. We can't understand what the emergency is, and it looks more like the fire is on this floor."

I agreed. I pointed to the exit sign and started for it with JP right behind.

When we opened the door, clouds of dark smoke hit us in the face. Coughing and choking, we grabbed the handrail and started down the pitch-black stairwell, feeling our way, step by step, to the next level down.

We had gone down about three floors when a door above us burst open and a crowd of men and women poured onto the stairs, pushing and shoving, crying and screaming. I was nearly knocked down the stairs, but JP grabbed my arm and pulled me against the wall.

"Let's let them go ahead of us, or we're going to get trampled," he said.

Coughing, I choked out some sort of affirmative answer but deep inside felt my own panic starting to build. The smoke seemed to be getting thicker, and it was becoming difficult to breathe. Maybe the air would be clearer down near the floor. I started to get on my hands and knees. JP felt me sag and grabbed my arm again.

"Come on!" he shouted. "If you stop now, the smoke will get you and you'll die!"

Some dim emergency lights flickered in the stairway, and for the first time I could see the swirling smoke. It was even thicker below us, and it made my eyes sting. I steeled myself, yanked off my jacket, and put it over my head, hoping that breathing through it might cut down some of the smoke I was inhaling.

Still gripping the railing, we felt our way to the fifteenth floor, where we decided to check the corridor to see if we were anywhere near firemen who might take us off the building with ladders. But before we could reach the door, it flew open and another group of panic-stricken people pushed into the stairway, again nearly trampling us in their haste to escape.

The announcement on the public address system was being repeated, and again we could not understand most of it, but we did hear "tenth and eleventh floors."

"Maybe that's where the fire is," I gasped to JP.

"If we can get below those floors, maybe it'll be easier to breathe," he gasped back.

The next few minutes will be forever etched in my memory, a montage of sounds and smells: the sounds of fear as people pushed and shoved by us, the smell of smoke that gagged and choked, and the thought that I might never see my home again.

Suddenly I felt fresh air.

I whipped my jacket off my head. Below us, the stairway was nearly clear of smoke. I looked up and saw smoke curling through the cracks from a door labeled "10." We were just below the fire. We were going to make it!

We arrived at the ground floor and pushed through an emergency door into a gray late afternoon in downtown Toronto. Pure, clean air was sucked into our lungs. In front of us, the street was filled with hoses and firefighting equipment. People huddled in blankets. We hustled to the other side of the street and saw smoke pouring from what must have been the tenth and eleventh floors.

We later learned that the fire had been set by an arsonist, who was caught when he tried to torch another hotel the next day. Damage was over $100,000, and at least two people had to be taken to the hospital for smoke inhalation.

I also learned from fire officials that we probably would have been safer staying in our rooms, placing wet towels under the door to keep out smoke, and opening outdoor windows for fresh air. But they also admitted they had no equipment that could have extended to the twenty-second floor to rescue us. We would have had only the prospect of trying to reach the roof, where they might have evacuated us with helicopters. Still, they emphasized that staying in the room and following instructions would have been the safest thing to do.

Since that day, I've disliked staying above the ninth floor in a hotel.

CHAPTER 7

Stunts

A REAL HUMAN FLY

"Our company sold several of them to Buckingham Palace in England," the man on the telephone declared.

"A personal fire escape system?" I replied.

"That's right," the salesman responded. "If your bedroom is above the first floor, you ought to have one."

When the man offered to come to Cleveland to give a demonstration by climbing down the front of a downtown building, I agreed to do a story on his product.

A week later, Charles Morgan arrived at our studios. He had some bad news. His arm was in a sling. Due to a sprained wrist, he would be unable to demonstrate the personal fire escape for me. But not to worry, he said, "This system is so easy to use that one of the princes at the palace uses it to sneak out of his room. Why don't you try it?"

"I get nosebleeds when I stand on a chair," I said.

"All you have to do is sit in this sling," he said, "and hang onto this rope. Just feed it out at the speed you want to be lowered to the ground."

He was holding up a series of sturdy-looking ropes and a wide canvas belt. The idea, he said, was to go up to the third floor of our building and find a suitable place to tie the ropes, then place the canvas sling around my rear end, step out a window, and lower myself to the ground.

Our boss, general manager Chuck Bergeson, was out to lunch. His office on the third floor of the old WJW building faced Euclid Avenue. We tied the rope to Bergeson's desk and draped it out the window to the street below.

My first concern came when I noticed Morgan looking at an instruction book that came with the fire escape. A puzzled look now and then crossed his face.

"Are you sure this is really safe?" I asked, looking over the windowsill and feeling butterflies in my stomach when I realized how far three stories could really be.

"Oh, absolutely!" he replied. "Our ropes are 100 percent guaranteed. If one should ever break, for any reason, we replace it, without charge to you."

I was just about to ask what good a new rope was going to do me if I fell three stories when I noticed a demonstration down on the street. Videographer Ralph Tarsitano, who had been assigned to film my descent, had organized a group of bystanders, who were chanting, "Jump! Jump! JUMP!"

Tarsitano, seeing me peering out of the open window, shouted, "Hey! Would you mind either climbing down here or jumping? It's just about time to go to lunch!"

Back on the third floor, Morgan was nervously strapping me into the harness. I noticed his hands were shaking. Just then, Chuck Bergeson strode onto the scene.

"You don't have to do this!" he said sternly. "Just remember, you don't have to do this, and if you get hurt there won't be any workers' compensation." And with that, he whirled and stomped off. I think he was sure I was going to fall, and he didn't want to be a witness.

With all of this support, I felt I just had to try it. I carefully pulled the rope taut and sat down on the edge of the windowsill. The chanting of "Jump! Jump!" was still going on with Tarsitano now leading it.

I closed my eyes and pushed off. I swung out and slammed back against the brick building. I wasn't going anywhere. I was just hanging there!

"You've got to let go of the rope so it will pay out the line!" shouted Morgan from above me, still holding the instruction book.

I gingerly let go of the rope and immediately dropped almost six feet before I again snatched the rope and checked my descent.

I was now hanging between the top of the building and the windows on the second floor. I opened one eye and saw fellow workers through the windows waving at me. I weakly smiled at them and then looked down. It was a big mistake. The bottom of the Grand Canyon would have appeared closer than the street.

A brisk wind was now whistling down Euclid Avenue, and I began to swing on my perch, blown back and forth. The word *terrified* would not adequately describe my feelings at that moment.

"PAY OUT THE ROPE!" Morgan shouted from above, still clutching the instruction book.

Inch by inch, I let the rope slide through my hands, suddenly realizing that I could control the rate of my descent. I had just reached the top of the first-floor windows when Morgan leaned over and shouted something I could not understand.

He was still shouting something as my trembling legs touched the sidewalk and I half-collapsed against the side of the building. I was greeted by a spattering of applause from bystanders and a few boos from those disappointed that I had not splattered myself over the sidewalk. I was still standing there when Morgan burst through the front door, still clutching the instruction book. His face was white as a sheet.

"Are you all right?" he gasped.

"Yeah, I'm fine," I replied. "What were you trying to tell me as I got near the bottom?"

"That the rope was breaking!" he said.

It turned out Morgan had never actually used the harness himself, and it was the first time he had ever had someone demonstrate it. When we strung the ropes over the edge of the windowsill at the top, he forgot to put a rubber pad between the rope and the sharp edge. Every time I swung back and forth on the rope, it grated across the lip, cutting the rope. Only a few strands of nylon still held it together as I reached the sidewalk.

Next time, I think I'll just take the elevator.

THE DAY THE CIRCUS CAME TO TOWN

"Do a feature on the circus that's in town," assignment editor Mickey Flanagan said.

"Like what?" I retorted.

"Oh, you'll find something to do," he said. "You know, like try out for the trapeze act or something."

"I think I'll do the 'or something,'" I replied as I went out the door.

The Circus Vargas was one of the last circuses still working under canvas and doing one-night stands across the Midwest. It was set up for a weekend run in the parking lot of a Willowick shopping center. The only problem was that the trucks carrying the tents and some of the rigging had broken down, and it was only a few hours to showtime. It looked like this circus would be a performance under the stars rather than canvas because, in the best tradition of show business, the show must go on.

The circus public relations man was understandably a bit harried, considering that his circus was about to put on a performance in the middle of a parking lot without tents.

"The only act that can talk to you right now is Vashock!" he announced as he led me through ropes and cables and around a lion's cage.

Vashock turned out to be a small blond man with a thick Czech accent who, I learned, did a high-wire act with his wife on a motorcycle. The motorcycle, which had no tires, was driven on its rims up a steel cable to a spot about forty feet above the lion's cage, at what would have been the top of the tent. I was asking him just what the rest of the act consisted of when he interrupted to tell me that we were using up his rehearsal time, and he wanted to make a couple of practice runs up the cable.

"Vy dahnt you come along," he said.

I gulped and looked at the steep cable that ran to the top of a huge pole over the cage where lions and tigers were now pacing. Videographer Gary Korb urged me on.

"Go ahead!" Korb said. "You know they want some reporter involvement in these stories."

"I don't think that looks too safe," I replied, again tilting my head back to see how far up the cable ran.

"You don't think he'd let you do anything dangerous," Gary said. "He'll probably just take you up a few feet and then come right back down."

Vashock stood there smiling, saying, "Yah, yah. Ve gif you short ride."

The motorcycle, already on the wire, set atop a wooden stand about six feet off the ground. Beneath it, attached to the motorcycle, was a steel trapeze with straps on each side. I sat down on the trapeze and Vashock immediately began strapping my hands to the sidebars.

"Why are you doing this?" I asked, nervously.

"Because I dahn't want you to be scared and jump off," he replied as he climbed onto the motorcycle above me and kick-started it. Whatever I said in reply was lost in the roar of the motorcycle. We started to move. I grabbed the steel bars with an iron grip as we went up, and up, and up. I finally opened my eyes and looked down. Below me was the largest lion I have ever seen. As he looked directly up at me, his mouth was open, teeth gleaming!

Just then the motorcycle shut off, and we sat there, gently swaying back and forth, balanced on a single, silvery steel cable forty feet over the lions and the blacktop parking lot.

"How you lak this?" Vashock shouted down to me.

I was too frightened to answer. I managed to look at him and open my mouth, but not a word would come out. Finally I was able to work my lips into a slight grimace, which Vashock immediately mistook for a smile of encouragement.

"Maybe we do a couple of loop-loops!" he shouted down to me as he started to swing the motorcycle in a crazy side-to-side motion. My weight was the only thing keeping the cycle on the wire!

"D-D-D-DOWN!" I finally managed to get out.

"Down?" Vashock said, perplexed.

"Yes, take me DOWN!" I shouted. "I forgot something on the ground."

"Okey dokey," Vashock answered as he fired up the motorcycle. We started coasting backwards, back towards the ground.

When we were finally back down and my hands had been pried from the trapeze bar, Vashock asked me, "Vot did you forget?"

"My courage," I truthfully replied. "Why did you take me all the way to the top?"

He smiled a bit sheepishly and explained, "Mine rigging is still on the truck that is not here, and I had to use someone else's cables, and mine wife is pregnant, and I didn't want her on board when I tested the cables. I think, if it don't break with you on board trapeze, it is safe for her to do the show."

TRAPEZE DAYS

The Al Sirat Grotto Shrine Circus was a Cleveland tradition for many years. A fund-raiser for the Masonic organization, it brought both professional and some semiprofessional circus acts to town. It was one of these part-time acts that attracted the attention of the WJW-TV newsroom and resulted in my taking a camera crew to Public Auditorium to interview one half of a husband and wife aerial duo.

I have forgotten their names, but they were schoolteachers who spent their off time traveling with the circus doing a trapeze act. The wife was a beautiful, shapely woman in her twenties. She did the interview standing on the bottom rung of a trapeze that had not yet been pulled to the ceiling of Public Hall.

She told me that one of the key ingredients in their act was the trust that she had in the strength of her husband as he hung upside down from the trapeze, holding her hands as she dangled beneath him doing somersaults. I asked how long they had to practice this act, and she admitted this was only their second season. But she assured me that the secret was to forget you were forty feet above the floor of the arena.

She asked if I would like to see what it looked like from on high. In a moment of sheer stupidity, I agreed. The next thing I knew, I was sitting on the trapeze, hanging on with both hands, while she stood on the bar beside me and a winch started hoisting us from the floor towards the rafters of the massive hall.

When we reached the top, we were directly over a large net spread below. I still have a photo of me looking down. The expression on my face pretty much tells what I was thinking at that moment. It is a look of sheer terror.

I had a death grip on the two cables supporting the trapeze as she dropped down to sit beside me on the bar. She said, "All you have to do is hook your knees over the bar and just go backwards, like this." And with that, she was hanging upside down from the trapeze bar. I fought the urge to cry like a small child in fear.

"Why don't you hook your knees and try this?" came a voice from beneath the trapeze.

Try hanging by my knees! I couldn't even work up the courage to look down to see where she was.

"Hang by your knees and put your arms straight down and I'll grab your hands and hang from them," she said.

"You'll hang from my hands!!" I nearly shouted in disbelief.

"It's okay. I don't weigh that much, and if I slip the net will catch me," she said.

"The net will catch you!! Who's gonna catch me?? You want me to hang by my knees and hold you on a trapeze at the top of Public Hall??" Although my voice was strangled, I managed to get the words out.

Very calmly she urged, "Yes. Let's try it."

I told her I urgently needed to get back down to the floor of the convention center for something I had forgotten.

She hesitated, then heaved herself back onto the trapeze beside me and gave the signal to the worker on the floor. The trapeze was lowered to the ground.

"What did you forget?" she asked as I jumped off the trapeze.

"My courage," I answered truthfully.

In those situations, I often remembered to forget it.

CLOWNING AROUND

It was a busy news night: The Cleveland Musicians Union had been on strike for several weeks and a rumored settlement was near; there was the usual crisis at City Hall, and the Al Sirat Grotto Circus was due to open that weekend.

TV8 assignment editor Mickey Flanagan had sent me with a camera crew to Public Hall, where the Grotto clowns were rehearsing, to do a standard fluff piece about the circus and the many wonderful charities that the Grotto supported. Most of the clowns were amateurs who just loved to entertain and especially loved making up as a clown.

We had interviewed several clowns and were getting ready to wrap up when photographer Lynn Chambers suggested that I put on some clown make-up for the final shot, and that I do the shot standing in a group of clowns. The idea was that no one would realize I was in the group doing my voiceover until the last few seconds, when I would reach down and pick up the microphone, revealing to the audience that I was one of the clowns.

It seemed like a cute idea at the time.

Several clowns raced to make up my face. They smeared white make-up on my cheeks, nose, and forehead, painted a large red mouth around my mouth, fastened a large red nose over my real nose, and slapped a wild red fright wig onto my head. A problem was that the nose and the wig kept sliding off when I moved my face or talked. One of the clowns rummaged around in a make-up kit and tossed a bottle of adhesive to the clown doing my make-up.

"Here, try this," he said. "It'll never come off."

The adhesive, whatever it was, was poured onto my head, soaking my hair, and the wig was tugged into place. More was spread on the inside of the bulbous nose, which was then pressed tightly over my real nose. I was ready.

The shot went just as planned. It went so well, in fact, that we all started to laugh and ruined the shot, and had to do it again and again. It took nearly twenty minutes to get everyone to keep their composure as I said, "This is Neil Zurcher, Newscenter 8. Just clowning around."

Then the telephone in the room rang. It was Mickey Flanagan. The musicians union had just settled, and he wanted me and my crew to stop whatever we were doing and get over to union headquarters ten minutes ago to cover a news conference that was about to start.

I ran to the bathroom and grabbed some paper towels to wipe off the make-up. I managed to smear it pretty good, mixing the red mouth paint, the white, and some other colors that gave me a ghostly look. But it was when I went to remove the wig that I got a real surprise. It wouldn't budge. It was glued onto my real hair. I called to the clown who had helped with the make-up.

"What's in this stuff? I can't get the wig off," I shouted.

After a long silence, one of the clowns shuffled into the bathroom holding a bottle of glue.

"Sorry," he said. "I thought it was a bottle of spirit gum. We'll have to get some alcohol to rinse your hair and see if we can dilute the glue."

The phone rang again. Flanagan was calling to see if we had left. The news conference was about to begin.

"We're on our way!" I shouted into the phone, grabbing my coat and running out the door after the camera crew.

I can't begin to tell you the stares we got when we arrived at the musicians union, and the chuckles and snide remarks from some of the newspaper reporters. I was forced to tell the story over and over.

We raced back to the studios to get the stories ready for the

11 p.m. news. Running in the door, I almost collided with Chuck Bergeson, the general manager.

"I hope that is not the way you came to work today," he said.

"It's a long story," I said, running past him for the editing room.

THE BIG BANG

Maybe because I have always had a problem with weight, news director Virgil Dominic came to me one day and suggested that I do a weeklong series on diets and how they worked.

I tried to think of a novel, attention-getting way to open the series, and suddenly it hit me: The Big Bang.

Everyone who goes on a diet knows what it's like when you have a refrigerator full of food. How do you avoid temptation? One way that would draw attention would be to have a big bang and blow the door off the refrigerator.

Okay, the concept might have a few flaws. But I thought if we could see a refrigerator with its door blown off the hinges, people might look at what I was trying to tell them.

The first problem was finding someone to donate a refrigerator to be destroyed. My good friend Dick Stammitti, who owned a towing service in Lorain, solved that. He had an old, nonworking refrigerator in his garage that he planned to junk. The bigger issue turned out to be exploding the door. We went to Stammitti's Garage and tried closing the door with a couple of big firecrackers inside, but nothing happened. Just a muffled *Whoompfff!*

Then I called Parker Miller, who was ranger chief at the Lorain County Metro Parks. Vermilion police called him each winter to dynamite the ice in the Vermilion River to prevent flooding.

I explained what I wanted to do. Parker said he had never blown up a refrigerator before but didn't think it would take much.

We met a couple of days later at the Amherst Dump on Quarry Road. Stammitti had placed the refrigerator near a tree in an open area of the dump.

Parker measured its interior and calculated how much explosive he'd need to blow the door off. He taped the dynamite to the inside of the door and attached a small lead wire from the explosives to a detonator behind a small hill about a hundred feet away. He closed the door and hid the wire as best he could, while we moved in with the cameras.

I stood in front of the refrigerator to do my standup.

I said, "Hi. I'm Neil Zurcher, and I'm fat. Have you ever thought the only way a diet might work is to blow up your refrigerator?"

With that, I moved out of sight, and photographer Bill Anweiler moved his video camera closer to the refrigerator.

Parker saw what he was doing and came out and said, "Uh . . . I think you better put it back a little further and just turn it on while you come behind the hill with me." Anweiler objected, saying he wanted to be sure he was in focus when the explosion went off. Besides, he was about fifty feet away, and all that was supposed to happen was that the door would be blown off its hinges.

Parker insisted, pointing out the danger of flying objects from the explosion.

Anweiler finally agreed. He set up the camera, turned it on, and ran to the ditch where we waited with the detonator.

Parker looked at me. I nodded. He pressed down the plunger on the detonator.

Nothing happened.

Parker looked at me in bewilderment. I looked back, just as confused.

He told everyone to stay put while he checked the wiring.

He followed the wire from the detonator back to the refrigerator. But before he opened the door, he warned us to keep our heads down. Slowly, he cracked the door open. Nothing happened.

The wire had apparently broken when they closed the refrigerator door. A new wire was installed, and a few minutes later we were huddled again behind the wall of the ditch as Parker again looked for my signal. I nodded my head, and he pushed down the plunger.

Kapowww!!!

This time, there was an ear-splitting roar and the refrigerator disappeared. I mean, it was totally gone. Shrapnel and bits of insulation rained down on us.

I finally looked up. Our camera and tripod was on its side. Where the refrigerator had been was just a scorched piece of earth.

Parker grinned and said, "I guess I put too much dynamite in there."

And that was the shot I used to open my series.

SANDUSKY BAY

I had the opportunity to get a true bird's-eye view of Sandusky Bay when some friends suggested that I try parasailing. That's riding a parachute attached to a boat, which tows the chute with you hanging beneath it—the chute, not the boat.

I had seen footage of poor, misguided middle-aged men and women who had been talked into similar rides. You see them running as fast as they can on a beach as a speedboat heads for deep water. A long rope tied to the person on the shore draws taut and then slams them, face first, into the sand, and drags them through the water.

"That's not for me," I told my friend.

"We don't do it that way," he insisted. "It's just like sitting in a rocking chair, only one that flies 300 feet in the air over the lake."

So one a sunny morning I found myself with videographer Bob Begany in the back of a strange-looking speedboat on Sandusky Bay. The rear of the boat was covered with a large square platform. I was told to put on a life jacket and a harness and to sit on the platform.

The boat sped up, and a crew member unfurled a huge parachute off the rear of the boat. Tow straps attached to two stanchions held the parachute down while it was filled with air.

The crew member then motioned for me to step up to the stanchions and to grab the straps. As I did, he transferred the snaps from the stanchions to my harness. Before I had time to ask what to do next, I felt myself lifted into the air by the parachute. An electric winch began to pay out the line, letting me go higher and higher as the boat picked up speed.

I quickly found myself floating hundreds of feet over Lake Erie, the boat now looking like some small water bug dashing across the lake below me.

It was very pleasant up there. I could even see the distant Canadian shoreline. I was still clinging to the straps above my head with a white-knuckle grip, but I was beginning to relax and almost enjoy the trip. Then I noticed that I was starting to sink towards the water. The boat was heading into the wind and unable to keep up enough speed to keep me aloft in the air, and I was slowly floating closer and closer to the surface of Lake Erie.

I was ready to take a deep breath before hitting the water when I stopped dropping and seemed to hover above the surface. My feet occasionally touched a wave as the boat gained enough speed to keep me airborne.

The boat turned and started running away from the wind, and I soared back into the sky. This time I noticed, as I rose higher and farther from the roar of the boat's motor, that I could hear only the creak of the nylon harness stretching and making strange noises as it adjusted to the pull of the rope and to my weight. I began to get a mental image of what it would be like if the harness suddenly broke and I dropped two hundred feet to the water below. It made me grab the straps all the more tightly over my head.

A few minutes later, I felt myself starting to dip again. But this time I was being reeled in by the rope, and I was headed towards the boat, not the water. In seconds I stepped softly down onto the surface of the boat, and the crew member quickly tied the chute onto the stanchions, releasing me.

More than a little proud of myself for having taken such a daring ride, I expected the young crew member to congratulate me on being so cool on the roller coaster–style ride. He turned and said, "You were a bit nervous up there.

"Last week I had an eighty-five-year-old lady up celebrating her birthday. You should have seen her," he said with admiration. "She insisted on taking her camera with her. She shot three rolls of film and changed film in the camera twice while she was up there."

SOME PEOPLE FLY, SOME DON'T

I was driving with a camera crew on Cleveland's West Side when, crossing a bridge, we spotted what appeared to be a huge kite sailing over the valley near the steel plants. We went to investigate and, on top of a cliff near West 11th Street, found a group of hang-gliding fans practicing their sport.

We watched for a while, did some filming, and were preparing to leave when the man in charge of the gliders, Chuck Slusarczyk, asked if I would like to try flying.

What they were doing was putting on a harness attached to a giant kite-shaped wing, hoisting it over their heads, running, and leaping off the edge of the cliff. Then, lifted by the wind, they would gently float and spiral down to a baseball diamond in the valley, several hundred feet below.

Slusarczyk assured me it was absolutely safe, that all you had to do was point the nose of the kite down to gain speed and point it up to slow or level out. Tip your body—hanging by the harness from the kite—to the right, and you would turn right. Tip left to turn left. The hardest part, he said, was carrying the kite back up the hill after you landed.

I suffered a total loss of good sense at that point. Egged on by photographers Dave Williams and Ted Pikturna, I somewhat reluctantly strapped on the hang glider and found myself running pell-mell towards the edge of a cliff, hanging onto a huge kite with white knuckles.

Just as I stepped off the edge into space, I realized this was not the best idea I'd ever had.

The hang glider plummeted about ten feet. And then, as I was closing my eyes to brace for impact with the earth below, I discovered I was soaring.

It was like being a bird. I leaned to the right, and the hang glider went into a tight turn to the right. Unfortunately, I was too close to the edge of the cliff to turn, and I slammed into a debris-littered slope. The impact dragged me over two discarded mattress springs and a patch of broken bottles before I stopped.

As I was counting my arms and legs to see if they were all there, Chuck Slusarczyk came sliding down the hillside.

"You turned too soon," he scolded me, as he helped me to my feet. "You go up there and try it again."

I looked down. My pants were in shreds, and a dozen cuts to my knees and shins were leaking blood into my shoes. He wanted me to go again?

"No way!" I said.

"Come on, skin will grow back," Slusarczyk said. "Besides, if you don't go now, you'll be spooked and never try it again. You almost had it. Try it once more."

As I said, I was suffering from a total loss of common sense at the time, because a few minutes later I found myself on top of the hill, shakily running again towards the edge of that same cliff.

This time I was expecting the sudden drop and was determined to soar straight across the valley to the baseball field. I tried to slow the speed by raising the front of the hang glider. It was too much and I began to stall. The hang glider peeled off to the right, and I found myself heading right back into the same patch of debris I hit on the first attempt.

I was still lying face down on a rusty bedspring when Slusarczyk and some friends reached me. My right pant leg was gone below the knee. I had bits and pieces of broken beer bottles embedded in my knees and shins, but otherwise I was unhurt.

Common sense finally returned. Despite Slusarczyk's pleas

that I try it one more time, I refused. Williams and Pikturna suggested that I might want to go to a hospital to get the glass out of my legs and to get a tetanus shot. They dropped me off at the emergency room at St. John Hospital and drove off to cover a fire.

Now, from the waist up I looked okay. It was from the knees down that I was hurting, and since I was standing in front of her desk, the registrar could not see the cuts on my legs.

"What's your problem?" she asked.

"I'd like to see a doctor about patching up some cuts."

"How did you get hurt?" she said, not even looking up from the form she was filling out.

"Uh, I don't think you would understand," I replied.

"Try me," she said with some smugness. "I've heard just about everything."

"Okay," I said. "I fell off a kite."

"Sounds to me like you want a psychiatrist instead of a medical doctor," she said.

You know, maybe she was right.

THE DAY WE ATTACKED MILAN

It reminded me of the famous scene in the movie *Apocalypse Now*, except this was no movie. We were just above the treetops. I was belted in and hanging out the open door of a Huey medevac helicopter as we screamed over the woods, suddenly coming upon an open area with several road crossings. Lumbering down the road below us was a sixty-ton M-60 tank, its 105mm cannon barrel swinging back and forth. The tank was followed by another tank-like vehicle from WWII called an M-42 "Duster," whose twin-40mm Bofors anti-aircraft guns were swinging menacingly towards our approaching copter. Over the headset in my helmet I heard someone yell at the pilot, "Ali wants you to make a pass over the M-60."

Ali was Ali Ghanbari, a photojournalist with WJW Fox 8 in

Cleveland. He had just traded places with me in the helicopter to get some ground shots as we shot a One Tank Trip segment, trying to capture the essence of the Firelands Military Museum of Norwalk, Ohio. The Firelands Military Museum was the brainchild of local businessman Dick Rench and his son, Dr. Tom Rench of Akron. It all started with a Korean War vintage military Jeep that Dick Rench received for a birthday present many years ago. What became a hobby developed into a full-fledged military equipment collection that the Renches have tried to share with northeastern Ohio. Their idea was to have a "living" museum with all equipment restored to operating condition. They would use it to demonstrate the capabilities of these massive weapons of war.

"We would like to be able to offer visitors the opportunity to ride in a real Korean War tank or fly in a Vietnam-era helicopter. To see how a World War II flamethrower worked," said Dick Rench. "We want to offer more than just a military steel museum where these machines sit silent and dead."

On this day, the Renches had agreed to demonstrate their equipment for our cameras. They had obtained permission to use an abandoned gravel pit near the historic town of Milan, where inventor Thomas Edison was born, on the Huron-Erie county line. The spot was perfect for putting the massive tanks through their paces while we flew above in the helicopter. But we soon discovered one problem: No one had bothered to tell nearby residents what was going on. All they knew was that a military helicopter was sweeping low over their homes, and that they could hear the roar and clanking of tanks. They called the police.

From my perch in the helicopter, I could see a white cruiser with flashing lights turn into the gravel pit and rush down a road to where we hovered. As the cruiser came around a blind curve, he could not see the other side of the hill, where the M-60 tank was headed right towards him. As the tank driver and the policeman suddenly realized they were on a collision course, each came to an abrupt halt, stopping just feet short of the tank's cannon barrel spearing the police car's windshield.

Fortunately for us, inside the police car was longtime Milan police chief Jim Ward, a good friend and an acquaintance of just about everyone involved in the demonstration. After seeing the TV cameras and hearing the Renches explain what was going on, he radioed headquarters and told his dispatcher to pass along the explanation to nervous callers and assure them that the city was not under siege.

Sadly, Dick Rench's dream of a living museum never came to fruition. He passed away in 2008, and new Homeland Security regulations grounded his helicopter and disabled his tanks. Today the remaining pieces of equipment are mostly in storage and only used infrequently at parades and festivals.

FRANK TAKES A RIDE

The temperature hovered near zero on a brutally cold winter day. Perfect weather for a ride on what was Ohio's longest and fastest toboggan slide.

East Sparta, Ohio, south of Canton, is home to Bear Creek Resort Ranch. Once the temperature started to hold around 40 degrees, Bear Creek started the refrigeration equipment to its half-mile toboggan chute. You'd ride a truck to the top of a 250-foot-high hill at the back of the property, where a small, two-story building is located. On the second floor is a platform that stretches out over the chute. You'd place your toboggan on this platform and then, when you were ready, an attendant would drop the front of the platform, plunging you down one story onto the frozen chute. During the ride to the bottom of the 250-foot slope, you'd reach speeds of up to 70 miles per hour.

If you were unable to stop when you reached the end of the chute, a 30-foot-long bed of straw and, beyond that, a stack of baled straw sat to stop runaway toboggans.

It was, quite simply, one of the most exciting outdoor rides in Ohio.

On the day we were taping our story up and down the toboggan run, we were alerted to a birthday celebration about to take place.

An elderly gentleman named Frank was about to take his first ride on the icy chute to celebrate his ninetieth birthday.

I asked Frank if he objected to our taping his ride. He did not. I asked why he had chosen such an unusual way to mark his nine-tieth year.

"I've always wanted to slide down that hill," he said, adding, "I thought I had to do it pretty soon or forget it."

Frank also pointed out that he wasn't going down the hill alone. His neighbor was going to ride with him. His neighbor was eighty-seven!

We watched as the pair was trucked to the top of the hill and as their toboggan was carried into the little shed and up to the second floor.

We could just see Frank and his neighbor climb aboard the toboggan, and we started our camera rolling.

The toboggan dropped and came flashing down the hill. The track was exceptionally slick that day, and they reached top speed quickly.

When they came by our camera position, nearly three-quarters of the way down the chute, they whipped past us at such speed that we were unable to focus on them.

We wheeled around just in time to see them reach the end of the chute, slice through the 30-foot bed of straw, and slam head-on into the pile of baled straw. Both men tumbled off the tobog-gan.

Everyone ran to them. Frank's neighbor was getting up, but Frank was not moving. He just lay there on his side, beside the capsized toboggan.

Several people called to him. "Frank! Frank! Are you all right?"

Frank opened his eyes and said, "Is it over yet?"

I asked Frank later if he was planning to take another ride.

"Not until I turn 100!" he answered.

Sadly, the economy caught up with the toboggan run. It was closed down when the campground could not negotiate a lease for the land where the toboggan was located. As of this writing, there are no plans to reopen what was once Ohio's most thrilling wintertime ride.

WRONG-WAY RIVER

"Hold it right there!" videographer Bill West shouted to me.

I was holding "it"—a canoe—by paddling frantically against the current in the Black Fork Mohican River here in Loudonville.

"Okay!" West shouted. "Paddle by me again and this time, SMILE!"

I gritted my teeth and sloshed the cold springtime water with my paddle. The current was so strong that I really had little to do other than keep the boat upright and steer it near the center of the river. I glided past West's photography position on the bank and once again started paddling hard against the current to stop the boat.

"Take it back up river again!" West called.

Once more I pushed and pulled on the paddle, battling the current as the canoe bucked and twisted. Finally, I worked my way about two hundred feet upstream, where I cautiously turned the canoe and grabbed an overhead tree limb to keep from scooting downstream again.

"You know, that water is cold," I said to West as he set up his camera in a different location.

"Just remember to smile as you go by me and we'll be done here," he prodded me.

On his signal I started paddling downstream again, trying to look like I did this every day and was an old hand at canoeing.

But just as I passed West's position, I felt the canoe rock. I grabbed the sides and hung on for dear life.

West shouted, "Aww, you screwed it up again! Take it back upstream."

The boat seemed to settle down, and I reached for the paddle I had dropped in the middle of the canoe. Then it happened.

My weight caused the boat to rock to the right, nearly overturning. I flung my weight to the opposite side, overreacting and overcorrecting, and the canoe started rocking the other way so violently that I knew I was going into the river.

I dropped the paddle and clawed at my hip pocket, flinging my wallet to shore as I tried, at the same time, to tear off my non-waterproof watch and hurl it, too. My arm was in midair when I went upside down into the cold river. Since the river is only about three feet deep in most areas, I hit bottom immediately and shot back to the surface.

"**&*%$#%&*&,*" I shouted, spewing a mouthful of brown river water into the air. I regained my footing on the slippery river bottom and started to wade to shore, just in time to see my wallet sinking beneath the surface. There was no choice but to dive for it. I managed to retrieve it and my hat, which had floated off my head in the capsizing.

Bill West stood on the bank with a funny smile and said, "I didn't have the camera running. If you did that intentionally, we'll have to do it over."

Between curses, I informed him that it was NOT intentional and we would NOT do it again. Frankly, I was grateful there was no footage of the embarrassing accident and that no one besides West had seen it. It turned out he was kidding. He had caught every embarrassing second of my splash into the river.

While he went to shoot some more proficient canoers, I slopped my way back to the parking lot. It had turned into a sunny day, and I noticed that the lot was empty, save one woman at the other end. I tossed my wallet onto the trunk of our car and spread out the sodden bills and cards. I peeled off my shoes and socks and laid them on the trunk to dry, and was just unbuttoning my shirt when I noticed the woman was taking pictures of me.

Jo Lemon of the Ashland newspaper had heard we were in the area and had come to interview me. The following week, there

I was, in all my wet and bedraggled glory, on the front page of the paper, wringing out my socks. It gave her readers a first-hand look at the "glamour" of television.

A footnote: Dick Schafrath, the former Cleveland Browns star, who operated the canoe livery where we did the taping, saw the segment. The next time I came asking for a canoe to use in a story, he offered me one with outrigger pontoons—sort of a canoe with training wheels!

JP AND THE SMOKY MOUNTAINS

Photographer John Paustian and I had set out on a One Tank Trip to the Smoky Mountains of Tennessee. We had decided to see if we really could make it all the way there on one tank of gasoline. We topped the car's tank as we left Cleveland and started south on Interstate 71. In the trunk, we had stashed a two-gallon can of gasoline—not that we doubted we would make it, but just to make sure we didn't have to walk if our calculations were wrong.

We drove steadily, hour after hour, as counties gave way to state lines, until we finally saw the magic words *Tennessee State Line*. Our gasoline gauge showed about an eighth of a tank left. We drove on, carefully observing the 55-mile-an-hour speed limit to nurse every mile, every yard, out of each drop of gas left until we reached the Sevierville city limits. Our destination of Pigeon Forge, Tennessee, was just one mile away. We were truly going to make it on one tank.

We were congratulating each other when the engine died. A quick glance at the gas gauge showed no movement from the needle, which rested against the "E" mark. JP swore under his breath.

"Better get the can out of the trunk," he said.

We were coasting over the crest of a small hill when we spotted an Esso station at the bottom.

"Might as well coast down there and fuel up," JP said.

We slowly crested the hill, then started down. Our news cruiser picked up speed as the hill unrolled beneath us. We were almost at the gasoline station, and I was thinking how nice it would be to stretch my legs, when I realized we weren't stopping.

"Hey!" I said. "What are you doing? Why don't you stop for gas?"

JP was hunched over the wheel, his eyes locked on something down the road.

Then I saw it, too, and started to cheer him on. Both of us were trying to use the power of concentration to will our now-dead car one last half mile to the sign that read: *Welcome to Pigeon Forge.*

We coasted closer and closer, but the road started to rise. Our speed, already only a mile or two an hour, slowed even further.

"No, you son-of-a-bitch!" JP shouted at the car. "You're not going to stop this close!"

He suddenly threw open the door, jumped out, and, keeping one hand on the wheel to steer, began to push the car the last fifty feet. Realizing what he was trying to do, I did the same on my side. Gasping and pushing, we crossed the corporation line and pulled off to the side of the road. We had made it to our destination in Tennessee on one tank of gasoline.

It was this kind of determination that made JP such a joy to work with. But there were times his enthusiasm almost got us into trouble.

On the last morning of our stay in Tennessee, I heard a buzzing sound. I thrashed around in the predawn darkness, groping around on my nightstand for an errant alarm clock, only to realize that it was not a clock but my phone that was buzzing.

I snatched it off the stand and growled, "HELLO!"

"Good morning, it's time for magic!" JP answered brightly.

"What time is it?" I mumbled.

"Three a.m." he responded.

"Three a.m.!" I shouted back. "It's the middle of the night. Have you been drinking?"

"Come on, get out of bed," he urged. "It's almost Magic Time."

"What are you talking about?" I demanded.

"I want to get up in the Smokies to see the sunrise and capture all that great magical color in the early morning," he replied. "Besides, you said you wanted to see the real Smoky Mountains, and this is your chance."

The memory of my words haunted me as I stumbled around the motel room getting dressed. The sting of the cool mountain morning helped to revive me as I crunched across the gravel parking lot, still illuminated by the moon, to our car.

A half-hour later, we were starting the winding climb up mountain roads into the Great Smoky Mountain National Park. The sky was turning to gold and purple in the east as we reached a lookout on the summit and pulled over.

JP was nearly dancing. He was like an excited child on Christmas morning. He leaped out of the car and yelled, "Come on Zurcher! It's MAGIC TIME!"

It truly was magic as we stood, he looking through his camera and I watching, mesmerized by the rainbow of hues evolving from the eastern sky as the first golden rim of the sun pushed up from beyond the horizon. Even more beautiful was the river of white fog that drifted down the mountain valleys below us. It truly did look as though the mountains were covered with smoke.

"You only get this golden light for about a half hour in the morning," JP said. "Come on, we've got to take advantage of it."

He started packing his tripod into the trunk of the car and wrestled his camera into the front passenger seat.

"Here, you drive," he said, flipping me the keys.

We had only gone a few hundred feet when he shouted, "This isn't going to work. Stop the car!"

I slammed on the brakes, barely in time, as he stepped out of the still-moving car. The next thing I knew, he was climbing onto the hood of the car, bracing his back against the windshield.

"Okay!" he shouted. "I can see now. Try to drive at a steady speed."

And so, down the mountain we went. Me driving, leaning out the side window to see where I was going. JP sprawled across the hood and windshield, chuckling and talking to himself. "That's beautiful! That's great!"

I noticed a tan pickup truck pass us in the opposite direction and the startled face of the driver, but I was too busy trying to keep the car on the winding road and worrying about JP falling off and being run over by his own news cruiser to pay any attention.

Suddenly, I heard a siren. I sat up and looked in the rearview mirror. Behind me was the pickup truck, which now had a blue flashing light on top of the cab. The ranger behind the wheel was motioning me to pull over.

"I've got a cop behind me!" I shouted out the window to J.P. "He wants me to pull over."

"Not now," JP hollered back. "This is a great shot! Let me finish it! Keep on driving."

"He looks pretty mad!" I shouted back. "I think I better pull over."

"No! Just keep driving for another couple of minutes while I finish this shot!" JP yelled.

I kept driving until we rounded another bend. At a wide berm on the road, I slowed, pulled off, and stopped.

JP lay back on the hood to relax, still euphoric about the beauty he had just captured. The ranger, about six foot four of him, marched up to my window and said, "JUST WHAT IN THEE HELL WERE YOU BOYS A-DOING?"

"It was magic, pure magic," JP answered from the hood of the car, his voice still full of wonder.

"What in the hell is that boy talkin' about?" the ranger demanded of me. "Is he high on some kind of dope or somethin'?"

It took us several minutes and some identification to convince the ranger that we were indeed sober and just a couple of nutty journalists who'd been carried away with the beauty of a Smoky Mountain morning.

My talented friend JP, who could get so enthused about the beauty of a new day, left us a short time later, losing a valiant fight with cancer. He was only thirty-seven years old. He left behind his wife, Kim, and their two sons, as well as a host of friends.

There is a little less magic in the world without him.

THE FREE SPIRIT ASSOCIATION CHURCH

Sometimes you had to be creative in the news business, especially when you had a slow news day. In some cases the reporter had to become part of the story, like the time I founded my own church.

It happened in the early 1970s, after assistant news director Ron Bilek showed me a magazine ad that offered to make anyone a legal clergyman for one dollar. It also boasted that becoming a clergyman might make you immune from the military draft and make you eligible for clergy discounts in stores. Bilek wanted me to investigate the people behind the ad and see if there was a local angle to the story.

So began a journey of several years.

The "church" in the ad had gained much publicity during the Vietnam War when some of its clergy, who had obtained ordination certificates simply by sending the "church" a dollar, had then used the certificates to avoid being drafted into the military. Some unscrupulous people had also used these instant ordination certificates to attempt to get tax breaks as well as business discounts that usually were given legitimate clergy.

I did a story reporting my findings, but the response from some viewers was disheartening. Many wanted the address of the "church" in California so they could send their dollars and be "ordained."

Bilek wanted to do more stories on the church scam, but he didn't want to enrich the bogus church's coffers.

A chance meeting with an attorney friend that weekend offered a solution. Elyria attorney Gary Carrothers and I were discussing the story and the problem it presented when Gary suggested that I could start my own church. That way we could explain the problems with the law without giving free publicity to any bogus groups. And if any viewers insisted that they wanted to join and be ordained, we could give out ordination certificates for free. He offered to check Ohio law to see what would be involved in setting up a religious organization similar to the one being run in California. It turned out that Ohio law was pretty fuzzy when it came to exactly who a clergyperson was or how he or she was ordained. For example: Just about anyone calling himself a member of the clergy could be licensed by the state to officially conduct weddings. I would prove it by becoming a licensed clergyman.

Bilek liked the idea, and with the approval of news director Bill Feest, Carrothers and I went to the state capitol in Columbus to file papers creating the "Free Spirit Association Church." I was listed as the presiding bishop, and my board of trustees included TV8 anchors Jeff Maynor, Jim Hale, and Jim Mueller, all of whom took on the "bishop" title. Dick Goddard offered to serve on the trustees but didn't want to be known as "Bishop Dick." He preferred to be "Vicar Dick." Other "bishops" of the new church included my friend Johnny Tarr, owner of the Hungarian restaurant The Bit of Budapest in Parma Heights. He offered us table 13, the large round table in the corner of the restaurant, as the headquarters and meeting place for our Board of Bishops.

Besides filing the papers in Columbus, I also registered with the state as a licensed clergyman, which allowed me to legally officiate at marriages in the state of Ohio. We casually mentioned this on one of the stories we did in the series about the newly formed Free Spirit Association Church. Right after the news that evening I got a call from a couple in Cleveland Heights, who were planning to get married and asked if I would officiate.

Their only concern was whether I could legally marry them. They already had the marriage license. I assured them that in the eyes of the state of Ohio, I could officiate at their wedding.

A few evenings later, I arrived at their apartment, where the ceremony was to take place in front of their families and a few friends.

The bride's mother was more than surprised to see me walk in. She had not been told who the clergyman would be.

"He's a TV newsman. How can he marry my daughter?" she kept repeating.

Throughout the brief ceremony she kept muttering, "I don't believe this. I don't believe this."

I wasn't sure she was talking about her daughter's choice of a groom or my presence as the clergyman.

My first public wedding came a few weeks later, when I received a call in the TV8 newsroom from a man who said that he and his fiancée were with a carnival that was set up on Rocky River Drive on Cleveland's West Side. They had called a local church that afternoon to see if the pastor would perform the marriage ceremony on carnival grounds so that their coworkers could witness the event. The pastor refused. The engaged couple happened to be watching TV8 that evening and saw one of my reports on the 11 p.m. news. He called me the next day.

After agreeing to perform the wedding, I learned they planned to wed on the portable merry-go-round where they first met.

Bilek suggested that if the couple was willing, we would cover the wedding "live" on our early newscast. They were willing, so photographer Gary Korb and technician Hap Halas joined me in our remote truck at the Rocky River Drive carnival site that afternoon.

The carousel was festooned with stuffed animals from the nearby game booths. The bride and groom sat side by side on wooden merry-go-round horses while I stood between the horses and conducted the wedding ceremony.

After I pronounced them husband and wife, their carnival friends, dressed in clean red coveralls, formed an arch of ax handles overhead as the happy couple disembarked from the merry-go-round. The crowd threw popcorn instead of rice.

I received many invitations to officiate at weddings over the next few years. One was in an unfinished log cabin out in the country. The bride and groom decided to get married before their new home was finished. Sadly, the roof was still not on. Just as I said, "Dearly beloved," lightning flashed, the skies opened, and the wedding party and guests had to run for their cars. We finished the ceremony in the hall the couple had rented for their reception. We all looked a little soggy and bedraggled.

Another memorable wedding was when my cousin, Nancy Rossi, who owns The Bride's World dress shop in Sandusky, asked me to host a large bridal show she was holding at a local hall. Two of the models, a man and woman, had been dating, and they decided that they really wanted to get married at the show, so as its big finale we held their wedding ceremony. The crowd looked a bit confused when I told the groom to kiss his bride and then turned to the audience and let them in on the secret that this was the real thing. There was some applause until the reality dawned, when they gave the newlyweds a standing ovation. As for the Free Spirit Association Church, we did several stories over the next couple of years about mail-order religion and even testified before a committee of the Ohio General Assembly about what we discovered. Some of the loopholes in Ohio law were changed, but the separation of church and state is a touchy subject, and lawmakers were reluctant to pass any laws that might step on the rights of people to believe what they want.

We continued to "ordain" anyone who requested it until one day when we realized we had several thousand clergymen all over the country and overseas. A project that started tongue-in-cheek had grown beyond my wildest expectations. The final straw came a short time later when I received a large brown envelope from Waco, Texas. A man who wrote he had been ordained by me said he had formed a church in Waco. He was sending me $147, which he claimed was his donation as a portion of his monthly collection. I immediately got a money order for the $147 and returned it with instructions that he donate it to a local charity and not send me any more money because I was "retiring" as head of the church. Our board of trustees held a meeting and voted to send any additional money that we received to cancer research. We also made a special fund for Cleveland wheelchair sports, which some of the members were supporting at the time.

A REAL GHOST STORY

When I wrote the book *Strange Tales from Ohio,* I was frequently asked if it was a book of Ohio ghost stories. It was not. It was more a collection of strange and unusual historic events that occurred here.

But I was involved in a story with ghostly overtones.

Franklin Castle, a historic gothic mansion on Franklin Avenue in Cleveland's Ohio City neighborhood, has been called the "most haunted spot in Ohio" by some paranormal investigators.

I don't know whether that is true, but this is what happened to me:

A group that owned Franklin Castle at the time was trying to promote it on the basis of its haunted reputation by arranging a séance with a well-known local medium. When I called the castle to ask about the event, I was invited to participate.

I arrived with a camera crew on the appointed night to join others sitting around a table on the mansion's second floor, in a room only lit by candles, as the medium began her efforts to call forth its ghosts. She was promptly interrupted when photographer Gary Korb's pager went off, signaling that WJW-TV was trying to reach us. We excused ourselves and ran down to the first floor to call the station.

Legendary bank robber "Fast Eddie" Watkins had earlier in the day attempted to rob a bank on Lorain Avenue near West 140th Street. The bank had recently improved its security set-up, and a publicity release bragged that even Fast Eddie couldn't get by it. So Eddie walked into the bank to prove that no security system could stop him. He claimed he had a bomb and was there to rob the bank. But the new security system worked perfectly to alert police. Trapped, Eddie took a group of people hostage. The standoff with police had been going for several hours, and now the station needed Korb to go to the bank to relieve the members of the camera crew, who had been there all day. A breaking-news story like a hostage situation took precedence over my feature story. Since my services weren't required at the bank, I told Korb to go ahead. I would remain at the séance and take a cab back to the station.

Korb left, and I returned to the second floor where the medium began the séance again. It was nearing 11 p.m. when she turned to me in the flickering candlelight and said, "Is there anyone on the other side that you would like to communicate with?" I was surprised by the question because I had only expected to observe, but I immediately came up with an answer:

"Yes there is," I said. "Marty Ross."

My good friend Marty, a longtime anchor at WJW, had only recently died after a long battle with leukemia.

"What would you like to ask Mr. Ross?" the medium intoned.

"I want to know what he did with my stopwatch," I replied.

Shortly before his death, Marty borrowed the stopwatch I used to time my scripts. He had never returned it. I thought this would be a good test of the medium's powers.

She began a long conversation, asking if Marty's spirit was present in the room, when we were interrupted again by the ringing of a doorbell on the first floor.

The medium motioned one of her young assistants to answer the door while the rest of us sat around the table in the near-darkness, the mood broken by the interruption.

I heard the young man's footsteps clunking down the stairs and then some muffled voices. Then we heard footsteps literally running up the stairs.

The young man burst into the room and nearly shouted at me, "Mr. Zurcher! Marty Ross is at the door and wants to talk to you!"

I was stunned. Then my curiosity kicked in, and I jumped up and trotted downstairs to the door, wondering what I was going to find.

It was something akin to a scene in a grade-B horror movie as I opened the large door to the mansion's side entrance. Streetlights burned sickly yellow through a light fog that drifted through the trees and utility poles along the street. Standing on the stoop were two figures. Two teenagers.

"Who the hell are you?' I blurted.

"I'm Martin Ross," the one nearest the door said.

It turned out his name really was Marty Ross, no relation to TV8's Marty Ross. An acquaintance of his was one of the hostages that Fast Eddie was holding at the bank. Ross and a friend had spent the evening watching the activities at the bank, where the standoff was still going on, but had become bored with the inactivity. They were standing near the WJW-TV camera crew outside the police lines when they overheard the photographers talking about me attending a séance at Franklin Castle. They instantly decided to leave the bank and come to see if they could join the séance.

The teenagers joined the group. We never did get a ghost to talk with us. I never found out what happened to my stopwatch. Fast Eddie gave up peacefully to the police after a twenty-one-hour standoff. No one was injured. Fast Eddie ended up in a federal prison from which he later escaped.

And, oh yeah—the ghost of the Franklin Castle.

After the séance ended, I was wandering around the second floor with my 35mm camera, taking some photos of the architectural features of the old mansion. I had just reached the bottom of an ornate stairway to the next floor when I noticed a suit of armor at the head of the stairs. I pointed the camera up the empty stairway and snapped a flash picture.

A few days later, my film was developed into 35mm slides. I was looking at them at home when the screen filled with my shot of the stairway with the suit of armor.

You can easily see the suit of armor and the stairway, but there is also a ghostly mist, which I did not see when I took the photo.

Was it just a reflection or a flaw in the processing? I don't know.

THE FAN CLUB

Believe it or not, I once had a fan club. I'm not really sure why. I think it had something to do with a badly designed T-shirt.

I was doing a program called "The Ohio Reporter" on WJW-TV. My good friend John Gullo, an artist, decided I should have a drawing of myself that represented my adventures, so he created a caricature of me with a microphone, interviewing a donkey. I went to the promotions department at TV8 and asked if they could have the color caricature made into a T-shirt that I could give as gifts as I traveled the state.

It was not the best time for such a request. There had recently been several budget cuts in the department, and money for such things was tight.

Instead of printing T-shirts, they suggested that they could find the money to print a decal that could be ironed on a T-shirt. I found it hard to get excited about the idea of handing someone an iron-on decal, but promotion is promotion.

I reluctantly agreed, and the Gullo painting was sent to a printing firm, which made several thousand T-shirt decals. I got a handful, bought some T-shirts, and tried to iron the decal to one. My first try looked as though the T-shirt had been worn for a couple of generations. It was so faded that you could barely make out the drawing or its message. I ruined half a dozen shirts before I noticed a small imprint on the back of the decal: "Works best on 100 percent polyester fabrics." I was using 100 percent cotton. We eventually learned by trial and error that a barely legible transfer could be made by using a shirt that was at least 50 percent polyester. But the end result still looked as though the shirt had been washed many times.

We made T-shirts for my daughters, Melody and Melissa, who were students in the Firelands School System in my hometown of Henrietta.

Melody apparently wore hers to school one day and, during band practice, took some good-natured kidding from classmates. Then someone suggested that if Melody could get them the free decals, they would also wear Neil Zurcher T-shirts. So one day about fifty band members showed up for practice wearing the T-shirts. The image, depending on the fabric of the shirts, ranged from awful to barely visible.

It might have been band director Gail Sigmund who decided they should form the "Neil Zurcher Fan Club" with an official song, sung to the tune of the jingle promoting Oscar Mayer wieners.

> Oh, I wish I were a Neil Zurcher T-shirt,
> That is what I'd really like to be.
> For if I were a Neil Zurcher T-shirt,
> Everyone would stop and stare at me.

The kids in the band invited me to come to school and hear the song. I accepted, trailed by a camera crew, and we found the entire band and even its director wearing Neil Zurcher T-shirts. When they burst into the official fan club song, I was laughing so hard I missed most of the lyrics.

The "fan club" never grew any larger, the TV8 promotions department had stacks of T-shirt transfers sitting in dark corners of closets for years afterward, and I suspect the fan club's T-shirts ended up as dust rags in many homes. But I still have fond memories of a group of high school students who gave me a very memorable afternoon and burned the memory of a song into my brain.

SEX SELLS . . . SOMETIMES

Cleveland Magazine honored me with a photo on the cover of their November 1995 issue along with a very nice feature story by Michael von Glahn about my career. The photo showed me dressed in a tuxedo, wearing my "One Tank Trips" baseball cap. Big letters beneath it proclaimed, "Sex sells but Neil Zurcher sells better," alluding to the sudden popularity of my local travel series on TV8.

The headline was obviously meant to tease potential readers into buying the magazine to learn why I was supposedly more popular than sex. Me? More popular than sex? It was so incredible a premise that even I would have bought the magazine.

But what I thought was even more humorous was what was not in the magazine article.

When I was first contacted by Linda Feagler of *Cleveland Magazine* and told they were considering an article on me, she asked if I would pose for a picture with my Nash Metropolitan. I said sure.

But when I met the photographer, *Cleveland* wanted something different than me in my usual attire. They wanted me to dress up. I pointed out that when people are on vacation, especially out of doors, they rarely dress formally. The photographer was insistent. He wanted something unique to go with the story. He wanted to see me dressed the opposite of what people might expect. Like wearing a tuxedo.

I told him I didn't have a tuxedo. Not to worry, he said, the magazine would rent one. They wanted to get shots of me in a tuxedo at sunset, standing beside my little red and white automobile with the skyline of Cleveland stretched out behind me.

On the day of the shoot, the first waterfront location they picked had too many shadows and didn't satisfy the photographer. So we packed up all the photographic gear, assistants, me and my car, and moved to a location off West 25th Street. That did not satisfy the photographer either.

By now the sun was getting low in the sky. If we wanted a sunset shot, it had to be taken soon, or we would have to reschedule for another day. Someone suggested shooting at a garden nursery in nearby Old Brooklyn. We quickly packed again and moved to the new location. It seemed to have all the right qualifications, but by now the sun was only a half disk sinking into the horizon.

There was a real sense of urgency as they posed me by my car. But something was still not right. The photographer wanted me to put on my red baseball cap with the tuxedo. I complied, and he took several test shots. He was now satisfied, but it was nearly dark. We had to pause as they brought out big box lights to illuminate me and the car against the purple and orange haze on the horizon, which was all that was left of the setting sun.

The photographer shot pictures until the light in the west was completely gone.

As we wrapped up the shoot in the dark, I promised to drop off the tuxedo the next day at the photographer's office, then started for home along Brookpark Road.

I probably made a strange sight, driving down the road in my red and white convertible with the top down, wearing a tuxedo and a red baseball cap. I noted that the van containing the photographer and his crew had fallen in behind me as we traveled west on the busy highway.

Near Cleveland Hopkins Airport, we came to an intersection with a stoplight near an industrial area. The light turned red and I slowed to a stop with the photographer's van still behind me. Out of the corner of my eye I noticed a young, scantily clad woman standing on the corner near my car.

She said, "Nice car."

"Thank you," I replied.

"Would you like a date?" she said.

"Uh . . . I beg your pardon," I stuttered.

"Would you like to go have some fun?" she said, walking towards the car.

Now I am not terribly sophisticated when it comes to some social contacts, but I was quite sure she was not trying to sell me Girl Scout cookies. The only other thought going through my mind was "God, I hope that photographer is not taking pictures of this encounter."

Just then the light turned from red to green. As her hand reached for the door handle, I took my foot off the brake, hit the accelerator, and shouted, "Thanks! But no thanks." As I drove off, I could hear the sound of uproarious laughter coming from the van behind me.

By the way, remember all that running around to get the right location to show me, my car, and the city at sunset? The photo that finally ran in the magazine was just a close-up of me and a tiny bit of the windshield and front fender of my car. No city skyline. No sunset.

LADIES DON'T SWEAT

My friend Wilma Smith likes to say, "Ladies don't sweat. They perspire."

That thought was brought home to me shortly before I retired, when I was assigned to interview the Rockettes of New York's Radio City Music Hall. They were in Cleveland on a nationwide tour of their fantastic holiday show.

The Rockettes, of course, are selected for their tall, leggy beauty and their talented dancing, which includes synchronized high kicking. I wanted to go behind the scenes and feature the talented ladies getting ready for their show at Playhouse Square. So photographer Mark Saksa, producer Lisa March, and I went backstage at the Palace Theater one morning to watch a rehearsal.

We walked into a very warm rehearsal room where forty young women had been practicing for some time. Wilma Smith's adage immediately popped into my head. These ladies were not only perspiring, they were downright sweaty. It reminded me of my high school days and the odor of the locker room after a hard-fought game. They work very hard for that beautiful precision they display on stage.

We had arranged for a quartet of the dancers to appear on the empty stage of the Palace in full costume to be interviewed and show me some of their steps. All four were beautiful in their Santa costumes, as the red and white short skirts showed off their long legs.

One of them demonstrated her high-kicking abilities by snapping her leg into the air, her foot clearing my head by a good six inches. Then the four invited me to join them in an impromptu chorus line for a few high kicks.

My rotund body was not made for this kind of activity. I did try mightily to join their high-kicking line, but while each of their kicks soared five or six feet into the air, my kick reached about knee-level. After the third kick, I started having pains in parts of my body that I didn't know had muscles.

As we finished the shoot, the four gathered around me for a photograph on the stairway to the Palace Theater lobby. I still have the photo and use it in some of my personal appearances. I don't have to explain or say a thing. As soon as they see the photo of me surrounded by the Rockettes, a chuckle sweeps the room.

I guess I was never meant to be a dancer.

CHAPTER 8

Planes, Trains, and Autos

THE CARS OF ONE-TANK-TRIPS

We used a variety of vehicles over the years to get to our One Tank destinations. In 1980, when the series started, I used my family car, a 1978 Ford. But we wanted a vehicle that would say "vacation," "travel," and "adventure," so we went to Bill and Bonnie Cutcher of Brownhelm and borrowed their vintage 1948 Chevrolet convertible. The Chevy became our official mascot for the next couple of years. But I decided that we needed a different type of car, something that would really stand out. Bill Cutcher answered my appeal by coming up with a classic 1940 American Bantam Roadster. That tiny car immediately caught the attention of my viewers.

For the next several years, the diminutive Bantam and I opened each One Tank Trip. But there was a problem. Since I did not own the car, I did not feel right in asking to drive it more than the few times each year when we would spend a day shooting generic scenes of it, giving the impression that I drove the Bantam to each trip. Also, every place I went, people would ask, "Where's your little car?" The only solution I could see was to buy my own vehicle.

A year-long search for the perfect car ended in 1989, when we found a 1959 Nash Metropolitan in a warehouse in North Canton. For the next eight years, whenever possible, I drove my Nash Metropolitan on the stories that we did and displayed the little car at car shows and other events.

The Metropolitan proved very popular and prompted a lot of questions, most often, "What is that car you drive?"

Sometimes, before I could answer, somebody would pipe up and say, "It's the car Lois Lane drove in the old Superman movies." Someone else might say, "Nah, it's one of those kit cars, you know, like you build yourself."

Wrong on both counts. Lois Lane drove a Nash Rambler, which is almost twice the size of my little car. And it is not a kit car. It was a production-line car for eight years before it drove off into automobile history.

Mine is a 1959 Nash Metropolitan, sometimes called the "Baby Nash." It was sold by the Nash Motor Company, which later merged with Hudson to form American Motors, which later was absorbed by the Chrysler Corporation.

The tiny Nashes were manufactured from 1954 until 1962. Probably the first truly international cars, they were built for Nash in England by the Austin Motor Company after a design by Pinin Farina of Italy. In eight years of production, fewer than 900,000 were built. Compare that with the millions of cars that major car manufacturers now produce each year! There were two models, a hardtop and a convertible. Both sold new for about $1,500—plus tax and title, of course.

Although a good idea, this tiny economical car came on the scene at the wrong time. In 1954, America was falling in love with big engines and even bigger tail fins. The Nash Metropolitan offered neither. It had a four-cylinder, 1,500-cc engine that could chalk up about thirty miles to the gallon. It could carry three people in the front seat and a couple of small children in a very small rear seat.

As near as we could discover, my car started life in Florida before ending up in North Canton, Ohio, where it was stored for a number of years before I bought it. It has about 72,000 miles on it, and it still has the original motor.

Did we really take it on all those trips? The answer is yes—and no. We drove it on many of the shorter trips in the earlier years.

But as time went by and the car became a favorite with viewers, we took it on fewer trips to preserve it. When we did use it, we shot extra footage of me driving the car for use in segments on longer trips, or during inclement weather. The car had become a symbol of our show—so much a mascot that at parades and at personal appearances, we have had small children come up to the car and pet it. One little girl thought it was alive and gave it a hug and kiss!

Does the car have a name? We never gave it one, but Dick Goddard referred to it as the "Neil-Mobile."

In 1996, we decided it was time I had another "new" car. Something different, something . . . unique. After a six-month search, we came up with a 1957 BMW Isetta 300. We found it in a small town near Grand Rapids, Michigan. I bought it sight unseen. The owners, a middle-aged couple, assured me over the telephone that the car was in excellent condition and had been "nearly restored." The only problem was a slight carburetor malfunction. I drove through a rainstorm to pick it up on the appointed day and arrived to be told again that there was a slight problem. The car, which they assured me had been running "like a top" only the night before, had developed the carburetor problem they warned me about, and today it just wouldn't start. Probably just the damp weather, they said.

I am a very trusting person, and I believed every word they said. How else could I have handed over a check for the full amount they asked for the car, pushed it onto a trailer, and hauled it through a rainstorm back to Ohio?

After three weeks of repair work and a couple of mechanics, the truth started to emerge. The car's motor and gasoline tank were loaded with sand, and the car had probably not been driven in months. A month later, friends Kevin Ruic, Scott Ruic, and George Kilburg, and my neighbor, H. B. "Army" Armstrong, who can usually fix most anything, had all taken a crack at making the Isetta run. A BMW Isetta is a strange little car. It has only one door, which opens the auto's entire front like a refrigerator door. Its four-speed transmission, located on the left side wall, is upside down.

George Kilburg finally put it back together late one night, hit the starter, and in a cloud of smoke it started. We were overjoyed. It ran! We were scheduled to unveil it the next day at the annual Dick Goddard Woollybear Festival parade in Vermilion. But none of us had ever driven it. We all agreed that since George had gotten the car running, he should have the honor of taking the first drive.

George is a longtime commercial airplane pilot who has also spent many years building and racing small cars. He is a man who can get into just about any car and drive it expertly. He proved it by backing the little Isetta out of his garage, turning it around, and roaring down his darkened driveway towards the front of his house. We saw the headlights turn to the left as he steered onto his front lawn in a large, sweeping circle. He came zipping back up the driveway, getting closer and closer to the open garage door without any discernible decrease in speed. Just as he whipped past me into the garage, I heard him yell, "Brakes! There's no brakes!"

George, thankfully, has quick reflexes. While we turned to watch in horror as the little car zoomed into the garage, George managed to pull the emergency brake, locking the back wheels, as the car skidded across the concrete floor, scattering tools, cans of grease, and nuts and bolts, and came to a stop mere inches from a workbench bolted to a concrete wall.

The next morning, with a new brake line installed, the car reluctantly started, and we loaded it onto a trailer, bound for Vermilion.

But the story doesn't end there. When we got to the Woollybear Festival that morning, we planned to have both the Nash Metropolitan and the BMW Isetta in the parade.

We had just arrived at the starting point for the big parade when the Isetta died. Despite frantic efforts by Kevin Ruic and other volunteers to get it going again, the cantankerous little car would not start. The parade was starting, and time was running out to debut my new car. Ruic, thinking more quickly than I was, ran to a nearby motorcycle club that was forming up for the parade and borrowed three nylon straps they used to tie the motorcycles to the trailer they used for transport. He knotted the straps together and had Bonnie back the Nash Metro to just in front of the disabled Isetta. He used the straps as a towrope, and we were off.

Towing the Isetta, Bonnie drove the little Nash with Kevin and his wife, Cindy, in the front seat and my son, Craig, and Kevin's son, Brandon, perched on the backseat. I crawled through the Isetta's moon roof and perched on top of the diminutive car, behind whose wheel was family friend Gary Rice.

We had just pulled into line to march in the parade when Rice tugged on my leg and said something. I ducked down inside, only to learn that Rice was trying to tell me the brakes had failed again. Somehow, we got through the parade without a collision.

After that inauspicious beginning, it was mostly downhill over the next year and a half. We learned quickly that the little car was not only temperamental, it was also dangerous to drive on a busy highway. Its small size caused other drivers to misjudge their distance, usually resulting in a near-collisions as they slammed on their brakes and skidded to a stop just inches from the Isetta's rear. And because its slow speed took too long to drive to our destinations, there was the need to trailer it almost everywhere we went. Rain or shine, snow or heat, we had to wrestle the car onto and off the trailer, sometimes in the dark. Skinned knuckles and bruised shinbones from night-time encounters with the trailer became a way of life.

The final straw was that when we took the Isetta to car shows, people would want to know why we quit driving the Nash Metropolitan, saying they liked it better. After fifteen months, I decided that retiring the Metropolitan had been a terrible mistake, and that the car that should be retired was the Isetta.

I went to the Crawford Auto Aviation Museum of the Western Reserve Historical Society in Cleveland and explained the circumstances to them. I had loaned them the Metropolitan, and they had displayed it in their lobby for a year. They graciously returned the car to me but decided they did not want the Isetta, which I also offered to loan for display.

Shortly after I put the Metropolitan back on the road and into our One Tank Trips series, I was doing a story at the Canton Classic Car Museum. Its director, Bob Lichty, asked what I planned to do with the Isetta. When I confessed I didn't know, he suggested his museum would like to borrow it for temporary display. Since I have always considered it one of the finest automobile museums in the country, I jumped at the opportunity and in a couple of days had the Isetta in Canton. It proved to be a popular exhibit. About a year later, Lichty asked if I might consider donating the car to the museum. My wife and I decided that even if the Isetta didn't work as the signature car in my television series, it was still unusual enough that a museum probably was the best place for it. So we turned the title over to the Canton Classic Car Museum, which is where you'll find the little car today, sitting proudly among some of the greatest cars ever built.

It seemed to naturally follow, when I retired from Fox 8 TV in 2004, that the little red and white Metropolitan should also go to a museum. We worked out a long-term loan agreement with the Canton Classic Car Museum, and today the car shares a gallery with some of the world's most classic and unique automobiles. Stop in and take a look sometime.

MY SIDE JOB IN TORONTO

I see a story every once in a while about some poor soul who goes to a theater or ritzy restaurant, and hands his or her car keys to a supposed parking valet, who turns out to be a car thief.

Funny how that can happen. I can report from experience.

Photographer Jim Holloway and I traveled to Toronto, Ontario, to do a story on the Broadway play *Ragtime,* which was running at the Fisher Theater near downtown.

Anyone who watched the segment remembers that I always

wore blue jeans, a sport shirt, and a baseball cap that said "One Tank Trips." It was my uniform, so to speak. But when we went to a fancy theater in Toronto, one where most folks wore suits and ties, it was pointed out that my usual apparel would not only be out of place, it would probably not be allowed inside. So we decided that I should wear a tuxedo for that episode. I didn't want to disappear among the other theatergoers, however, so I insisted I would wear my baseball cap with the tux, at least outside the theater while we filmed.

When the night arrived, Jim Holloway and I stood outside the theater, waiting for a crowd to show up as the background for my report. I wore my shiny black tuxedo, bow tie, and my red "One Tank Trips" baseball cap.

A short line formed at the door, and we started filming. But no sooner had Jim turned on the portable lights than the battery went dead.

"I'm going to run back to the car and get a fresh battery!" Jim shouted to me as he jogged to the parking lot behind the theater.

I was standing with my hands in my pockets at the edge of the turnaround in front of the theater when the loud, nearby sound of an automobile horn startled me. I turned and was blinded for a second by headlights that had stopped just in front of me. It was a large, expensive Mercedes, and a man in a tuxedo and his lady, in furs and a gown, got out of it. The man walked towards me and tossed me the keys.

"You don't peel the tires! You don't change the radio! And you don't change the bloody seat settings! Understand?" he barked at me.

I stood there somewhat bemused until it dawned on me that, in my tux with the red baseball cap, he had mistaken me for the valet.

"And you better not be smoking in my car," he added. "I'll have your job if I smell any smoke in there!"

At this point, Jim came jogging back with his TV camera on one shoulder and a new light pack on the other.

"Hey Jim, look!" I said. "This nice gentleman just gave us the keys to his Mercedes. Who says Canadians aren't hospitable to Americans?" I held the keys high so Jim could see them.

Jim looked puzzled, but I was watching the Canadian's face as the truth of the situation dawned on him. Before I could put my arm down, he snatched his keys from my hand and rushed his wife inside the theater as I called after him, "Does this mean we can't use your car?"

The real valet came out of the theater a few minutes later, saw Jim and me standing by the Mercedes, and said, "I don't know what you did to that old man, but he was sure upset."

I told him the story, and we could hear his laughter even as he made the tires squeal, driving away in the Mercedes.

ACROSS THE LAKE

There are three ways to get to Canada: fly, drive, or take the ferry. The Pelee Islander has been a mainstay in international travel for years, running daily during the summer from downtown Sandusky to Pelee Island, Leamington, and Kingsville, Ontario.

When cameraman Grant Zalba and I went to Canada for a week-long series of reports on what was on the opposite side of Lake Erie, we drove. WJW had only a limited number of radio-equipped news cruisers in those days, so we used a rental car instead of a company car. And we decided to return home on the Pelee Islander. It turned out to be a trip neither of us will forget.

Our week in Canada was enjoyable. We met a lot of nice people and saw the sights on the northern shore of Lake Erie. One of the first stories we did was on the dock at Kingsville, Ontario, where we met a man from Lorain, Ohio, waiting for the ferry. He carried a box containing the cremated remains of a friend. He told us the man spent many summers on Pelee Island, and it was his last wish that his ashes be buried there, the largest island in Lake Erie. He had no living family, however, and the courts were ready to have him buried in an old family plot. The friend, remembering the man's wishes, appealed to the court. On this beautiful, early summer day, he was fulfilling a last request and taking his friend to his final resting place in Lake Erie.

On our last evening in Erieau, the tiny fishing village directly across from Cleveland, we filmed a pair of bagpipers from the Chatham Post of the Canadian Legion standing on the rocks on the edge of Lake Erie, piping down the sun. A beautiful sight.

On the final day, we arrived in Leamington to board the Pelee Islander for the ride back to Sandusky. It was a hot, muggy June day. Large cumulonimbus clouds were forming in the west as the boat departed, packed with early vacationers headed for Pelee. A deck hand sandwiched our rental car between two other cars on the open part of the deck. The space was so tight that when we wanted to retrieve something from the car, we had to crawl in and out of an open window because there was no room to open the doors.

The weather got worse as the first hour on the water passed. Grant and I had not paid much attention because we were interviewing the crew and taking footage of passengers. But a sudden bolt of lightning that struck the water only feet from the boat and the almost immediate clap of thunder did get our attention. We headed for the enclosed cabin on the first deck to escape the torrential downpour that followed.

The ferryboat, although a sizeable craft, began to toss and pitch as we entered the full fury of a Lake Erie thunderstorm. I had always wondered what it would be like to ride out a storm on the lake. It only took a few minutes for me to decide that I wished I were on land instead of in this pitching craft.

In the cabin, passengers looked worried and pale. Many were becoming seasick. Grant went to help a young mother traveling alone with two children who were terrified by the storm. I struggled up the ladder to the pilot house and found many passengers hanging on to the rails on the second deck. The crew confirmed that the very strong storm was slowing our transit, but they had seen many storms on the lake and didn't seem worried. Reassured, I lurched out onto the second deck just in time to see what looked like a large fiery basketball strike the water and start bouncing towards the ship. About fifty feet away, it exploded like a bomb. One crew member told me it was "ball lightning." I decided to go back to the enclosed cabin on the first deck.

It was two hours of howling wind and pounding sea as we pushed our way through a veritable wall of water before finally reaching the dock at Sandusky Bay. The passengers were a damp and pale-looking lot as they filed off the boat to go through customs. Grant and I were still on deck, waiting for our car, when we saw a young crew member walk to it, open the door, and jump back as a gush of water poured out. The storm had nearly filled the auto with water through the window we had left open.

Grant and I sponged as much water as possible off the seats so he could drive it off the boat and through customs, where we learned we had just ridden out a storm that spawned tornadoes, doing some damage in nearby Fremont.

The car? We couldn't turn it in for several days. We left it setting in the sun with the doors and windows open until it dried out. The folks at Hertz did ask if we had carried fish in the car.

YOU DON'T MESS WITH THE OPP

I am second to no one in admiration for the abilities and talents of my colleague and sometime traveling partner, photojournalist Ron Mounts. Down through the years, Ron and his camera have often added much beauty to an otherwise average One Tank Trip. When the occasion warrants, he has even risked life and limb to provide just the right video to accompany my words. He has just one problem: Canada.

When the new Windsor Casino was about to open in the spring of 1994, Ron accompanied me, my wife, and my son across the border to do a story not only on the new casino, but on what else was across the lake from Cleveland.

Our problems started the first day, when we arrived to discover that the construction work, supposedly finished, was still going on, and it would be another week before the casino opened. And, even though it was spring, the city of Windsor was hit that night with a large ice and snow storm that played havoc with our plans to set out for Leamington, Ontario, the next day.

We were late and on QE3 (Queen Elizabeth Highway 3) just outside of Windsor. Ron was driving the GMC Suburban we were using. A string of traffic was ahead of us, and Ron was just keeping up. Suddenly we passed an OPP (Ontario Provincial Police) car, which made a U-turn and started after us. We heard a siren and saw the lights go on atop the cruiser. Since we were the last car in a line of autos, we assumed he was signaling us to move over so he could take off after a speeder he clocked up ahead of us. It turned out we were the ones he was after.

A pleasant-faced, gray-haired officer approached our car and asked Ron for his driver's license. Ron asked him what we had done wrong.

"A bit of a hurry, eh?" the patrolman declared. "I clocked you at 118 kilometers."

"I was only going sixty!" Ron protested. "Besides, all those other cars were pulling away from me."

"Looking at the miles per hour instead of kilometers, eh," he said. "Most of you Americans forget that we don't use that system here. Here we use the metric system, and the speed limit is 100 kilometers, eh."

"But what about those other cars I saw pulling away from me?" Ron protested. "They were certainly going faster than I was."

The Canadian officer smiled a Cheshire-cat smile and replied, "But you're the one I stopped, eh?"

He wrote out the ticket and handed it to Ron with this advice: "If you decide not to pay this, I suggest you not come back to Canada, eh, because this will be in our computers, and if you get stopped for any other offense, I can guarantee you'll be spending some time in Canada as our guest."

Realizing he wasn't going to win this one, Ron accepted the ticket with tight lips, and we slowly pulled back into traffic and crawled on toward our destination with the policeman watching.

But our Canadian adventure wasn't over. That evening we were to videotape the Chatham, Ontario, Royal Canadian Legion Pipe Band piping down the sun on the rocks at the edge of Lake Erie in Erieau. Although it was April, the temperature was in the teens. There was snow on the ground, and a brisk wind was coming off the lake. The pipers were arrayed across large boulders, silhouetted against the setting sun, playing a beautiful rendition of "Amazing Grace." The haunting sound of the pipes was accompanied by swooping gulls, which added their shrill cries to the sound of the bagpipes.

Ron was transfixed by the sight. He dashed around the beach trying to get the best angle of the sun's rays bouncing off the polished pipes, the swinging drumsticks of the drum major, the kilts blowing in the breeze. What he wanted was a shot from the lake that would show the water in the foreground and the pipers on the seawall. There was one way to do it: Ron had no boots with him, but he waded into the freezing lake and squatted down, holding his camera (which weighs nearly fifty pounds) just inches above the water. The shot was glorious. It was magnificent! From his cold, wet, uncomfortable position, Ron caught the last rays of the sun side-lighting the band, their ribbons and kilts blowing in the wind. The pipe major lifted his large silver-topped staff to the heavens, and sunbeams reflected in every direction.

I was watching from a rock, just out of camera range, taking some home video of the scene, and when I saw the pipe major's baton go up, I could almost read Ron's mind. It was one of those times when you open your mouth to scream a warning, but nothing comes out. I saw everything in slow motion. Ron, seeing the light reflecting from the baton, started to run from the lake toward the rocks. I could see his wet feet slipping in the sand, and as he leaped for a rock to get his camera in closer range, his foot landed on the stone and slipped off. Ron pitched forward, slamming his camera and his chest into the next boulder.

The drums stopped. The bagpipes stopped, with what sounded like an animal's dying scream. All eyes were riveted on Ron and his camera. I was halfway to him when he climbed to his feet, picked up the camera, and looked through the eyepiece.

"It's okay," he said, motioning the pipers to continue playing. I took a deep breath of relief that Ron was all right, as was his camera. Then I saw Ron's face. It was a study in concentration as he punched and punched the camera's off/on switch.

Things were not all right, after all.

"I think it's broken," he admitted as we looked at the huge dent in the lens cover. There were no friendly whirrs or beeps or little lights to signal that it was recording anything. Cleveland, we have a problem.

We were on the other side of the lake, in a foreign country, it was eight o'clock at night, and we still had a day and a half of videotaping to do before we could start home. The nearest television station was more than an hour's drive from where we were, and even then, there was no guarantee they could fix whatever had broken. We had a choice: pack up and go home without our final day's shoot, or improvise.

Ron Mounts is a professional, and while he owns one of the little 8mm home-video units, he wants to feel the heft of a professional camera when he's on the job, one that uses professional tape and takes pictures that can be shown on TV. What I suggested to him was probably like asking Picasso if he could paint with a broom. I suggested that he take our tiny home camera and use it to finish our Canadian shoot. It was as though I had just suggested that he sell his wife and children into bondage.

After he called several TV stations and was told they were unable to help us with our broken camera, the reality of the situation began to sink in. He reluctantly agreed to try the little camera. With it taped it to the top of his tripod, he seemed a bit embarrassed each time we set up in a public place, where people would gather to see what we were doing. We staggered through the last day of our trip and were able to use some of the home-video footage in our final product.

As for that speeding ticket, Ron vowed not to pay it and never did. His wife, Sandy, fearing that some day they might go to Canada and discover that the Canadian police had long memories, sent in the fine without telling him.

WATCH WHERE YOU PUT YOUR HANDS

The Cleveland National Air Show was slated for Labor Day weekend, and WJW's irascible assignment editor, Mickey Flanagan, asked me, "Z, do you like flying?"

I assured him that I enjoyed watching planes but had never piloted an aircraft.

"Go over to Burke Lakefront Airport and do a story with some navy guy who's going to take you for a ride," Flanagan said as he continued to rip copy coming in on the UPI News printer.

The "navy guy" turned out to be a lieutenant with the famed Blue Angels, and the plane he planned to give me a ride in was the F-4 Phantom II that the navy was using at that time. The pilot told me that the aircraft was a two-place supersonic fighter plane that could reach speeds of Mach II, or twice the speed of sound. It was capable of carrying 16,000 pounds of rockets, bombs, missiles, and guns.

Most of my flights up to that time had been in the waning days of piston-driven airplanes. It was a time when cabin attendants were called "stewards" and "stewardesses," when they still served free drinks and meals, and when pillows and blankets were readily available at no charge. No matter how many amenities they offered, however, the airplanes were noisy and slow.

I wanted to fly in a jet airliner but had never had the opportunity. Now the navy was giving me a rather strange initiation into the world of jet propulsion.

They helped me get into a green flight suit, and the pilot told me that the trip we were taking was just going to be a short take-off, a few passes over the airport, and a return to Burke Lakefront Airport.

"It's going to be a ride you won't soon forget," he assured me. "My crew chief will take you out and get you strapped into the airplane."

A chief petty officer grabbed my arm and hastily walked me to the big blue and gold plane. "You ever flown in a jet before?" he asked as he pulled me along.

"Uh, no," I replied.

"Shit!" he said. "Don't you get sick in my airplane."

"Why would I get sick?" I asked as we reached the shade under the wing.

"There's a barf bag tucked in the back of the pilot's seat. You feel like you're gonna hurl, you use it," he insisted, pushing me toward a short ladder that took us up on the wing.

"You get sick in there, I gotta clean it out," he said in a low, threatening voice as we reached the open cockpit.

At his direction, I climbed into the rear seat of the big fighter. A clear canopy was tipped to the rear. The cockpit was small and filled with switches, screens, and instruments. I could barely squeeze into the seat. As he started attaching a harness over my shoulders and between my legs, he snugged up the straps so tight I winced.

"If anything goes wrong and you have to eject, you'll be glad these seat belts is tight," he chortled. "And don't you get sick in my airplane."

He handed me a large helmet with a dark visor that pulled down over my face. With the helmet on, I could barely hear him as he continued to point out the bag I was to use in case I got sick. I was getting pretty excited. Suddenly, in my earphones, I heard the pilot's voice.

"Are we all ready to go?"

He was standing in the front cockpit, and he quickly folded himself into the seat and put on his seat belt harness.

Within moments we were bumping down the taxiway. Aside from the chatter of the control tower in my headphones, all I could hear was the whining sound that got louder as we turned and started down the main runway. In seconds the bounce of the wheels stopped and the ride became smooth. The skyline dropped away, and we suddenly seemed to be heading straight into the sky at a speed that was curling my lips away from my teeth.

"How you doing back there?" the pilot asked.

"Just fine," I replied. "Just like sittin' in my grandfather's rocking chair."

"We're going to do a couple of turns. You let me know if they make you uncomfortable," he said.

Over the next few minutes we turned, dipped, went screaming into the clouds, and then leveled out with the clouds below us. It was an incredible sight, and I must have been babbling about the vista when I heard the pilot again.

"You seem to be really enjoying this," he said. "Would you like to experience weightless flight, like the astronauts?"

He explained that astronauts in training are taken up at a high speed in a plane that suddenly levels off. The forces of gravity take over, and for a few seconds they're weightless in the aircraft. He took us into a climb. As we reached the apex, I saw the ballpoint pen I had tucked loosely in the breast pocket of my flight suit float out in front of my face! It was an incredible feeling.

"Still having a good time back there?" he asked

"Yep!" I answered. "And I haven't felt airsick at all, so the chief doesn't have to worry about me messing up his airplane."

The pilot chuckled and said, "Since you're having so much fun, would you like to do a few eight-point rolls like we do in the show?"

Would I? Absolutely.

So off we went, rolling through the sky—first in a barrel roll, where the sky and the ground quickly changed places, over and over, then in slow point-by-point rolls, ending with a screaming climb towards the sun, a roll over the top, and then a descent at incredible speed that pulled my face towards the back of my head. He flipped the plane upside down, and suddenly I was looking up at the runway as we rocketed over it about two hundred feet in the air.

"How you doing back there?" the pilot inquired again.

"I'm hanging on, but I'm having a ball!" I replied.

"Uh . . . hanging on to what?" he asked.

"This yellow and black handle above my head. I grabbed it when we did the run down the runway."

After a few seconds of silence, the pilot's voice came back in a very deliberate tone.

"Very carefully remove your hand from that handle. That is the ejection handle for both of us!"

When we got back on the ground, the pilot was a bit irritated with his crew chief, who was so intent on warning me against getting sick in his airplane that he had forgotten to explain what the ejection handle did, that it allowed the rear passenger to eject both himself and the pilot if the pilot became incapacitated. Especially, he was upset that the chief had not told me to keep my hands off of it.

BECOMING A SILENT BIRDMAN

One of my early problems after joining WJW-TV was occasionally having to jump in an airplane or a helicopter to fly to the scene of a disaster or major breaking news story. I did it, but usually with a sweaty brow and white knuckles. I learned I was afraid to fly. Oh, I had flown in airliners and even small planes, but they were usually happy events on nice flying days that I selected. I couldn't get used to climbing into a single-engine aircraft on a day of freezing rain and snow and then flying across frozen Lake Erie to the scene of a plane crash that killed several hunters.

On that particular flight, winds buffeted our small craft, bringing occasional white-outs, when the snow became so thick we could not see the lake beneath us. The flight only lasted about ten minutes before we landed on Kelleys Island, but then we had to arrange ground transportation and get to the scene of the crash. The only thing I could think about was that, once we finished a story on the recovery of bodies from a downed airplane, I would have to get back on a similar aircraft and fly into the same winter storm we had come through to get here.

It did little to cure me of my growing fear of flying.

Fortunately for me, I was sent one Sunday in the early 1970s to Middlefield, Ohio, to do a feature story on how the Amish gathered at the Middlefield Airport to watch sailplanes. Sometimes called *gliders,* sailplanes are highly maneuverable aircraft that have no motor and rely on air currents to remain aloft.

My first thought on seeing the craft was that there was no way I would ever get into one. It was bad enough flying small aircraft with motors. I thought these people flying sailplanes were all nuts.

Then I met Mike Nemes.

Mike was one of the instructors that day. He had a thick Hungarian accent, and I asked where he had learned to fly. He told me he learned in Hungary as a boy, and later was a pilot in the Hungarian branch of the German Luftwaffe in World War II. He had flown the famous Messerschmitt 109 fighter plane, was shot down and captured by the Russians, and spent some time in a cruel Russian POW camp. When the war ended and he was repatriated, he moved to the United States and eventually purchased a sailplane trainer and started a program to teach young people to fly.

After our interview, he urged me to put down my microphone and climb into the plane so he could take me for a ride and show me how easy it was to fly. I demurred, saying I got enough flying when stories required me to get somewhere in a hurry. Just going up to fly around a field held no appeal for me.

But Mike was persistent. He promised that if I got into the aircraft we would only go up for ten minutes, and I would see in that short time that this was unlike any aircraft I had ever been in.

Whether it was because of Mike's salesmanship or the teasing I was getting from photographer Peter Miller, who stood behind me clucking like a chicken, I finally gave in and climbed into the front seat of the trainer. Mike Nemes climbed into the rear seat. A long cable attached to a propeller-driven plane was hooked on to the front of our sailplane. Mike told me to place my feet gently on the pedals in front of me and to lightly grasp the control stick between my legs so I could feel what he was doing while flying the craft.

He suddenly wiggled the control stick, and the plane we were attached to started to taxi. The rope pulled taut, and we briefly bumped across the grass. Then there was a lift, and soon we were smoothly flying a few feet above the grass.

The tow plane slowly gained altitude, and we followed at the end of our long tether. When we reached two thousand feet and the airport beneath us looked like some toy, I heard Mike tell me to reach to the dashboard and pull the large red knob. I hesitated. Mike said, "Go ahead; we won't fall out of the sky."

I pulled the knob, and the rope towing us fell away. All I could hear was the whish of air sliding past the canopy. I could even hear the sound of auto horns far below.

Mike said, "Step on the left pedal and push the stick to the right, gently."

I did, and the plane started a gentle, graceful turn.

"Now bring the stick back level and ease back on the pedal," Mike instructed from behind me. I did. The aircraft straightened out, and we were now headed in a different direction.

"We're going to head for that plowed field to the north," he said. "Now you'll feel like you're in an elevator when we find the thermal."

I had no idea what he was talking about, but sure enough, a few seconds later as we passed over the sunlit field below, I felt a sudden strong upward motion in the aircraft. Mike threw the control stick to one side, and the plane was standing on one wing, turning in a tight circle over the field.

Chortling in the rear seat, Mike said, "We've found a really good thermal. We'll ride this up a couple of hundred feet."

The dizziness I first experienced when we started "thermaling" passed, and we spiraled up another fifty feet or so. Then Mike righted the craft, and we started back in the direction of the airport.

"That is what we live for," Mike said, "to see how long we can stay up here by locating and riding the thermals."

We went lower and lower as we approached the airport.

I called back to Mike, "What do you do if you don't have enough altitude to get back to the airfield?"

"That means you are not a good pilot," Mike joked back. "If that happens, you have to land in some farmer's field and then take the airplane apart and truck it back to the airport."

"What if you're coming in too fast or too high? How do you go around to try it again?"

"You can't go around, so you have to make a good landing the first time, every time," he replied as we got closer to the landing area.

"Take the stick and follow what I do," he ordered. "Just do exactly what I tell you."

I put my hand on the stick and for the next few seconds followed each correction that Mike calmly gave me from the backseat. Then we were just inches off the grass, and I felt a soft bump as we landed, rolled a few feet, and came to stop nearly in front of the crowd that had been watching.

Mike said, "Turn around and look at me."

I turned in my seat. He had his hands over his head and his knees doubled under his chin.

"You did that landing all by yourself by just following my instructions," he announced with a satisfied smile.

I was astonished and didn't really believe Mike until I later talked with Peter Miller, who assured me that he saw Mike hold both of his hands against the top of the canopy as we approached the landing. *I* flew the craft.

It was one of the most thrilling rides of my life. With no experience and only the guidance of an experienced pilot, I had actually flown the craft on my very first ride. I was hooked on sailplanes.

I became a member of Mike Nemes flying club that met on a farm field near Belden in Lorain County each weekend.

He had no tow plane on a regular basis there, so they often used a motorized winch to launch the sailplanes. The winch was a partially dismantled automobile with an exposed axle. A two-thousand-foot-long steel cable was wrapped around the axle, which would wind the cable quickly and powerfully enough to pull the sailplane and its passenger off the ground and more than a thousand feet into the sky, where they would disengage the cable and go in search of a thermal.

Being launched from the winch was like a low-tech rocket ride. As you sat strapped into the cockpit, a ground crew member lifted a wing, held it steady, and gave the signal to the winch operator to launch. With a snap that pushed you back into the seat, you started down the field, rapidly gathering speed as you pulled the control stick back as far as you could. Suddenly you found yourself pointing almost straight up at the sky until you reached a thousand feet, where you leveled off, pulled the cable release, and were on your own. It was a quick and thrilling way to get to flying altitude.

Most of that summer I took lessons from Mike Nemes at the little Belden grass strip. Sometimes the weather was perfect and offered lots of thermals that kept us flying in circles over nearby farms for nearly an hour. Other times we would go up and only manage one or two circles of the landing area, losing so much altitude that we had to return to the grass strip.

I wasn't a very good pilot, but I was learning. I started looking forward to the day I would "graduate" and make my first solo flight in the two-seat trainer. I started wearing old shirts to my lessons because of a tradition: When you made your first solo flight, the instructor and other pilots would cut off your shirt tail and hang it in the clubroom, marked with the day of your flight.

Mike never told you when you would make that flight. It would happen when he was satisfied you could do it without hurting or killing yourself.

I went to the field one Saturday in late August not expecting to fly, but just to help out as a ground crew member, as we were all expected to do—running the cable back and forth, up and down the field, hooking up the glider, and keeping track of each member's time in the air. One student failed to show up, and Mike called me over and asked if I would like to take his time. I jumped in the front seat while Mike climbed into the rear. By now, he had to say little as I ran a preflight check of the cockpit, checked my seat belts, and nodded to the ground crew that I was ready.

We took off smoothly and flew for about ten minutes when Mike tapped me on the shoulder and said, "Let's take it back down." I gently brought the sailplane back to earth and made a smooth but long landing. I had just unhooked my seat belt when Mike tapped me on the shoulder again."Leave it on," he said. "It's time."

Without another word, he climbed out of the plane and took the place of the ground crew as they turned the sailplane around and pointed it towards the winch operator.

Mike leaned over me, looked into my eyes and said, "Do you remember everything I have taught you?"

I nodded yes, and he continued, "Just take it up, make a couple of circles of the field, and land. Don't try anything fancy. It's going to feel faster and more responsive with just you alone. And one final thing: Don't you dare bend my airplane."

With that, he stepped back and waited for me to give him the signal that I was ready to take off on my first solo flight.

My heart was in my mouth. I was nearly shaking with excitement. I so much wanted to do this, but I also wanted Mike in the backseat so I could hear his calm voice telling me what to do when something didn't go just right. I also had a rather strange thought: I was wearing one of my favorite shirts, and when I completed this ride it was going to be cut to shreds.

I checked my seat belt for the third time, snugged the shoulder straps a little tighter, checked the cockpit, tapped the variometer and other gauges to make sure they were working, and then took a deep breath. I looked at Mike and gave him an almost imperceptible nod. He raised the right wing as a signal to the winch operator, and just like that I was shooting down the field and nearly leaping into the air.

The next few minutes were a blur. I pulled the release lever at fourteen-hundred feet, and the plane instantly seemed to climb even higher. I brought it under control, made two giant circles of the airfield, and started getting into position to take the plane back to the ground. I lined the field up perfectly as I flew in over a woods at the end of the field. When I saw the winch operator flash by below me, I realized I was coming in way too fast. I was eating up the runway and was still fifty feet in the air. Ahead of me was State Route 83, and across it was a barbwire fence and about fifty curious, grazing dairy cows. I had to get the plane on the ground where I could apply the brakes.

I could hear Mike's voice from similar landings, telling me to push the stick forward gently until I was just above the grass and then to pull the "spoiler," a lever on the left side of the cockpit that would raise two panels on the wings, breaking the lift created by air flowing over the craft's wings. The effect would be like an elevator, pushing me onto the ground.

It worked, but I was still going far too fast, and the runway was just about gone. Mike and some students ran frantically toward the highway to stop traffic because it looked like I was going to barrel across the road into the fence. With only fifty feet left between me and the highway, and still traveling at about 30 miles per hour, I heard Mike's voice saying, "Ground loop, ground loop!" I pushed the stick to the side, lowering the wing, while standing on the right rudder pedal. The wing dipped, and a small wheel on the end of the wing for just such situations hit the grass, slowing my forward motion and causing the craft to go round and round in a circle, creating a large cloud of dust at the edge of our parking lot. I stopped just yards from the busy highway.

Everything was quiet. All I could hear was the wild pounding of my heart. Mike slowly walked over to the plane and opened the canopy.

"That wasn't exactly the smoothest landing I have ever seen," he said dryly. Then he said, "Do you think you can take it back up and do it right this time?"

The last thing I wanted to do right then was to take that aircraft back into the sky, but I gulped and nodded yes.

I was airborne again in a few minutes, and this time I made a picture-perfect landing to the cheers of my fellow students. They rushed over, pulled me from the cockpit, and held me while Mike cut the back off one of my favorite shirts.

Mike later asked me what happened on that first landing. I told him that, as he had cautioned, the glider was faster and more responsive with only person aboard, and I forgot to watch my speed on landing. Had it not been for his yelling at me to ground-loop the plane, I might have plowed into the cows across the road.

Mike looked at me with some confusion and said, "I didn't yell anything to you; we were too busy trying to stop traffic."

His "voice" that I heard apparently was in my subconscious, from the many times during training when I used too much runway and Mike gave me that same command.

I flew sailplanes every chance I had for the next several years. And my fear of flying? I can't say I felt comfortable on every flight I had to make, especially in bad weather. But my sailplane experience made me more knowledgeable about how airplanes worked, and I even grew to enjoy many of the flights.

WINGS OVER NEW YORK

There was a time when I talked so much about the joy of soaring that friends would walk the other way when they saw me coming. I was fascinated with the silence of flight without a motor. I took advantage of any and all chances to fly. In the early years of One Tank Trips, one of the first attractions I thought to show viewers was soaring. It is considered one of the safest forms of aviation, at least for the pilot.

Videographer Jim Holloway and I drove to Elmira, New York, the cradle of America's soaring industry. This is the home of the Schweizer Aircraft Company and of the National Soaring Museum, on Harris Hill. An airport on top of the hill offers sailplane rides and instruction, and we had made arrangements for an instructor and me to take up a sleek new low-winged, high-performance sailplane while Jim went aloft in the tow plane. The plane would fly in formation with us after we cut loose so Jim could photograph me at the controls.

The first problem was that the regular pilot was not available for the tow plane, so a retired pilot was contacted and agreed to fill in. When he arrived, however, we began to have a few doubts. He was in his eighties! He had flown during World War II. The instructor assured us that he was well qualified. Besides, he pointed out, he was the only pilot available.

Jim Holloway, a good friend and a Vietnam veteran who stayed alive in combat by following his instincts, told me he had misgivings about our white-haired, very senior pilot, but he finally agreed to go.

They took the door off the plane so Jim could sit tethered in the doorway with his camera to do some plane-to-plane photography. The towrope was hooked onto the sailplane and, with a wiggle of the tail rudder, I gave the signal that I was ready for takeoff.

We taxied smoothly across the top of the hill. I was already airborne, holding my sailplane about two feet off the ground, as the tow plane, still earthbound, bore on toward the end of the runway. Finally, slowly, he lifted off just before the end of the pavement. It was a good thing, because less than a hundred feet beyond the end of the runway was a cliff that dropped off into the Chemung Valley, nearly two thousand feet below.

As we climbed, the umbilical cord connecting us dragged me again and again into the turbulent wake of the power plane. I was very happy when we finally reached an altitude of about five thousand feet and the instructor, sitting behind me, said I could disconnect the towrope.

I pulled the lever, pushed the stick forward slightly as the rope dropped away, and started to build some speed to do wingovers while Jim's plane caught up with us to start taping.

I noticed that they had flown back to a spot just above and slightly in front of me. I saw Jim, sitting in the open doorway, his legs dangling out of the plane, point his camera at me as I moved my stick to the right and gave it full right rudder. I tipped up on one wing and turned away from them.

It would have been a beautiful shot: the gull-winged aircraft I was piloting against a backdrop of the mountains of western New York.

What I didn't see was that the pilot of the tow plane had decided to stay with me, apparently forgetting that Jim was sitting in the open doorway. He performed the same maneuver, with his plane going up on one wing. The movement left Jim hanging from his belt in the doorway, dangling five thousand feet over the Chemung Valley!

I looked above me as I leveled out and was shocked to see Jim's legs churning in empty air. He seemed to be trying frantically to climb back inside. The pilot finally appeared to realize what he had done and brought his plane level, making it easier for Holloway to work his way back into the cockpit. A few seconds later he made it, and the plane suddenly veered away from us and started descending toward the airport. The pilot radioed us that Jim had just told him he would prefer to shoot the rest of the scenes from the runway—on the ground!

CHAPTER 9

Mishaps

NORTH TO ALASKA

I have been asked many times what my longest One Tank Trip was. That question is easy to answer in just one word: Alaska.

We really did take a one tank trip to Alaska in the early 1990s— although in a 747 airplane, not in a car—because WJW was then owned by a company that tried all kinds of ways to increase revenue.

I first heard a rumor that I was going to be assigned to such a trip from the TV8 photographers. The photo department at TV8 seemed to have advance notice on just about everything. If there was a rumor, true or false, you could be sure the photographers were on top of it.

I learned about it officially a few days later from my boss, news director Phyllis Quail. She casually asked if I had ever been to Alaska. I replied in the negative and she said, "How would you feel about leading a tour there and doing a series of reports on a visit to Alaska?"

Now I had heard stories for years from colleagues who, for a free vacation, spent their vacation time leading tour groups to places like Hawaii. I had also heard the horror stories. When Marty Ross was an anchor at TV8, he and his wife led such a tour to the South Pacific, only to spend most of the time settling arguments between husbands and wives. They were even rousted from bed early one morning to go to the local jail and bail out someone in the tour group who was arrested for too much drinking the night before.

I had visions of playing nursemaid to forty or fifty unhappy tourists while trying to line up stories and do location shootings. I said, "No thanks."

A few days later, Phyllis called me into her office and told me that our parent company had formed an alliance with Holiday Tours, and that I would be going to Alaska for two weeks with a group of tourists and photographer Bill Wolfe to document the trip. Before I could object, she told me that the tour company had promised to provide a trip leader who would take care of any problems we had along the way. I would serve in name only as the guy in charge.

She sweetened the pot by saying I could also take my wife, Bonnie, all expenses paid. We would fly to Anchorage where we would board a tour bus and head to Fairbanks, travel into Canada and the Northwest Territory, and finally head back to the U.S. at Skagway, Alaska, an old gold-mining port. There we would board the *Crown Princess* for a leisurely, four-day trip down the inland passage to Victoria, British Columbia, where we would catch our plane home.

It sounded like a dream assignment, but I had one problem: Our son, Craig, was then 13, and we had no one to stay with him while we were gone. The sales department must have been desperate to do this trip because a day later we were told that Craig would accompany us.

The plan was for photographer Wolfe and me to shoot a day-by-day special of everything we did and what we saw. A five- or even ten-part series would run on our news shows for a week or two, and we might also air a half-hour to hour-long special on the trip, a sort-of "super" One Tank Trip.

It turned into a wonderful, fun-filled journey. Our tour group, folks from all over northern Ohio who paid thousands of dollars to join us, were absolutely wonderful. Everyone seemed to get along. No matter what went wrong or what schedule wasn't met, there was little or no complaining. By the end of the journey, we felt we had forty new friends.

It was a trip of sights, sounds, smells, and memories that my family will never forget. Alaska is known as "The Great Land," and from the first sight of the Alaskan mountains and wilderness to eagles flying over Glacier Bay to the majesty of Mount McKinley rising out of the mist and clouds over Denali National Park, it lived up to its name. We had a wonderful time, and it even got better when we reached Skagway to board the "Love Boat."

As we sailed down the inland passage, a pod of whales joined us, accompanying us for hours on our journey. Wolfe shot cassette after cassette of videotape, capturing the whales, new icebergs being born at Glacier Bay, and the simple beauty of mountains and towns drifting by. As soon as we got back to the station, I grabbed the nearly forty hours of videotape from the trip and took it to my office to view and to start writing.

A word here about how WJW-TV edited videotape in those days. We were unionized, which meant I could not go into an editing suite and look at tape unless a video editor from that union was available. These were the same video editors who were extremely busy doing the daily news shows. Because this was an ongoing problem, management had solved it by negotiating with the editors' union to allow two or three of the oldest video playback units that were no longer needed in editing suites to be set up around the newsroom. Reporters could look at their tapes on them, but since the machines only played back video and did not record, it would be impossible to do any editing. The way we worked was to look at the tape, log all the shots, and make notes for the video editor where we wanted edits to occur. It usually worked pretty well.

Since I usually had more tape to view than other reporters, I had one of the playback machines just outside my office cubicle. I came in early and started logging the hours of tape, which was going to take several days. I screened about half of the tapes and turned them over to the video editors with my notes, asking them to start cutting the tape while I continued to view more and write.

I was at my computer terminal, happily tap-tap-tapping away, when I sensed someone standing behind me. One of our best video editors, Nancy McCasson, was standing at the doorway to my cubicle with a funny look on her face.

"That Alaska tape," she said. "Did you notice any problems with it?"

"Nope," I replied. "Bill Wolfe got some beautiful stuff up there. Just beautiful."

"Uh . . . I think you had better come and look at it," Nancy said as she turned away.

"Uh?" I said, as I stood up and followed. "I don't like the sound of *uh*."

We went into the editing suite, she flipped a couple of switches, and there was our footage of whales leaping out of the water alongside the *Crown Princess*. It was beautiful except for an electronic line right through the middle of the picture.

She turned a knob to advance the tape, and the line continued splitting the picture in half.

"Most of the tape is just like that," she said flatly.

My heart was in my mouth as I frantically handed her tape after tape and found each one ruined.

We later learned that the old playback unit outside my office was the culprit. Something had malfunctioned in it. As the picture passed the recording head, something scratched the tape, damaging it beyond repair. Of the forty hours of tape that we shot, I had accidentally destroyed almost twenty-two hours in that blankety-blank machine.

If you think I felt bad, you should have been around when I had to tell Bill Wolfe what had happened to his hard work. Let's just say he wasn't very happy.

The trip wasn't a total loss. We did salvage about twenty hours of tape I had not put through the suspect video player and managed to put together a five-part series. We were just starting to write the hour-long documentary when I learned that our connection with the travel company had ended, and there was now little interest in the documentary.

So. My longest One Tank Trip? Alaska.

The trip with the most problems? Alaska.

But it also became one of my most unforgettable journeys, with memories of a steam locomotive making a ghostly appearance out of a morning fog, the majestic sight of a grizzly bear romping with two cubs in a mountain meadow, and days when the sun refused to set—just a few of the incredible sights we caught on tape. It was one of my most memorable One Tank Trips, and one that very few of our viewers had the opportunity to share.

MY BRUSH WITH ROYALTY

I had a couple of encounters with royalty during my years as a journalist.

The first was in 1977, when it was announced that His Royal Highness, Charles, the Prince of Wales, would visit Cleveland. Because America had seen the assassinations of John F. Kennedy, Bobby Kennedy, and Martin Luther King, Jr., in the previous decade, security was tightened everywhere, and when any world leader traveled, a reporter was usually assigned to duty we called "the death watch." The reporter's job was to be as close to the leader as possible, with a camera ready to go, in case someone made an attempt on the leader's life. It was a macabre situation but one that governments understood and at least tolerated.

So when it was announced that the heir to the British throne was coming to Cleveland at the invitation of the English Speaking Union, word came from Scotland Yard and the U.S. State Department that only "pool" reporters could travel with the prince throughout the day. One reporter and photographer would represent all the TV stations in town, and others would service newspapers and radio stations.

Several weeks prior to the royal visit, WJW assignment editor Mickey Flanagan told me that it was TV8's turn to be "pool reporter." I had been picked with photographers Peter Miller and Lynn Chambers to travel with the prince, once we cleared our respective background security checks.

In addition to staying close to the prince all day, I was expected to share with all the TV stations in town our video and audio recordings, my impressions of the prince, and anything he might have said that we didn't capture on video. And, oh yes, I needed to be there to record any attempts on his life.

We were gathered on the chosen day in the terminal of Burke Lakefront Airport to await the royal party's arrival and get last-minute instructions from the Buckingham Palace advance team. We were told that while we would be close to Prince Charles, we were not to speak to His Royal Highness unless he spoke to us first. And we should never, ever attempt to shake hands with him unless he first offered his hand.

I had, of course, seen many pictures of the prince and read many articles about him, but seeing him in person as he stepped off his plane was a different experience. He was a tall, smiling young man, much more handsome than he appeared in photos. He seemed to genuinely enjoy meeting the gaggle of Cleveland officials gathered to welcome him.

We jumped in our news cruiser to follow the royal limousine and police escort on a whirlwind day of nonstop activities. From a visit to NASA Lewis Research Center to a tree-planting at Public Square, our small band of reporters and photographers was part of the royal party and at the prince's side. My good friend, legendary UPI photographer Ron Kuntz, was the pool still photographer. Ron wore his trademark beret. Several of us noticed that the prince seemed fascinated by Kuntz's beret and frequently stared at him.

At Public Square, we joined the rest of the local and national media in town to cover the royal visit. While we may have stood cheek-by-jowl with the prince at private gatherings, here we were just members of the herd of reporters jockeying for position to shout questions or get a picture of him planting his tree. Since the other stations were on hand, plus another camera from WJW-TV, Peter Miller, Lynn Chambers, and I had a chance to observe from the edge of the crowd.

But Ron Kuntz had to cover for newspapers all over the country. He was fighting to get close for a good shot, but the prince was surrounded by dozens of cameramen and curious onlookers struggling to get closer. One more aggressive woman gave Kuntz a shove and knocked him to the ground. As he glanced up, he saw the prince, who was just about ready to dig the obligatory shovel of dirt, looking directly at him. With no time to spare, Kuntz grabbed his shot from the ground. The photo shows Prince Charles looking at Kuntz and his camera through the branches of a tree.

Later, our small entourage moved with the prince to the Cleveland Clinic, where he was to take a look at an artificial heart they were using and visit a then-new sports medicine complex. By this time we had been on the road all day without a break, though we had been furnished tea and coffee and other beverages at each stop with the royal party. So by the time we got to the clinic and its "nonpublic" appearance—meaning just the prince, a few dozen security people, clinic officials and doctors, and the pool journalists—my bladder was bursting. I kept looking for a restroom as we entered the research area but noticed that most were closed, probably as a security measure. Finally, while the prince was trying out a piece of exercise equipment, and we were in a well-guarded room, far from the public, I bolted out the door to try the handles on restroom doors marked "closed." The first one was open. It was a small bathroom, just a toilet and sink. After I finished and washed my hands, the door suddenly flew open, and there stood a rather large man who I assumed was from Scotland Yard, because behind him stood a rather bemused Prince of Wales. Apparently it had also been a long day without a bathroom break for him. I was a bit embarrassed to be caught peeing in what was probably set aside as "The Royal Toilet" and, remembering our instructions not to speak unless spoken to, was trying to slink out of the bathroom when Prince Charles, smiling, asked me, "Did you wash your hands?"

Startled because he had largely ignored the pool reporters' presence all day until then, I replied, "'Uh . . . uh . . . Yes . . . Your Highness."

"Good," he said, walking into the bathroom and shutting the door.

After several more stops we ended the day as we gathered, at Burke Lakefront Airport, and the prince said his good-byes to local officials. Again we noticed him staring at Ron Kuntz and his beret. The prince sauntered over to him and asked, "Do you sell onions?" Nodding at Kuntz's beret, he explained that onion sellers in Brittany wear berets like his and carry baskets of onions on their bicycles.

Before he left, Prince Charles paused at the door to his plane to greet the lone piper playing for the departure. The piper, in the regalia of a pipe major of the famed Black Watch, was Sandy Hain, who retired to Cleveland from the 2nd Battalion, 42nd Royal Highland Regiment, Black Watch of the British Army. Sandy had once been the bagpiper for Prince Charles' grandmother, Queen Mother Elizabeth.

My second royal encounter, in 1983, followed a One Tank Trip to London, Ontario, where we visited the museum of the Royal Canadian Regiment at Wolseley Barracks. We learned that later that summer His Royal Highness Prince Philip, Duke of Edinburgh, husband of Queen Elizabeth, was coming to Canada to help celebrate the regiment's 100th anniversary. It would be a huge event, with all the elements of the regiment returning home for the first time in many years, replete with the pageantry of a royal visit.

Since London was just across the lake from Cleveland, I decided it would be an interesting piece of history to witness and a wonderful One Tank Trip. Our executive producer at Newscenter 8 at the time was Grant Zalba, a Canadian by birth. He agreed with me, and credentials arrived for cameraman Bill West and me after a couple of weeks of dealing with the Royal Canadian Mounted Police and Scotland Yard. It turned out that we were the only American TV crew accredited for the visit.

We gathered with Canadian journalists at London's airport to await Prince Philip's arrival. Also on hand were the red-coated band of the Royal Canadian Regiment, with their distinctive white colonial pith helmets, and a couple of platoons of paratroopers to form an honor guard. Two paratroopers unrolled a long red carpet to the area where the plane was to stop.

It was a beautiful summer day, hot and very windy. We saw a plane approaching on the horizon. Since all traffic at the airfield had been held up for the prince's arrival, it had to be him. The large, twin-engine aircraft landed, and almost immediately a small flag popped out on top of the cockpit, the royal colors, to denote that Prince Philip was on board. As the plane drew closer, we could see his familiar face in the pilot's seat. We were told later that he was a qualified pilot and sometimes liked to fly the aircraft personally.

As he wheeled the craft in front of the crowd, the propeller blast picked up the waiting red carpet and sent it skittering across the runway. An officer sent several paratroopers running to retrieve it and place it up to the door of the now-stopped aircraft.

The Prince appeared in the doorway, still buttoning his coat as the band broke into "God Save the Queen" and "O Canada," the Canadian national anthem.

Just then a gust of wind picked up the red carpet and again sent it sailing across the tarmac into the legs of a nearby honor guard. The music stopped. Everyone froze.

The prince paused and went back inside the aircraft as a red-faced sergeant major and two young privates ran across the pavement to retrieve the carpet again. It was quickly laid back in place, and the band started to play again as the wind again picked up the carpet and took it dancing into the nearby troops.

I could see the veins popping in the sergeant major's neck as he shouted commands at a platoon of paratroopers, who double-timed with him to the troublesome carpet. They grabbed it and hauled it back in place, but this time the sergeant major ordered a trooper to stand on each side of the carpet every dozen feet. Then he cued the band again.

This time the prince made his walk down the carpet, ignoring the troopers standing every few feet, and went to a podium to deliver some remarks. He finally climbed into an open convertible and, with an RCMP escort, left the airfield for the regimental headquarters.

I'm happy to report the pageantry the next day with companies of red-coated soldiers, pipers, and drummers in kilts went off without a hitch at the stadium in London. But I didn't notice any more red carpets.

PRESIDENTIAL ENCOUNTERS

I have always identified with President Gerald Ford. Not because of my politics, but because he and I suffered from a reputation for clumsiness.

When Mr. Ford was still in office, for example, he came to Cleveland, and I was assigned to do what is called a "one-on-one" interview. In other words, I was the only reporter in the room asking questions of him.

My camera crew and I arrived at his hotel suite at the appointed hour, and we were ushered into the parlor, where a gaggle of local officials and Secret Service agents were milling around. In the center of the room was the president. A press aide escorted me across the room and introduced me to Mr. Ford.

As he turned towards me to shake hands, I stepped forward, misjudging the distance, and immediately stepped on his foot! Now consider how you would feel if you accidentally stepped on the foot of the President of the United States. I was terribly embarrassed, but Mr. Ford was gracious. Wincing a bit, he waved off my apologies and limped to a nearby easy chair that my videographer, Cook Goodwin, had moved to a position near the center of the room.

The press aide indicated we would have only a few minutes

for the interview and emphasized that we should hurry with our preparations.

While Cook set up the tripod for the camera, I grabbed one of our tall light stands and walked quickly behind Mr. Ford to set up the light. As I ran the cord to a wall outlet, I did not notice that it was wrapped around the light stand's legs! The shout from an alert Secret Service agent alerted me. He caught the light as it toppled over, nearly striking the president.

I got several glares from agents. Cook took over setting up the lights while I seated myself across from Mr. Ford, stammering yet another apology for my clumsiness.

Again Mr. Ford was gracious enough to wave off my apologies, and we launched into the interview. I remember very little of it, other than that some of his answers were rather long and that we changed film at least once before his press aide indicated our time was up.

As I stood to say good-bye to the president, I realized that both of my feet had gone to sleep—I had no feeling in either one. As I tried to step forward to shake hands with the still-sitting Mr. Ford, I stumbled and fell to my knees, my head landing in his lap. Mr. Ford said nothing for a moment as startled agents reached to pull me up. As they lifted me to my feet, the president looked intently at me and said, "Young man, by any chance do you vote Democratic?"

Another time President Ford came to Cleveland, he was slated to meet with some officials at the studios of WJW-TV.

A camera crew and I were assigned to follow him while he was in the station. We had to undergo a rigorous background check by the Secret Service because this was soon after the two assassination attempts on Mr. Ford's life. We were each issued a tiny metal badge by the presidential security detail that we had to wear in our lapels. Without them, we could not even be on the same floor of the building as the president.

It actually turned into a rather boring assignment. We filmed the president and his motorcade arriving at 5800 South Marginal Road. We accompanied him into the station and dutifully taped him meeting with station manager Chuck Bergeson, and we followed him down the hall to TV8's executive conference room. As he entered the room, two burly Secret Service agents barred my photographers and me from following.

"This is not for publication," the agent said as he turned us away.

So we walked down the hall and sat on the floor to wait for him to come out. Problem was, he didn't come back out.

First minutes crept by, then a half hour, then an hour.

I started bugging the two Secret Service agents guarding the door.

"Who is he meeting with in there?" I asked.

"Can't tell you," answered an agent.

"Will he be out soon?"

"Can't tell you."

"What can you tell me?" I asked in desperation.

"The president is taking a nap."

And that is exactly what he was doing. Apparently the president was suffering a bit of jet lag and had decided to use the comfortable couch in the conference room for a nap.

Mr. Ford was retired when our paths almost crossed again. I went to Grand Rapids, Michigan, his hometown, to visit the Ford Presidential Museum. This beautiful edifice contains not only many mementos of his career in Congress and the White House, but also a personal office that he used when he visited Grand Rapids. It just so happened that the day we were slated to do a One Tank Trip to Grand Rapids, Mr. Ford was also in town to give a speech. He was expected in the museum sometime that afternoon to do some work in his office. Museum officials were glad to have us there to do a story on their facility but were understandably distracted by the presence of Secret Service agents checking out the building. They indicated that we could wander through the museum on our own while they escorted the agents on the upper-floor security check.

We had been videotaping for about fifteen minutes when we

came to the centerpiece of the museum, an exact replica of the Oval Office, just as it was in the White House when Mr. Ford was president. Velvet ropes blocked each doorway. Videographer Bill West and I stood there looking, Bill taking some shots of the presidential desk and chair through the doorway. I turned to Bill and said, "I wonder what it would feel like to sit behind that desk."

"Don't do it," warned West. But I already had unhooked the velvet rope and was walking across the room to the chair.

I pulled it out and had just settled into it, waiting for West to focus his camera on me, when Gerald Ford's voice boomed through the room: "This was the desk and chair that I used as president of the United States."

I leapt, red-faced, from the seat, believing I had just been caught by the former president. But no one was there. There was just the sound of the running feet of security guards. I had tripped an electronic beam that turned on a recording of Mr. Ford's voice and alerted guards that someone was inside the exhibit, where they were not supposed to be.

Museum officials, although polite, were not happy with me, and we had an escort for the rest of our short visit. If you get to Grand Rapids, be sure to see the Ford Presidential Museum, but *don't* try to sit in Mr. Ford's chair.

EMMY AWARDS AND ONE TANK TRIPS

You would think that a TV series like One Tank Trips, having survived on the air for twenty-five years, would be a certain winner of the coveted Emmy Award from the National Academy of Television Arts and Sciences. But it never happened.

Oh, we were nominated several times over the quarter-century that we were on the air, but when the big night came, it was always somebody else who got to run up on stage, stand in the spotlight, and thank everyone they have ever known or hope to know.

Perhaps I never got to have that moment of fame for One Tank

Trips due to a situation that happened at an Emmy show many years ago. I was invited to go on stage—*not* to receive an award, mind you, but to announce the winner in some category.

I even went out and rented a tuxedo for the big night. I arrived backstage at the awards dinner just in time to be told I would be co-presenting with a well-known local disc jockey. I had never met her. She turned out to be about a foot taller than I was. She was lovely. And she was having a hard time concealing her displeasure at being paired with me rather than, say, Dick Goddard or Judd Hambrick. She gave me an icy greeting and then pretty much ignored me until seconds before we walked onstage. At that point she whirled around and said, rather forcibly, "I'll announce the nominees, then you open the envelope and announce the winner and I'll hand them the statue."

I really didn't care. It was just kind of fun being in the spotlight on such a night, so I nodded my head. We heard our introduction and walked out to a smattering of applause, looking like the cartoon characters Mutt and Jeff.

I believe the category was "Best writing of the introduction to a commercial-break," or something equally esoteric. In any event, the glamorous, tall lady DJ read off the nominees and then looked down on me as I fumbled to open the envelope. I read the winner's name and applauded as the lucky recipient squealed and ran to the stage. As she approached, a model on the stage picked up a statue from the table where all the Emmy statuettes were lined up. Unaware of the tall DJ's plan, the model tried to hand it to me. Just as I grasped the rather heavy statuette, the DJ also reached for it, bumping my hand. The Emmy fell to the floor and broke into three pieces. Everything seemed to move in slow motion from that point on. I stared down at the broken trophy, wondering whether to pick it up and just hand the pieces to the winner. The lady DJ looked like she wanted the stage to open up and swallow me. The winner stood in front of me, a confused smile plastered across her face, her hand still outstretched for her award. Trying to salvage the embarrassing situation, I turned and grabbed a second Emmy off the table and at the same time saw Emmy officials offstage frantically waving their hands and shaking their heads back and forth. But it was too late. I had already brought the statue close to the winner's outstretched hand, and she snapped it away from me, probably afraid I might drop this one.

I could still see officials slapping their heads and stage-whispering, "No! No!" But the winner had already pushed me away from the microphone with her hip, and from the bodice of her dress had pulled out three pages of names that she was starting to thank for this magical moment in her life. There was nothing I could do but stand behind her and smile. The tall DJ stood next to me with a forced smile, both of us aware of the consternation that we could hear offstage, where a group of officials was now whispering and pointing in my direction.

The music was starting to play, indicating to the winner that her time was up, but she was only through the first page of her multipage acceptance speech. She started to read faster, the music got louder, and the host of the show started to walk towards the microphone, which only seemed to make the woman more determined to get all of her speech in. She was fairly shouting now, " . . . thankmysister,brother,aunthelen,unclejoe,cousinsMary,Ethel . . ." The host leaned over her shoulder, said, "Thank you very much," and took her arm to lead her off stage. The tall lady DJ and I followed. I was met by Emmy officials who whisper-screamed at me, "WHY DID YOU GIVE HER THAT OTHER EMMY??"

"What did you want me to do? Give her the broken one?" I responded.

That was when I learned that I had missed an earlier briefing: If anything happened to a statue, we should just announce we would send the recipient another one because each Emmy was already engraved for the category. So I had not only broken one category, but I had inadvertently snarled the awards for the rest of the evening.

I slunk back to my seat, hoping someone else would drop a statue, but it didn't happen. It was many years before I was asked to be a presenter at the Emmy Awards again, and this time they kept me well away from the award statuettes.

READ THE FINE PRINT

"Remember, you have a speech tomorrow in Warren, Ohio," my wife reminded me.

"On a Monday morning?" I asked.

"Check the calendar," Bonnie replied as she walked out of the room.

I walked to the desk, and there it was, circled on my calendar: tomorrow's date and "Packard Music Hall, Warren, Ohio, 9 a.m. Speech."

The alarm clock rang at six o'clock on Monday morning. Outside, a late winter snow was falling, and radio newscasters were warning motorists to prepare for a long drive to work.

I drove across the Ohio Turnpike wondering if the weather would affect the turnout at my speech. Spun-out trucks dotted the median strip, and it was a white-knuckle trip every mile of the way.

At 8:45 a.m., I reached the Packard Music Hall parking lot. It was empty. My tire tracks were the only ones in the fresh snow. I drove to the rear of the building. No cars there. Perhaps I was early. I waited.

Fifteen minutes later, when the speech was to have started, I was still the only one in the parking lot. I picked up my cellular phone and called Kevin Salyer at TV8, who had set up the speech.

"Kevin," I said, with some sarcasm, "I just drove through a snowstorm to Warren, Ohio, and no one is here."

"Let me check the invitation," he replied. "I'll be right back."

There was a short pause, and then he came back on the phone.

"Do you have the copy of the invitation I gave you?" he asked, a sarcastic tinge in his voice.

"Certainly!" I replied. "It's right here on the seat beside me."

"Read the date to me." "Just like I told you," I began, "March 19th, 9 a.m."

"No," he said, "the WHOLE date."

I looked at the letter again and read, "March 19th." But I had arrived too early. In fact, I was one year early. My speech was for March 19th of the following year.

CHAPTER 10

Animals

MY ADVENTURES WITH ANIMALS

I am not an animal person. Never have been. Never will be.

Animals and I do not get along. When I was starting out as a journalist, for example, I was driving one day past the Town Hall in Henrietta, the community where I lived. There on the front steps were at least a dozen goats. No one else was near. Obviously, the goats had escaped from a nearby farm. But what was their fascination with the local seat of government?

I stopped the car, grabbed my camera, and jumped out to take a picture. But these goats apparently had an aversion to being photographed, as three of the larger ones with large curved horns went "Baaaaaaa!" and put their heads down to charge me. Laughing, I jumped back inside the car as the first goat slammed into the door. The other two started to investigate the car by jumping on the hood and staring me down through the windshield.

I blew the horn. I yelled at the goats, but to no avail. I started the car's motor, and the vibration caused those on the hood to leave. But the first one was still butting my door.

I finally wound down the window, took a quick shot of the remaining goats gamboling on the front steps, and drove off.

And then there was my duel with a pregnant raccoon.

I was living in an apartment in Rocky River. As I prepared to leave for work early one morning, I approached the carport behind the apartment where my car was parked. I heard a hissing sound and saw a large female raccoon on the hood of my car. I clapped my hands and said, "Scoot!" but all it did was make her angry. She reared up on her hind legs and bared her teeth at me, making a loud hissing noise.

I looked around for some kind of a stick to push her off the car. Not finding one, I decided to try to get into the car, figuring that starting the motor would drive her off. But when I started to reach for the door, she leaped onto the roof of the car and started towards me. I backed away. We had a standoff.

The clock was ticking, and I was going to be late for work. No one was around to help, and calling the animal warden would surely make me late, so I went back into my apartment to see if I could find some type of equipment to remove a large, pregnant raccoon from my car.

The first thing that caught my eye was a fencing foil I bought at a flea market. It was about four feet long and had a soft rubber tip. I grabbed it and ran back to the carport, where the raccoon was happily washing herself on the hood of my car. She reared up again as I approached, made that hissing sound, and again showed me her teeth.

I assumed what I thought was a fencing stance and timidly lunged forward, hoping to push her off the hood. But she was quicker than I. In a lightning move, she grasped the tip of the sword and bit off the rubber tip.

So now I had a sword with a sharp point. I used it to keep her at bay as I edged over to the car door. Giving her one sharp poke, I wrenched the door open and jumped inside. Seeing me inside only seemed to infuriate the furry critter. She launched an attack at my windshield, clawing at the glass trying to get to me. I started the car and threw it into reverse. But the raccoon held on to the edge of the hood as I rocketed out of the parking garage, then slammed on the brakes and stopped. As her claws loosened, I put the car in reverse again and floored it, rocketing backwards across the driveway and up onto the lawn. The raccoon finally slid off the front of the hood and dropped off the car. As I watched through the windshield, I saw her saunter back to the car port. That was one mean raccoon.

Even my wife, Bonnie, who loves animals, has had her problems with critters from the wild.

Bonnie had gone into the bathroom off the library in our home to comb her hair. Standing at the sink, she saw movement out of the corner of her eye. A small, furry creature suddenly ran across her bare foot. She let out a blood-curdling scream.

Sitting at my desk, I jumped at her cry and ran to the bathroom, where Bonnie stood shaking.

"What happened?" I asked.

"Ani—ani—animal!!" she finally gasped.

"Mouse?" I asked.

"N—no . . . little . . . f-f-furry . . . cute."

"A chipmunk?"

"Yes. Yes. A chipmunk."

How a chipmunk got in our house we did not know, but he had disappeared somewhere in our library. We searched for hours but saw no trace of the little critter.

Days later I began to notice a bad smell each time I entered the library. But a search turned up no cause. We had a lady, originally from Romania, who cleaned for us once a week. I mentioned it to her, and she walked into the library and started sniffing.

"Eet is thee smell of death!" she announced. "I know eet well."

She looked at a furnace vent in the floor and said she thought it was coming from there.

A furnace repair company sent out two men who removed the furnace piping from the furnace to the library and found nothing. When they looked at where the pipe connected with the furnace, however, they found the barbecued remains of our missing chipmunk.

THE ISLAND

WHOP! WHOP! WHOP!

Whop! Whop! Whop!

Through closed eyelids I saw the shadow of the propeller flashing over my head. It was like a movie scene, but this was not a movie—this was real, and I was lying on my back on a small island while a real helicopter hovered only a few feet above me.

What had brought me to Starve Island, a tiny spit of sand jutting out of Lake Erie off South Bass Island, was an idea that Bill West and I had cooked up to emphasize the joys of an island One Tank Trip. Starve Island is about thirty feet long and six feet wide. We pictured a final shot that would show me sleeping in the sun and then, as the helicopter lifted higher and higher, would reveal me on a tiny spit of land in the middle of the lake.

Helicopter pilot Andy Overley had outfitted his craft with pontoons for this shoot, and we waited until late afternoon, when the sun would be in just the right position.

It looked like everything was going to work perfectly. We circled the tiny island a couple of times before starting down. We noticed several seagulls take off but gave them little thought. Andy was more concerned with the number of rocks sticking up at uneven angles. He finally decided that it would not be possible to set down on the island, but that he could hover a foot or so off the rocks. I could sit in the doorway and step out. When I got in position, he would lift straight up.

The downdraft from the helicopter blades set up a veritable whirlwind of feathers and sand as we sat hovering over the rocks. I shielded my eyes from the wind, quickly stepped out, and lay down on the greenish rocks with a child's inner tube beneath my head for a pillow. I heard the "Whop! Whop! Whop!" of the blades as Andy applied more power to lift off. I peeked out of one eye and could see that the lens on Bill West's video camera, now two feet away from my face, was starting to lift away.

As the helicopter soared into the sky and the wind from the propellers lessened, I became aware of some new sensations. The rock was wet and slippery. It also smelled. Just then I heard it: the sound of angry sea gulls! Opening both eyes, I saw them fill the sky above me. This looked like a scene from the Hitchcock movie *The Birds*. I was lying in the middle of a smelly seagull rookery, and around me were several nests! I scrambled to my feet and frantically waved at the helicopter, which was now two thousand feet in the air and headed towards the edge of South Bass Island. We had agreed that after they took off, Andy and Bill would shoot the outline of the bigger islands before coming back to retrieve me.

For the next fifteen minutes I used the small plastic inner tube and my hat to scare off angry gulls that zoomed in closer and closer, scolding me with their raspy squawks. I also realized that I was covered from head to toe in slimy bird dung. It was just about the longest fifteen minutes of my life.

The helicopter finally came back, and I clawed my way back inside, much to the amusement of Overley and West—at least until the smell of my guano-soaked clothes intensified in the heat of the helicopter's bubble cockpit. We made a high-speed run to the nearest landing strip in Port Clinton.

ELEPHANT TROUBLE

"You're gonna ride in an elephant race," said Mickey Flanagan, TV8's assignment editor.

"A *WHAT?*" I replied.

"An elephant race," he said with some finality as he turned to ripping copy on the large newsroom desk.

"But Mickey," I pleaded, "you know I hate animals."

"You'll have fun," he said without looking up from his work. "It's just a promotion thing. There will be elephant keepers walking alongside controlling the animal, and you just have to sit up there and go around in a circle."

So, with a great deal of reluctance, I found myself on a balmy spring day at the Cleveland Zoo. But instead of the enclosed elephant pavilion, I was on the large field in the center of the zoo. Instead of letting us ride their elephants, the zoo staff had decided to bring in some privately owned pachyderms.

My colleagues, "Big Chuck" Schodowski and Bob "Hoolihan" Wells, already were mounted on two of the smaller elephants when I arrived. A huge elephant with the unlikely name of Pansy was waiting for me.

A rather grubby elephant handler, with one leg shorter than the other, prompted some immediate speculation in my mind as to just how his leg had gotten shorter. Perhaps the elephant had eaten it!

The handler barked "DOWN!" and I was already lying on the ground when I realized he was talking to the elephant, who ponderously squatted.

"Just step on her leg, grab her ear, and pull yourself on top of her head," he ordered.

"Won't stepping on her leg make her upset or something?" I asked timidly.

"Nah," he grumbled at me. "She won't even feel it."

Stepping on her leg was like stepping on a rather soft rock. Pansy's ear felt like dusty leather as I tentatively grabbed and tried to jump onto her neck. She snorted softly a couple of times as I tried repeatedly to crawl, jump, or pull myself up her side and onto her neck. Finally the handler, still grumbling, walked over. As I desperately pulled Pansy's ear and had one leg nearly onto her neck, he placed a hand on my rear end and pushed with such force that I flew up onto the neck and right off the other side.

To the laughter of the assembled crowd, I picked myself up and sheepishly walked around the front of Pansy, who, at that moment, raised her trunk and snorted right in my face, giving me the full benefit of elephant morning breath—a cross between sewer gas and the scent of skunks.

With a reeling stomach, red face, and grim determination, I again stepped onto Pansy's spongy knee and, this time, was able to spring clumsily onto the elephant's neck. There was no saddle, just a sort of halter that the elephant wore over her head. A large leather strap was the only thing to hang onto.

"Grip your legs just behind her ears and hang on tight to that halter," the grumbling attendant said.

I was trying to figure out how to pinch my legs around something that large when the attendant barked, "UP, PANSY. UP!" The elephant lurched to her feet, nearly putting me on the ground again as I grabbed the leather strap and hung on for dear life, a scream of terror bubbling up in my throat.

I suddenly found myself towering twelve feet above the ground, looking down on the hundreds of people who had gathered to watch the spectacle. It was also at this point that I realized straddling the neck bone of this elephant was like straddling a rip-saw blade.

Swaying on top of the beast, I watched as the limping keeper herded Pansy into a line with the elephants that Big Chuck and Hoolihan were atop.

We posed for pictures. I wore a nervous smile, trying both to watch the cameras and keep an eye on Pansy's handler down below to make sure he didn't decide to go off and leave me alone on top of the elephant.

Chuck Voracek, the zoo's public relations director, told the crowd that they were about to witness the first-ever elephant race at the Cleveland Zoo. I was looking around to see what elephants were going to race when, with a feeling of terror, I realized he was talking about the elephant I was astride and the other two. Before I could utter even a gurgle of protest, someone raised a starter's pistol and fired a blast into the air. We were off.

We lumbered at a fast walk across the field. My limping handler seemed to be keeping up with some difficulty. I turned to see where the other two elephants were and realized that I was far out in front. I turned to call down to the handler to suggest we might slow down and, to my shock, saw no one there.

I swiveled the other way, bringing a sharp stab of pain to the area between my legs, and to my dismay saw Pansy's handler limping and running and swearing as the elephant steadily left him in the dust. I was on board a runaway elephant!

Many thoughts raced through my mind in the next few seconds, most of them concerning death and dismemberment. How do you stop a runaway elephant? I tried "Whoaa!" Pansy was oblivious. I pleaded with her, "Stop! Please Stop!" No good. Pansy lumbered on, heading towards the flamingo pens on the other side of the field, her speed increasing. With each stride I would fly up several inches and then slam back down on her razor-sharp back. Each time that I flew into the air, I could see her massive feet below. My imagination went wild with thoughts of how I would look if I flew off and ended up squished between her toes.

Over my shoulder, Pansy's keeper and the other elephants were getting farther and farther away. I debated trying to jump from the top of the elephant, but then I would run the risk of being trampled by her back feet. Just as I was about to give up hope, Pansy suddenly stopped. I almost tumbled headfirst to the ground as her head went down and she started grazing on some flowers planted along the edge of the walk.

This gave her swearing, limping keeper a chance to catch up. Relief washed over me. I was almost giddy with the thought of getting off that elephant's back. The keeper placed his elephant hook in her harness and gave a command.

"UP PANSY!" he shouted.

I was expecting the animal to kneel so I could get off, not to raise up on her hind feet. I suddenly found myself hanging by both hands from her harness, fifteen to twenty feet in the air, as the keeper yelled to me, "SMILE AND WAVE AT THE CROWD!"

I was incredulous! Here I was hanging straight down the elephant's back, clinging to the harness with such ferocity that it would have taken three men to get my hands loose, and he wanted me to wave to the crowd! In fact, when Pansy finally did kneel and they told me I could get off, he did have to pry my fingers from the harness. It took three weeks for the bruises on my inner thighs to fade.

To this day, when I walk by the elephant exhibit at the zoo I get a little nervous. I have never had the slightest desire to ride another elephant.

CHAPTER 11

Holidays

BUT NEVER ON TUESDAY

One of southwest Ohio's hidden gems is the historic Clifton Mill in Clifton. It's one of the largest water-powered gristmills in the world still operating. The waters of the Little Miami River are diverted through the base of the mill, powering the grinding wheel as it has for almost two hundred years.

In addition to offering freshly ground flour and meal, the mill has a gift shop, which sells its product and other souvenirs, and a small restaurant where the breakfast fare is legendary. They make pancakes here. I mean, they make *real* pancakes here. Pancakes that are almost the size of manhole covers. They boast that rarely can anyone finish a stack of three of their flapjacks. For dessert, if you are still hungry, they offer their signature oatmeal pie.

The mill really shines during the Christmas season. The day before Thanksgiving, they turn on more than two million lights that outline the mill, mill wheel, and adjoining valley. There is also a display of three thousand animated Santa Claus figures and a miniature village of Clifton that has electric trains and even an animated Christmas parade. There is also a Santa Claus workshop where a real Santa practices for the big night every fifteen minutes by running up and down his chimney and waving to appreciative families watching from below.

Not surprisingly, the mill at Christmastime attracts thousands of people each evening. A sizeable staff is required to serve the crowd and to keep people from wandering too close to the illuminated mill wheel or from falling into the valley of the Little Miami River.

But the first year they decided to light the mill and invite the public caused quite an uproar: The lights were to be on at the mill each evening, *except Tuesdays*, until New Year's Day. On Tuesdays, the mill was closed and the lights were out. It said so in all their advertising. Signs posted all around the front of the mill said, "Closed on Tuesdays."

Tony Satariano, the owner, put the lighting display on a timer so the lights came on promptly at 6 p.m. and went off at 9:30 p.m. On Tuesdays he just turned off the timer so the lights would not come on.

Christmas happened to fall on a Tuesday that year, and so the mill was closed. On Christmas night, Tony and two of his kids were moving one of their gifts, a canoe, from their home to a storeroom in the darkened mill. But when they pulled up the street to the mill, they found it choked with cars and people. It was about 5:45 p.m. Darkness had just fallen, and people were waiting for the lights.

Tony tried to explain to the crowd that there would be no lights tonight, that the mill was closed on Tuesdays, and, for safety reasons, he could not turn on the lights because he had no staff to make sure people did not stray too close to the gorge. The crowd was not happy about this. In fact, they became downright surly. They started to shout at Tony and his family. The trio, with their canoe, beat a hasty retreat inside the mill.

"Don't turn on any lights!" Tony warned his kids. "If they see a light on, they'll think I changed my mind and that we're open."

He told one of his daughters to toss him the mill keys so that he could make sure the door was locked. She tossed the keys, which went sliding under a counter. The three were searching for them on the floor of the blacked-out room when, suddenly, *WHAM!* The night was flooded with lights. Tony had forgotten to turn off the timer, and all the millions of lights outside had sprung to life. The crowd of nearly two hundred outside cheered and surged forward onto the grounds. Realizing that the three of them could not control so large a crowd, Tony ran to the light switch and turned it off, plunging the mill into darkness again.

For the next half hour, Tony and his family huddled on the floor in the dark as people pounded on the door. Occasionally they peeked out of the windows to see if the angry crowd had gone. After that, they decided during the holiday season to stay open seven days a week.

'TIS THE SEASON

After all the holiday stories I have done through the years, I still believe that one of the best places to get a holiday boost is in the restored canal town of Roscoe Village in Coshocton.

They begin the season with an outdoor candle-lighting ceremony about the first weekend in December. I was invited one year to be the "official candle lighter," and I arrived on a very cold and dark December night. The town looked like a page from a Dickens novel, with frost painting the edges of windows. Guides from the village's various attractions were dressed in nineteenth-century frock coats or hoop skirts. Streetlights from another era illuminated the walks and roadways, where thousands of people milled about, waiting for the ceremony to begin.

A stage had been placed halfway down the main street, White-woman Street. Beside the street, on one side, was a steep hillside that led upwards to the next street. On the other side were the stores that serviced canal boats and their crews a hundred years earlier.

A brass ensemble wandered the streets playing Christmas carols, while small groups of carolers strolled in front of the stores, singing the songs of the season.

My duties were simple. I was given a brief introduction to polite applause, and as I stepped forward to the podium, the lights along the streets went out. I struck a match and lit a candle I was holding. For a moment, as I wished the crowd a Merry Christmas,

I held in my hand the only light on the street. In the darkness, several thousand people stood crowded around the stage. The flickering light from my candle reflected on the faces around the edge of the stage.

I walked across the stage and, leaning towards the crowd, started to light other candles held by their outstretched hands. The light spread outward from my candle and, in moments, pinpoints of light climbed the hill behind me and ignited a river of candles in the street on both sides of me. I led the crowd in singing "Silent Night." Never before had the song seemed so real and so personal as it did on this magical night in Roscoe Village, where I stood bathed in the light of thousands of candles.

PEACE ON EARTH AND GOODWILL TO ALL

Videographer Bob Begany and I traveled to Charleston, West Virginia, to do a holiday season One Tank Trip segment on the West Virginia state capital and its giant sternwheeler, the *West Virginia Belle*. We wanted to get a nighttime shot of the *Belle*, all lit with holiday decorations as she sailed down the Kanawha River, past the imposing state capitol building, and toward downtown Charleston.

The first problem was that the boat moved faster than we had anticipated, so we appealed to one of the owners to accompany us with a walkie-talkie to a site on a college campus, located directly across the river from the capitol building. The walkie-talkie was for communicating with the boat's captain to slow him down a bit while we got the camera set up.

We discovered the second problem when we arrived on campus: All of the streetlights ended at the edge of a row of buildings a hundred feet back from the river's edge, leaving the last hundred feet to the river in total darkness—and none of us had thought to bring a flashlight.

The boat had already gone upriver and turned for its run past the capitol by the time we found a parking place and began running through inky blackness towards the river's edge.

Across the river, the West Virginia capitol glowed in the light of the moon that was just rising over a mountain behind it. The capitol's lights were reflected in the water, and upriver we saw the merry lights of the approaching *West Virginia Belle*. The captain told us by radio that he was going as slowly as he could, but a strong current was carrying him faster.

In the darkness, Begany and I fumbled to set up his tripod and to mount his camera by touch. But in minutes the camera was locked on, and the eyepiece with its tiny monitor was glowing.

It was going to be an absolutely beautiful picture. Christmas carols cascaded from the *Belle's* loudspeakers as she glided serenely down the river, all aglow. Begany was just starting to focus in on the ship when his eyepiece went black.

Renowned for his ability to curse, Begany filled the air with expletives as he grappled in the dark with the camera's battery container. He ripped it open and reached for the spare battery in his belt. I urged him on as the ship got closer and closer.

In his haste to replace the battery, he dropped it—just as I stepped closer to see if I could help. My foot met the falling battery, booting it off into the pitch blackness.

Begany's cursing hit fever pitch as we dropped to our knees and started feeling around for the battery in the grass. The ship's owner, who happened to be with us, tried to shed light by firing up his cigarette lighter. The *Belle* was only minutes away from passing us.

"WHY ME, LORD? WHY ME?" Begany implored, as we frantically felt the ground. Struck by sudden inspiration. I jumped to my feet and called to the owner with the walkie-talkie.

"Use your radio to call the ship and ask them to hit us with their spotlight!" I yelled.

In seconds, I saw crewmen running out to the bridge of the ship and its huge spotlights. A million-candle-power beam shattered the darkness, froze us on the lawn, and momentarily blinded both Begany and me.

Whatever hope we had of finding the battery and saving our shoot was gone in the flash—except that the ship's owner, anticipating the lamp's glare, had turned his back on it. He scanned the ground and spotted the battery.

"HALLELUJAH!" Begany shouted as the man pressed it into his hand. The night was illuminated again, this time with an explosion!

We had been so intent on the approaching boat that we did not notice lightning behind us. The first drops of rain fell and thunder rumbled as Begany put the battery into the camera. In seconds it was pouring, and in the downpour we got one water-logged shot of the *West Virginia Belle* as she sailed past the capitol building. Drifting back to us in its wake, above the rain and Begany's swearing, we could hear the words, "Peace on earth and good will to men."

Sadly, the *West Virginia Belle* has since moved on to the more lucrative service of riverboat gambling in another state, and only a much smaller tourist boat remains to offer the impressive view of the state capitol that can be seen only from the water.

AKA CUPID

I have been called upon to do some rather silly things during my fifty-some years as a journalist, including taking my clothes off when visiting a nudist colony and climbing a rope down the side of our station.

One of the silliest was in 1995, when we decided to run a contest with my weeklong series about romantic getaways. The promotions department wanted to dress me up as Cupid to plug the contest at the end of each night's segment. I immediately balked at the thought of running around in public wearing nothing but a diaper and carrying a bow and arrow.

"Wear anything you like," said Kevin Salyer, who headed promotions. "Just be sure you look like Cupid."

I took the problem home to my wife. Bonnie, when she stopped laughing, suggested that maybe she could make a costume. She started out with a large pair of red pantyhose. Then she recycled an old gray sweatshirt of mine by gluing hot pink felt hearts of assorted sizes all over it. She did the same for an old pair of gray flannel gym shorts, and topped off the costume with a pair of wings—fashioned from wire coat hangers and plastic wrap—sewn to the back of the sweatshirt.

I added a couple of my own touches: a pair of cowboy boots and my battered old red-and-white "One Tank Trips" hat. But what to do for a bow and arrow?

My friend Gary Rice of Lakewood is a teacher. He is also a pack rat and a flea market maven who, if he doesn't have some object in his house, knows where to get it.

"Gary," I said over the telephone, "I need a bow and arrow like Cupid carried."

Gary didn't even ask why. "Let me think about it," he replied. "I'll call you back."

A half hour later, he walked into my kitchen carrying a long package in an old duffel bag.

"I couldn't find exactly the type of bow and arrow that Cupid carried," Gary said as he unwrapped the package, "but I think this will do." He held up a large toilet plunger with feathers affixed to the handle and a large steel object.

"I didn't have a bow," he apologized, "so I took the top part off a crossbow and put the string from an old bass fiddle on it."

My costume was complete.

The next day, videographer Jim Holloway and I went to Sell's Candy Store in Bay Village to shoot the segments with me in my Cupid costume.

First, I discovered that trying to stand on one foot to assume the classic Cupid pose is hard work. (I also discovered that I looked like a fat flamingo.) I could stand on one foot for about thirty seconds before losing the pose. Just when Jim got focused, I would drop down to two feet, ruining his shot.

Then there were the customers, who would walk into the store and see me standing on one foot, wearing red pantyhose and carrying a steel bow with a toilet plunger for an arrow. Some snickered, some laughed out loud. One woman ran screaming from the store.

Finally, we finished with the taping, and several bystanders said they wanted their picture taken with me. We clustered together as Jim took their camera and aimed it at us. As we stood, arms around each other, beaming at the camera, one of the women reached back and pinched me on the rear end. The shutter clicked as I jumped in shock.

Later, on the air and to laughter on the news set, TV8 anchor Robin Swoboda christened me "Doctor Love." I still get hailed by strangers who want to know where my bow and arrow are. I blush and say I left them in my Nash Metropolitan.

CHAPTER 12

Friends and Colleagues

BILL WEST

I had the good fortune to work with some of the best motion-picture photographers in Cleveland, if not the whole country. As is the case with many talented individuals, they could sometimes be a bit eccentric.

Take Bill West, probably the only person I ever knew who carefully raked the gravel in his driveway each day to make sure it was uniform in appearance. My garage at home is a repository for all kinds of clutter, including cars, and it usually has a few weeds growing through cracks in the floor. West, on the other hand, keeps his garage so spotless you could perform heart surgery in there. And the cars? Most news cruisers are like police cars, badly abused and frequently filthy from spilled coffee, forgotten sandwiches, or french fries that wedged between the seats during a hurried meal. West keeps his cruiser immaculate. He shampoos the carpet at least once a week and even keeps air freshener in the vehicle. On our way to an assignment in Columbus one day, I spilled a can of grape soda on the passenger-side carpet. West insisted we stop at a service station for seltzer water to put on the carpet and paper towels to blot it up. From that point on, I was subject to dirty looks if I attempted to bring food or drink into his cruiser.

West was usually a gregarious individual who loved to talk about cars, his family, and his home, but he could be moody at times. I well recall the morning he picked me up at my home in

Bay Village for a One Tank Trip to Detroit. As I got into the car, I said, "Good morning, Bill." No response.

As we got underway, I asked how his day had been yesterday. Again, no response. We drove on in silence for a half hour before I tried again.

"Do you think it will rain today?" Silence.

Okay, I thought—if that's how you want to be, I won't talk with you either. We both sat in silence, watching the miles go by. Finally, as we reached the outskirts of Toledo, West broke the silence.

"Do you want to stop for coffee?" he asked pleasantly.

"Oh, so now you're going to talk to me?" I challenged.

"What do you mean?" he said.

"Since we left Cleveland you haven't said anything to me."

"I just didn't have anything to say," he replied.

That was Bill West.

SOME OF THOSE TV PEOPLE

One of the longest friendships I had during my years at WJW was with the late Ed Bates.

Ed and I met when I hired him at WEOL in the time I was news director. Soon after I joined WJW-TV full-time in the late 1960s. Ed was also hired, first as a booth announcer and later as a reporter.

He was physically challenged, but you never would have known it. He had lost an eye in a childhood accident and wore a glass eye in the empty socket. He didn't mention it to me the first time I met him, nor did he note it on his employment application at WEOL. This resulted in a strange occurrence the first night he went on the air there.

As the newest man in news, he drew the long afternoon and evening shift at the station's Lorain studio. After spending the morning moving into his apartment he came straight to work. By late evening, his long day had caught up with him.

I happened to be in downtown Lorain on business that evening and was listening to the station on my car radio—perhaps more closely than usual because it was Ed's first night on the job and I wanted to hear how he sounded.

When it was time for the 9 p.m. news, Bill Fenton in the Elyria studios introduced Bates in Lorain. Silence. Fenton introduced him again, got no response, and said, "We're having some technical difficulties. Ed Bates will be along with the news just as soon as we can correct the problems."

I was only a block from the Lorain studios in the Antlers Hotel, so I sped to the station to see what the problem was. As I pulled into the parking lot, Fenton was still getting no response from Bates. Nothing but silence came from Lorain.

I ran into the studio and stopped short at a terrifying sight.

The studio door was open. Bates was lying face down on the news desk, and one of his eyes was in the middle of the desk, staring back at me. Some demented listener must have come to the station, caught Ed with his back to the door, and somehow killed him and torn out his eyeball!

I rushed to Ed's side to see if he was still breathing and started frantically calling his name.

He suddenly sat up and wheeled around at me.

"What's the matter?" he asked sleepily.

I was speechless. Not knowing about his missing eye, all I could do was stare at him while his vacant eye socket stared back at me.

"What...uh...Oh!" he said as he noticed the eyeball, picking it up and popping it back into his eye socket.

"You . . . You . . . have an artificial eye!" I nearly shouted in relief.

"What? Oh, yeah," he said nonchalantly. "Didn't I mention that?"

Over the years he often used his artificial eye in other ways, such as the night we were drinking in a bar. He popped out his eye, dropped it into a martini glass, and handed it to an unsuspecting woman he was with.

"Here's looking at you," he said.

YOU NEVER KNOW ABOUT THOSE TV PEOPLE

We had set up a booth at the annual outdoor sports and travel show at the giant I-X Center to hand out One Tank Trips booklets to visitors. It was about the end of the fifth day I was there when a friend, Lieutenant J. P. Allen of the Ohio State Highway Patrol, stopped by. J. P. looks like a recruiting poster for the state police—six foot one, sandy-haired, handsome. He was off duty and wearing a flannel shirt and dungarees. I invited him to join me in the booth so we could chat between visits by viewers.

We had been talking about ten minutes when I got occupied with several people who had questions. J. P. stood beside me, watching the crowd, when he noticed an elderly lady studying him.

She would first look at J. P., then study the display on the back of the booth, where we had large color photographs of our leading anchors: Tim Taylor, Dick Goddard, Casey Coleman, and Tana Carli. Tana, from Alliance, had been Miss Ohio and runner-up for the title of Miss America. She was also the first female evening anchor hired by TV8.

After several minutes of looking at the pictures and J. P., the lady stepped up to the counter.

"Which one are you?" she said, nodding towards the wall of pictures.

"Oh, I'm Tana Carli," he said, joking.

"No, you're not," the woman declared. "You're a man."

The challenge in her voice was just enough to trigger J. P.'s sense of humor.

"Yes, I am Tana Carli," he replied, moving back to stand beside Tana's picture.

"That's impossible," the woman said. "You're a man."

"Take a good look and use your imagination," J. P. said, holding Tana's picture next to his head. "Picture me with a woman's wig, false eyelashes and some makeup, and wearing a dress."

He smiled at the lady with his best Tana Carli smile.

She stared at him and the picture in confusion.

"But you're a good-looking man, why would you want to dress up like a woman?" she finally blurted.

"Well, it's this way. I wanted to get into television, but they didn't have any openings for men at the time, and so I decided to apply as a woman," he answered with a straight face.

She still wasn't buying his story.

"If you're Tana Carli, let's hear you say something like she says it," she said.

Without batting an eye, J. P. raised Tana's picture in front of his face and said, in a falsetto voice: "The attack of killer parakeets, next on Newscenter 8."

J. P. does not sound a bit like Tana Carli, but the power of suggestion must have been at work. The woman's mouth dropped open, and she exclaimed, "MY GOD! You really are her!"

From behind the picture, J. P. gave me a wink.

"I just can't believe this is really true," the woman said.

I was struck by a fit of coughing and excused myself from the counter.

J. P. was just warming up.

"Did you like that sweater I was wearing on the news show last night?" he asked the woman.

"Uh, yes," the lady replied. "It was quite attractive."

"I bought that at Value City," he said. "I just love bargains, don't you?"

The more they talked, the more convinced the lady became that J. P. was indeed Tana Carli.

Finally, an elderly man, obviously the woman's husband, wandered up to the booth.

"You ready to go yet?" he asked her.

"You're never going to believe who this man is," the woman gushed at her husband.

Before he could guess, she blurted out: "This is Tana Carli, on TV8!"

"Go on!" her husband responded.

"No, really," she said. "He wears a wig and a dress when he's on television."

"Woman, have you lost your mind?" he retorted.

The woman turned to a smiling J. P. and said, "Put the picture in front of your face and talk to him like Tana."

J. P. complied, and once again the power of suggestion apparently overcame reason. The man stepped back, studied J. P., and said, "I'll be damned!"

As the couple wandered off, shaking their heads, we could hear the man telling the wife, "You just never know about those TV people."

THE CBS YEARS

During most of the years I worked for WJW-TV, we were an affiliate of the CBS Television Network, and we were often visited by some of the biggest names in television news.

Whenever a really large story broke in northern Ohio and the network sent in reporters, they would come to WJW-TV to edit and feed their stories to CBS headquarters in New York. People like Mike Wallace, Ed Bradley, Daniel Schorr, Dan Rather, Roger Mudd, Charles Osgood, and Bill Plante were frequent visitors to 1630 Euclid Avenue.

Once the story had been fed and assignments confirmed for the next day, we would all adjourn to "the Swamp," Seagram's Tavern, two doors west of WJW.

How can I describe the Swamp? It was a neighborhood bar transplanted to Playhouse Square. It always seemed to be half full, never crowded. A black-and-white TV was above the bar, always tuned to WJW. It only showed other stations when regular Mickey Flanagan demanded that the bartender change the channel so Mickey could see what the competition covered that day.

The Swamp also served the greasiest hamburgers in Cleveland. Many nationally known journalists shared a beer and a grease-kissed burger with us. CBS's Ike Pappas, the man Jack Ruby shoved out of the way to shoot Lee Harvey Oswald in the basement of Dallas police headquarters, relived that experience with me over a beer and a burger at the Swamp.

Bill Plante and I shared a helicopter to fly into and out of the embattled Kent State campus after the May 4th shooting in 1970. Our day also ended with a review of its events at the Swamp.

During that time, I anchored the Newscenter 8 morning newscast that was part of the CBS morning news hosted by Charles Kuralt. My final line each morning was, "And now back to Charles Kuralt in New York."

Viewers frequently asked if I had met Kuralt, who was also the original host of "CBS Sunday Morning" and had his own series, "Charles Kuralt on the Road." In fact, though I became acquainted with his producer, Bernie Birnbaum, and though Kuralt did several promotional spots for my segments on the news, I never met or talked with the man.

I considered him one of television's finest writers, a true poet with words. I am truly sorry I never got to meet him—if for no other reason than to tell him how to pronounce my name.

I was always on the road somewhere and missed him when he occasionally passed through Cleveland and stopped at the station. He would be asked to do the promotional material and graciously agreed, but he just couldn't wrap his tongue around my name. He would say, "Be sure to tune in at 6 p.m. for One Tank Trips with Neil Zur-chur."

No matter how many times the producer reminded him my name was pronounced "Zur-kur," he would apologize, repeat the promo, and get to my name and say, "Zur-chur."

After two or three takes, and because he was usually in a hurry, they would just tell him, "We'll try to correct it in editing." He would go on his way. And they never corrected it.

THE UNFORGETTABLE PEOPLE YOU MEET

Johnny Tarr from Parma Heights was many things: chef, restaurant owner, raconteur, and friend to many people.

I first met Johnny when I received a call in the WJW newsroom one weekend. Parma Heights was in the midst of a gar-bage collectors' strike, and we were preparing to do a story on the debris piling up on the streets and behind businesses. The call I received was from a man with a thick Hungarian accent. He introduced himself as the owner of the Bit of Budapest Hungarian Restaurant on Pearl Road. He said that he had asked his waitresses to come in early in their bathing suits on this hot July day, to help him load the restaurant's garbage to be hauled to a landfill. He obviously was looking for free publicity, but I recognized an unusual twist to the story, so we agreed to meet in an hour at his establishment.

As photographer Ralph Tarsitano and I pulled into its parking lot, we saw no women in bathing suits, only a short man in an old-fashioned torn undershirt with a dirty butcher's apron over it. On his feet were some old shoes whose toes had been cut out. I figured we were early, and this was the janitor taking out the rubbish.

To my surprise, the janitor turned out to be restaurant owner Johnny Tarr.

"Where are the girls in bathing suits?" I asked.

"Ha!" he said. "If I had told you I was loading up my truck with rubbish, would you have been as interested in the story as you were when I told you I was going to have beautiful girls in bikini bathing suits?"

He had me there. And that was my first meeting with Johnny Tarr. Little did I know it was going to turn into a long friendship, and that he and I would grow as close as brothers.

A few days after the story appeared on TV, I got another call from Johnny. He told me he was having a party at his restaurant and that I was invited as his guest. That was my first experience with Johnny as a chef.

Despite his disheveled appearance the previous time I saw him, this time he wore immaculate chef's whites with a chef's hat. His kitchen was spotless. You could practically eat off the floor. Wonderful smells emerged from the ovens and kettles that were bubbling on the stove. Johnny was commanding his staff like a Prussian general, barking orders as he flew through the kitchen like a whirling dervish, tasting this, checking that, stirring a kettle. In quieter moments he would dash into the dining room of the restaurant to greet his guests and kiss each woman's hand, telling her how beautiful she was.

This was the suave Johnny Tarr, who started his life apprenticing in some of Budapest's finest restaurants when he was just a boy. The cooking skills he learned there would later save his life and eventually bring him to the United States.

In 1945, when he was a teenager, he was conscripted into the German army in his native Hungary. The Germans were nearing defeat, and one indelible memory from that time was marching long distances on little or no food. His most frightening memory was watching the fire-bombing of Dresden, Germany, on February 13, 1945. Allied forces bombed the city so heavily for fourteen hours that a firestorm broke out, destroying the town and killing, some estimates say, tens of thousands of people. Tarr was among the German troops who marched into the ruins the next day to search for survivors. He never forgot the dead—many of them only charred skeletons—on every corner.

By April 1945, with German resistance crumbling and food getting scarcer, Tarr decided he had enough. He took off his German uniform, stole some civilian clothes, and fled to the Hartz Mountains of Austria. He lived off the land for nearly a month, discovered an American army encampment at the foot of the mountains, and decided to surrender.

Problem was, because he was dressed in ragged civilian clothes, the Americans were not interested in his surrender. That was how John learned the war was over. He offered to wash dishes in the Americans' field kitchen just for some food. They agreed, and as the days passed, he noticed the cooks got lots of complaints. He started offering them advice, which led them to have him do some cooking. His food got great reviews, and he soon found himself cooking only for the officers.

His cooking skills and those contacts he made in the first days of peace eventually led a high-ranking American officer to help him to emigrate to the United States and pursue his dream of owning a restaurant that would capture a little of the Budapest that he remembered as a boy. He named his new establishment The Bit of Budapest.

John never forgot what it was like to live hand-to-mouth as he had after he fled the German army. When a huge fire destroyed some apartments on Cleveland's West Side, John filled his pickup truck with soup and sandwiches, drove to the scene, and started feeding the homeless tenants. Many people over the years were recipients of John's random acts of kindness and his caring.

He also helped preserve a Cleveland landmark. Although the USS *Cod* submarine had been on Cleveland's lakefront for years, the navy was considering scrapping the World War II sub. I casually mentioned one night to Johnny that I had volunteered to make public service announcements, trying to do what I could to help the committee formed to save the *Cod*. I also mentioned that the committee had run out of money, and that without help, the sub was likely to be turned into scrap.

Tarr immediately swung into action, scheduling a wild-game dinner at his restaurant that would feature ice sculptures of the *Cod*. He arranged for a twenty-foot long replica of the submarine to be placed in front of the restaurant. He hired a band to play patriotic music in his parking lot, and he invited officials from all over the county to be his guests for dinner. All proceeds were donated to the Save the *Cod* Committee. The dinner raised needed funds, and it attracted citywide publicity that led others to join the battle to keep the *Cod* as a part of the city.

Rear Admiral Richard Freundlich, then-chairman of the committee, said, "While many people were responsible for the saving of *Cod*," Admiral Freundlich said later, "Johnny Tarr's action at a crucial time contributed a much-needed push that brought many of us together to successfully complete our mission of preserving the submarine."

The admiral later presented John with an oversized dolphin insignia, the symbol of the submarine service, which he proudly displayed on the wall of his restaurant. When he died several years later, the *Cod* Committee paid him tribute by lowering the sub's flag to half-mast on the day of his funeral.

OF CUCKOO CLOCKS AND KOMAR

One of the most endearing people I met during the years that I traveled for Fox 8 Television was Vernon Craig of Wilmot, also known as "Komar the fakir." Vernon appeared to most people as a kindly, middle-aged, balding man with an Amish-style beard, who managed a cheese and gift shop at a restaurant known as Alpine-Alpa, located in Wilmot, which was also home to the world's largest cuckoo clock.

But Vernon Craig had a secret identity. When his workday was finished, he donned a turban and silk pantaloons and became Komar, an Indian fakir, a man who could walk across fiery hot coals in his bare feet. A man who would lie down on a bed of nails and, as the nail points pierced his skin, would hold a large rock on his chest and allow the strongest man present to take a sledge hammer and break it.

He came to the attention of the *Guinness Book of World Records* in 1971, when he spent twenty hours lying on his bed of nails. It was to be the first of many world records that Vernon "Komar" Craig would hold.

In 1976, at an international festival in Maidenhead, England, Komar walked his way into the *Guinness Book* by strolling an incredible twenty-five feet across a fire pit in his bare feet. The temperature of the fire was recorded at 1,494 degrees Fahrenheit— the hottest fire any human had ever been able to walk through without serious injury.

It all started, according to Craig, when he was doing some volunteer work for the Board of Mental Retardation in Wayne County in 1963.

Asked to give a speech at an annual meeting, he decided instead to demonstrate his theory that most people don't use the full power of their brain. Craig said he always seemed to have the ability to withstand or control pain just by thinking about it.

Wearing an old Halloween costume that consisted of a turban, a vest, and some oriental pantaloons, he walked into the meeting and mixed his message by climbing a short ladder made of sharpened knife blades without cutting himself. For his big finale, he drove hundreds of nails into a piece of plywood, their spikes forming a bed on which he lay down. He then allowed a volunteer from the audience to take a sledge hammer and break a cement block placed on his unprotected chest.

I first met Vernon Craig when I was doing a story on "The World's Largest Cuckoo Clock" in the 1970s. Alice Grossnicklaus, the owner of the Alpine–Alpa Swiss Restaurant, wanted another attraction to draw tourists to her Alpine-themed restaurant and Swiss cheese factory. Having decided to build the world's biggest clock, she had moveable figures of Swiss dancers, half life-size, hand-carved in Switzerland. A Swiss clockmaker created the clock movement, and the entire timepiece was so large it had to be assembled outdoors. The clock stood twenty-three feet, six inches tall. It was twenty-four feet wide, and thirteen feet, six inches deep. Besides the cuckoo bird that popped out of the top of the clock every fifteen minutes, a door would open at the base of the clock, and a four-piece Swiss musical group would slide onto the stage while two dancers, a woman in a dirndl and a man in Alpine clothing, did a short animated dance to their music.

The clock was an immense success as a tourist attraction. To get to it, you had to pass through the cheese shop, pay a quarter to go through a turnstile, and climb to a patio on the second floor of the building where the clock stood. Thousands of families traveling through Ohio's Amish land would trek to Wilmot to have their photos taken in front of the big cuckoo clock.

Vernon Craig became the keeper of the clock. To capitalize on its popularity, he started a small clock shop, located inside the restaurant–cheese factory complex, that exclusively sold European-imported cuckoo clocks. He became the second-largest dealer of cuckoo clocks in America. I knew him as the man I talked to at the Alpine–Alpa Cheese Shop.

Then one day I got an assignment to cover an unusual spring celebration at Wooster College. The main attraction was Komar. As I watched his performance of knife-climbing and lying on a bed of nails, I searched my mind, trying to figure out where I had seen him before.

My photographer, Peter Miller, and I were very close to him as he sat up on the bed of nails. We could actually see the tips of the nails pulling out of his skin and blood seeping from some of the holes. But as we stood there filming, the holes seemed to close, and in seconds there were only dimpled impressions of the nails left on his skin.

I saw it. To this day, I cannot explain how or why it happened.

A few minutes later, we caught up with Komar in the college library where he was autographing copies of a book he had written called *Life Without Pain*.

As we chatted, I said he looked very familiar. Had we met before?

With a twinkle in his eye, he said, "Do you remember doing a story on the World's Largest Cuckoo Clock?"

Even then it took a few seconds to hit me.

Komar explained that he kept the two identities separate. He worked by day in Ohio's Amish Country as a cheesemaker and store manager, but he traveled the world in his off-time as Komar. He visited over a hundred countries worldwide, appearing on television, lecturing at colleges, and demonstrating his skills for diverse organizations.

The *Guinness Book of World Records* has museums all over the world where they display artifacts of some of their record holders. Komar has been selected, along with four other attractions, including the Beatles, to be represented in every one of the museums. They even had life-size statues of Komar placed in their operations in places like London, New York, and Niagara Falls, Canada. I was there when the Niagara Falls statue was unveiled and Komar posed beside his fiberglass image.

But I also witnessed the practical application of Vernon's abilities.

In the early 1980s, when One Tank Trips had just started, we gave out free booklets describing some of the trips at the annual Sports and Travel Show at the I-X Center. I invited Vernon to be a guest host with me in the TV8 booth. He agreed and said he planned to bring along some of Alpine-Alpa's baby Swiss cheese to give away.

He was late in arriving, and I noticed a slight limp. When I asked him what was wrong he said, "Oh, I tripped and think I broke my ankle." I thought he was kidding. But later that evening he pulled up his pant leg, and I saw that the ankle was an angry shade of red and *very* swollen. I suggested that he should see a doctor and have the ankle put in a splint.

"Maybe tomorrow when I have more time," he replied, which was the last thing he said about the leg that evening. I later learned that he had indeed broken his ankle. However, he had walked on it from the parking lot to our booth, stood on the leg throughout the evening, and walked back to his car. That was the day I started thinking that instead of "Komar the fakir," he should be "Komar the invincible."

The big cuckoo clock is gone, sold when the restaurant and cheese-house business failed under new ownership. The clock was sold at auction to a Walnut Creek businessman, but its future at this writing is uncertain.

Sadly, my friend Komar passed away in March of 2010. I shall miss him.

AND THE EMMY GOES TO . . .

Elsewhere in this book I have bemoaned the fact that "One Tank Trips" never received a coveted Emmy. In the interest of full disclosure, I should point out that I *did* win an Emmy for some of my other work—though I almost lost it the same night to an English singing star. It was 1970, and I had just received the award for a piece I wrote about Vietnam prisoners of war entitled, "Does Anyone Remember Me?"

It was a happy evening at the old Hollenden Hotel in Cleveland. Broadway and movie star Celeste Holm served as one of the award presenters, and after the show, she and her husband celebrated with us and "Big Chuck" Schodowski and his wife, June, at a table in the hotel's ground-floor nightclub. Celeste mentioned that Tom Jones was in town, appearing at the Palace Theater and staying at the Hollenden.

We had all had several celebratory drinks. I believe our thinking might have been clouded. Chuck suddenly stood up and said to me, "Let's go say hello to Tom Jones."

It seemed like a great idea. The two of us, me still clutching my Emmy statuette, marched from the bar to the front desk to find out which room Tom Jones was in.

Tom Jones, of course, was an international star at his peak. Women crowded his concerts and threw their underwear at him. Teenage girls tried to sneak into his hotel room. So security was tight.

Ordinarily, the front desk might have politely refused us any information, but the young woman clerk recognized Big Chuck. When he smiled at her and said, "Neil and I just want to stop up and say hello," she immediately scribbled his room number on a piece of paper and handed it to him.

On the elevator, we found that the floor he was on had been locked out. So we went to a stairway and found police holding a group of teenagers at bay.

Chuck was not to be deterred. We went back to the elevator, took it to the floor below Tom Jones, and walked up the stairs to his floor. We opened the door to the hallway and found ourselves face-to-face with a uniformed Cleveland police officer, escorting away two girls who had apparently tried the same thing. But he and other officers recognized Chuck and me, and when we explained we were just dropping by to say hello, they had no objections. So we knocked on the door to the suite.

A burly man with a cockney accent opened the door and glared. "'Oo are you?"

Chuck introduced us and said he wanted to talk with Tom Jones.

"'Ee's not seein' anyone," the bodyguard replied with some hostility.

Chuck, thinking quickly, snatched the Emmy from my hands and proffered it to the bodyguard.

"We wanted to give him this award."

"We'll see about this!" the guard said as he grabbed my Emmy and turned and slammed the door.

"Wait a minute!" I protested to Chuck. "That's my award!"

Before he could answer, the door opened. The guard tossed my Emmy at us and said, "'Ee don't want it," slamming the door again.

We went back to the bar.

THE ELBERTA INN CAPER

A large group of us worked nights at TV8, and we sometimes went out after work to have a few drinks and unwind. One night I mentioned the Elberta Inn in Vermilion, a nightclub that offered good food, drink, live music, dancing, and also exotic dancers. Several of the group said we should get together some Saturday evening and go there.

It proved to be a popular decision. For a time, a number of us including Big Chuck, photographer Bob Kasarda, director Chuck Lorius, reporter Ed Bates, and I became regulars. We also became acquainted with the owners and one of the exotic dancers, Rusty Belle.

To help relieve the stress and tension of our broadcasting jobs, we played many practical jokes on each other. We decided that the Elberta Inn would be the perfect place to play a practical joke on another coworker, director Bill Turner. We got Rusty Belle and the club's owners to cooperate, and we reserved a large table on the dance floor for the following Saturday night.

We invited Turner to join us. He was unaware that we also invited TV8 film editor Ralph Gertz, who frequently did roles on *The Hoolihan & Big Chuck Show* and was skilled at disguise. For this evening, Ralph dyed his red hair and beard to a Santa-like whiteness. Wearing a thick pair of glasses and a rumpled suit, he sat at the bar with a large bottle of vodka—actually filled with water—from which he drank frequently.

We called Turner's attention to Gertz, and Bill apparently did not recognize him. Besides, Rusty Belle was working close to our table during her show, flirting with Turner and distracting him by urging him to assist in removing some of her clothing.

When her act was finished, a small dance band began playing, and customers took to the floor. Rusty, on cue, came to our table, claiming she wanted to meet Big Chuck. When she was introduced to Turner, she grabbed his hand and pulled him onto the dance floor. She was wearing a fur coat with very little beneath it, and she allowed it to fall open while they were dancing. She also told Turner that the old man drinking at the bar was her jealous "sugar daddy." Gertz periodically would turn from his seat at the bar to glare and wag his finger at Rusty and Turner.

When Turner returned to the table and told us this, we of course encouraged him all the more to return her overtures. We kept telling him that Gertz appeared to be getting more intoxicated and looked ready to pass out.

The big moment came after the next show, as planned. Rusty came back to the table wearing her fur coat, and Turner needed no encouragement to get up and dance with her, though he did give a nervous look at Gertz, who now was slumped over the bar. As Rusty snuggled up against Turner on the dance floor, her coat again came open. Turner was mesmerized. But the music was interrupted by a roar from Ralph Gertz as he staggered onto the dance floor towards the couple, waving his empty vodka bottle.

Turner literally jumped away from Rusty and stood frozen by

our table. Gertz suddenly clutched his chest, moaned, and fell to the floor. Though she may have been a wonderful dancer, Rusty's acting skills needed a little work, but even so, she rushed to Gertz's side, coaxing Turner to join her on the floor beside the seemingly unconscious body and urging him to give Gertz mouth-to-mouth resuscitation.

We were biting our lips to stifle our laughter when our elaborate practical joke was almost destroyed by a well-meaning customer who tried to shove her way through the crowd, shouting, "I'm a nurse, let me through."

Turner, meanwhile, was cautiously approaching Gertz on his knees, and at Rusty's urging he carefully reached out to check for a pulse. Gertz suddenly reached up and grabbed Turner. Turner almost had a real heart attack before he realized it was all a joke.

DICK GODDARD

Dick Goddard is one of the most recognized people in all of northeastern Ohio. It was a privilege to work at the same station with him for forty-two years. He's the dean of Ohio television weather forecasting and a best-selling author, and his good deeds are legendary: his work with homeless animals, his charity appearances, and, of course, the biggest single-day festival in Ohio, the Woollybear Festival, which Dick co-founded.

Years ago, however, one of his many good deeds almost got him into trouble, and made him the target of a practical joke.

I had been working full time at WJW for just a short while when a school group in the Firelands School District, where I lived at the time, held a benefit auction. Unbeknownst to me, they had contacted Dick and asked if he would contribute original artwork. Dick, an accomplished cartoonist with a degree in art, drew a caricature of me and sent it to the school. I did not learn of this until the night of the auction when, much to my surprise, they announced they were selling an original caricature of me drawn by Dick Goddard.

I am no judge of artwork, but I thought the drawing more closely resembled a humanized Goodyear blimp than me. Nevertheless, it went up for sale. Nobody offered a bid. I sat trying to hide my head in embarrassment. Nobody would offer anything for a drawing of me, a local son! Someone in the back of the room finally said, "You say that was drawn by Dick Goddard?" The auctioneer assured him it was, and that it depicted local resident Neil Zurcher. The man responded, "I never heard of that Zurcher guy, but I guess I'd bid seventy-five cents for a Goddard drawing." He added that his wife watched Goddard all the time. The auctioneer swiftly brought my embarrassment to an end by hammering the table, shouting, "Sold! For seventy-five cents!" and moving on to the next item.

I was crushed. Here I was, a reporter for a big-time television station, and the local folks didn't even seem to care. I slunk out of the auction without buying anything.

It took me a day or two to start seeing the humor in the situation, and by that weekend I was laughing about it. I was relating it to my longtime friend, Elyria attorney Jack Zagrans, a man who loved practical jokes. We sat in his office laughing as I told him the drawing fetched only seventy-five cents. Suddenly Jack got a twinkle in his eye and said, "You are going to sue Dick Goddard." I almost choked.

"For what?" I said.

"For holding you up to public ridicule and for defamation of character," Jack replied with a big grin. "He drew the picture without your knowledge, right?" he asked. I nodded. "People were laughing at you that night, weren't they?" he asked.

"Yeah," I responded, "but *Dick* didn't mean to embarrass me; it was the fact that people didn't want to buy the picture that was embarrassing."

"Doesn't matter," Jack said. "We aren't really going to sue him; we're just going to have some fun."

Over the next few days Jack had a real lawsuit drawn up. He brought both the Lorain County recorder and the county sheriff's department into the joke. The recorder put official-looking seals on the suit, making it look as though it really had been filed, and an off-duty sheriff's deputy agreed to come to Cleveland in uniform to serve the bogus lawsuit on Dick.

I had clued in everyone in the newsroom about what was going to happen. Anchors Doug Adair and Martin Ross were at their desks across from Goddard. Behind some curtains in the news director's office, at Jack's request, we had set up a camera to capture the scene because he wouldn't be there to witness Dick's reaction. At 4:30 in the afternoon, when we were sure Dick would be in the newsroom, the deputy arrived in full uniform with a gun, walked up to Goddard's desk, and asked, "Are you Dick Goddard?"

Goddard looked up, smiling curiously as the deputy placed the bogus lawsuit in his hand and said, "You have just been served with a lawsuit." With that he turned, keeping a straight face, and walked out of the newsroom, leaving Goddard with his mouth hanging open. He opened up the papers and read that I was suing him for $200,000. When he saw my name, he started to laugh, thinking it was some kind of joke. Then he saw the official seals and the filing stamps and stopped laughing.

At that point, on cue, I walked out of the news director's office right in front of Dick. He looked up and said, "What's this all about? Why are you suing me?" I cut him off by replying, "Sorry, Dick, under instructions from my attorney I cannot discuss the matter." With that, I swept out of the office into the hallway where the deputy and those in on the joke were waiting. We were bent over with silent laughter. When Dick came running around the corner, apparently looking for me, he suddenly saw the crowd and realized he had been had.

Our joke really worked because, unknown to us, Dick had recently been served with an actual lawsuit, and he knew what the procedure was. He said later that it was the deputy and the stamps on the suit that convinced him I was seriously going to sue him for that caricature. We all had a big laugh, and I assured Dick the suit wasn't real, just payback for a drawing that no one wanted.

I don't think Dick was mad. Of course, it was many years before he asked me to be grand marshal of the Woollybear Parade, I haven't gotten a Christmas card from him in years, and he has never tried to give me a homeless cat or dog. And he has never drawn another picture of me.

But I meant what I said at the beginning of this chapter: It has been an honor and a privilege to work with Dick for all those years. I have always thought of him as both a colleague and a friend.

THE WOOLLYBEAR FESTIVAL

Goddard has often said that I was instrumental in the founding of the Woollybear Festival.

The truth is, it was a very minor role. This is what happened.

In the early 1970s, Goddard and his daughter Kim were guests at the annual Valley City Frog Jump. They discussed festivals on the way home, and Dick opined that the woollybear caterpillar would be a great subject to celebrate because of its legendary weather-forecasting ability. The fuzzy orange and black worm supposedly grows one band of color larger than the other when it is going to be a bad winter.

The next day at work, Goddard mentioned to me that he was looking for a group that might be interested in celebrating the woollybear. I gave it little thought since I, unlike Goddard, spend little time thinking about worms, fuzzy or otherwise.

But, as luck would have it, when I arrived home from work a few nights later, my then wife, Gay, was hosting a meeting of the Parent Teacher Association at Birmingham Elementary School, where our daughter Melissa was a student. The PTA was trying to raise funds for school activities, and as I walked through the living room, one of the ladies asked if I had any ideas. Goddard's comment popped into my mind. I said, "If you host a Woollybear Festival, Dick Goddard would probably come out and take part in it."

They voted that evening to offer to sponsor the festival at their school that fall. I took the message to Goddard. The rest, as they say, is history.

That first Woollybear Festival in the fall of 1972 attracted perhaps a couple of thousand people to the tiny community of Birmingham. The parade was short; it just wound around a couple of blocks and back to the school. But we were all having so much fun that we took the parade around the block twice to make it last longer. Goddard's stage was the back of a fire truck, and they held woollybear races in the school yard.

But with Goddard's continuing support and mentions of the festival on his weather segments on TV8, the festival grew. On Woollybear Sunday, the little community would be packed to capacity.

The parade also got bigger. Goddard loves to tell the story of those early years when a truck driver passing through Birmingham on State Route 113 got caught up in the parade and accidentally became one of the parade units.

And there was the year that George Voinovich, then Ohio's lieutenant governor, was the grand marshal. The crowd was so big that both main roads leading into Birmingham reached gridlock. With nothing moving, Voinovich could not reach Birmingham by car and had to be helicoptered into the school baseball diamond to lead the parade.

It began to dawn on Goddard that year that the festival was outgrowing its home base. That, along with some opposition from prominent local residents who didn't appreciate thousands of people descending on their quiet community, led him to start searching for a new home for the event.

Several communities offered themselves as the new home for the Woollybear. In the end, it seemed to boil down to two choices: Wellington, a historic town in southern Lorain County that, as home to the county fairgrounds, had facilities for big crowds; and Vermilion, the quaint lakeshore community just north of Birmingham. Needing the original team that Goddard dubbed the Woollybear Ladies, who did the real work of organizing the festival each year, Vermilion became the logical choice.

While I don't play a role in the festival planning, for more than three decades I have attended it and ridden in the parade. My grandchildren, Allison and Bryan McCallister and Ryan and Jason Luttmann, have occasionally ridden with me. Because of my job I have seen a lot of festivals, and the Woollybear Festival is one of the best in the state and probably the nation.

One of the little-known facts about the Woollybear Festival is how its date is chosen each year. Goddard has worked for many seasons as the statistician for all home games of the Cleveland Browns. He waits until he sees the team's schedule each fall, then picks the Sunday in late September or early October that the Browns are playing out of town. That becomes Woollybear Sunday.

OPERATION OPEN HEART

I first met David Harper when he was a young patrolman assigned to the Elyria Post of the State Highway Patrol. An air force veteran, he was raised in the Summit County Children's Home in Akron, and he asked me if I would help him take some of the youngsters from the home on a day of fishing. Remembering his lonely childhood in the orphanage, he tried to spend as much time with them as his duties allowed, giving the kids individual attention and helping them create some good memories.

I agreed to help and suggested that some other law enforcement people in Lorain County might like to participate. I called Parker Miller, then chief ranger of the Lorain County Metro Parks, park ranger Bob Hartle, and Vermilion police chief Harry Lechner to see if they could arrange a picnic pavilion, fishing gear, and a boat ride for the kids. They did, and the idea seemed to keep expanding.

Before long, the simple fishing trip had grown into an overnight campout at the Bacon Woods of the Lorain County Metro Parks. Other police from around the county, like Amherst police chief Art Koppenhafer and South Amherst chief Tom Snizek, also pitched in, collecting food and working on the outing. The project got a real boost when local attorney and humanitarian Jack Zagrans joined the group, coming up with some much-needed funds to make sure we had everything we needed for the boys.

Don Miller of the *Elyria Chronicle–Telegram* gave our fledgling group its name while doing a story on the outing.

"What do you call this project?" he asked me.

"We really don't have a name for it; we just referred to it as Dave Harper's fishing trip."

Harper said, "How about Project Cooperation?"

"Nah," said Miller. "These cops have really opened up their hearts to these kids. It ought to be something that reflects that feeling."

He thought a moment and said, "How about Operation Open Heart?"

By August 1962, when the date arrived for the afternoon fishing trip that had now grown to a two-day outing, more than twenty youngsters from the Summit County Children's Home were to be joined by a dozen kids from Green Acres, the Lorain County Children's Home in Oberlin. Operation Open Heart would be hosted by nearly every police department and law enforcement agency in Lorain County, as well as community leaders and volunteers like "Tiger" Wilms, Jay Savage, and Roy Jensen.

Andy Ortner, who operated a small airport near Birmingham, Ohio, volunteered to fly his DC-3 passenger plane to Akron to pick up the Summit County kids, while a police delegation and a custom-made camper bus owned by Hudson industrialist John Morse and his wife Helen went to Green Acres for the Lorain County youngsters. Both groups met at Ortner's, and a caravan of nearly twenty police cars with flashing lights and sirens set out with the kids across back roads to Bacon Woods.

The kids spent the afternoon fishing, swimming, riding with officers in police cars and on motorcycles, taking jaunts around the park on top of a historic fire truck, playing softball against the adults, and then joining together in a picnic shelter for a steak fry provided by the police officers and cooked by Parker Miller and Tiger Wilms. After dinner there was an appearance by Cleveland TV personality Ron Penfound, the popular kids' show host known as Captain Penny, who sat talking with the kids around the campfire. The day ended with Dave Harper leading the boys and the cops in a sing-a-long as the fire slowly died.

The next day was filled with more swimming, a boat ride on Lake Erie, and miniature golf in Vermilion—a memorable two days for youngsters who rarely had much fun.

None of us would have guessed that this outing for orphaned children would continue not only for years but for generations.

One of the more memorable days was in the early 1980s, when the police officers decided to show the kids an up-close look at a real police chase. They proposed to have police follow a car of criminals into the park, with siren and lights going, and then chase it out of the park and up to the top of the cliff along the Vermilion River, where it would be out of sight to the youngsters in the park below. After a few minutes, with all eyes searching the top of the cliff, the criminals' car would crash over the edge of the cliff and drop a couple of hundred feet into the shallow Vermilion River. The car was rigged with fireworks, so when it hit the river it would also explode.

Looking at it today, it was a bad idea ecologically. But this was the 1980s, and no one said no. The kids loved it, as did a crowd of visitors to the park. But in the crowd was also the director of the park system, Henry Minert, and to put it mildly, he was not happy. It was the last time Operation Open Heart dumped a car in the river.

Another favorite of the kids was Ralph Gertz, the TV8 film editor at TV8 who frequently played character roles in skits on the "Hoolihan & Big Chuck Show." He was to join the kids' outing in the role of an old hermit who made his home in the woods along the Vermilion River. The youngsters were told that the hermit had agreed to come out of his cave and tell ghost stories around the first night's campfire.

Ralph was working at the station all day. He planned to arrive just after dark, and a couple of us agreed to meet him and surreptitiously take him to a back entrance of the park, where he would don a hooded robe. He would carry a lantern and a long staff as he emerged from the woods.

Larry Wickham, a ranger at the park who loved wild animals, had recently captured a six-foot-long black snake to show the kids. He suggested that he and I should meet Ralph and give him the snake in a burlap bag that he could carry to surprise the kids. I agreed. Larry got the large but harmless snake, put it in the bag on the floor on my car, and we drove up to North Ridge Road and our rendezvous with Ralph.

Two things went wrong: The first was that I did not know Ralph had a serious fear of snakes. When he got out of his car and Larry pulled the snake from the sack, Ralph took one look and passed out. He collapsed right on the spot. Larry put the snake back into the bag, placed it in my car, and we both went to assist Ralph.

He came to almost immediately and calmed down after we promised not to bring the snake within ten feet of him.

We led Ralph to the back of the park. While he was putting his hermit costume on, Larry went to get the snake from my car. But the bag was empty. Larry had forgotten to tie the top of it after stashing the snake when Ralph collapsed.

We got flashlights and spent the next half hour searching my car and trunk without success. We had pulled out the backseat, as Larry speculated how the snake had made its getaway, when we found it curled up in the springs. Although I have no great fear of snakes, I was relieved to have it out of my car.

David Harper, the man who started it all, later resigned from the force and left Ohio. He returned in 1987 as guest of honor at the outing's twenty-fifth anniversary at Bacon Woods Park, where it all began. John and Helen Morse also returned for the festivities.

Now, nearly fifty years after it began, a new generation of police officers still holds the outing each year at the Bacon Woods in the Vermilion River Reservation. Hundreds of orphaned and neglected children have been exposed to a kinder side of law enforcement and life that they might never have seen—all thanks to a trooper who wanted to give a few homeless kids the chance to go fishing.

NAKED ON THE PHONE

Jane Lassar is in charge of publicizing my books. She is like an adult camp counselor, lining up radio, TV, magazine, and newspaper interviews for authors. She gives them praise, pep talks, and even argues and convinces them otherwise when they don't want to do an interview or personal appearance. The night before an author is slated to do an interview or give a speech, Jane is on the phone like a proud parent, offering advice about everything from what to wear to things that to say and not say. Usually she does this with great skill, warmth, and kindness. Every author should be so lucky as to have Jane Lassar promoting his or her books. But I have one problem with Jane: I rarely talk to her when I have any clothes on.

I think she has a third eye that can see over telephone lines into my home.

It started in 1995 with my first book, *Favorite One Tank Trips*. I realized that almost every time Jane called me at home, I was in a state of undress. It didn't matter what time of day it was. The phone would ring; it would be Jane, and she would catch me just as I shed the last item. I have talked to Jane naked in my bathroom, naked in my shower, even naked in my bedroom.

Down through the years and for the half-dozen other books I have written, the pattern has continued: Me naked. Jane phoning my house.

Now I want to point out that Jane is a lovely, happily married lady with a family. But I secretly think that if there is such a thing as reincarnation, that Jane and I had a "thing" going in another life. What else would give her the instinct to call just as I take off my clothes?

It has become a standing joke in our house. No matter what

time of day I go to take a shower, it's pretty certain that Jane Lassar will call and insist she has to talk with me.

In fact, I recently mentioned at a speaking engagement that there is "this lady at Gray and Company whom I usually speak to only when I am naked." You should have seen the reaction.

Now I am beginning to feel like a pervert. I know Jane doesn't do it intentionally. I know it is just coincidental. I know she can't see me. I know it's impossible for her to have a third eye.

Isn't it?

PEOPLE WE MEET ALONG THE ROAD

As you may have no doubt perceived, this book is not so much about me as it is about the people I have met along the road.

One thing I have learned is that, as our lives intertwine and mingle, we touch each other in ways we may never realize. One of my earliest memories illustrates this point.

In 1942 I found myself at age six in the backseat of an Elyria police cruiser, but I am getting ahead of the story.

My parents had planned a Valentine's Day excursion from our farm home in Henrietta to Elyria in order to have some work done on my father's company car and to do some grocery shopping.

I rode to the Elyria Ford agency with my father in his shiny white 1941 Ford. My mother followed in our family car, a blue 1939 Packard. After dropping off the Ford, we all climbed into the Packard and drove to the Fisher Foods store on West Broad Street.

I got bored walking with my parents and their shopping cart. I started to run ahead of them, hiding behind stacked cans of food and jumping out to scare them when they caught up. I'm sure I looked like a typical spoiled brat to the other customers, who frowned at my antics. But the attention only spurred me on. I began to run up and down aisles to see if my mother or father would look for me. But they just kept shopping, acting as though they were ignoring me.

After waiting several minutes behind a stack of Campbell's soup cans, ready to jump out and surprise them, I suddenly realized that they were not coming. In fact, I had not seen them for several minutes. I felt a small bubble of panic. I wanted to find them and to be reassured they were looking for me.

I ran up and down the aisles, searching, and the bubble of panic got larger and larger. Each time I rounded the end of an aisle and did not see their familiar faces, the panic worsened. It was no longer a fun game of hide and seek. I convinced myself that my parents, having become angry with me for running through the store, were punishing me by hiding themselves. Now frightened, I ran out the store's back door, forgot that we had arrived in my family's blue Packard, and frantically began to search the parking lot for my father's white Ford. When I didn't find it, I used the logic of a frightened six-year-old: I convinced myself that I had so angered my parents that they had abandoned me and driven off, leaving me to find my own way home.

Inside the store, my parents were growing concerned as they went from aisle to aisle looking for me. Apparently, as I ran searching for them, we had just been missing each other.

Outside in the parking lot, I considered my options. Although I was only six, I had made the trip from Henrietta to Elyria many times and was familiar with the route. Because I was convinced my parents had abandoned me, I set out to walk thirteen miles home.

My parents, meanwhile, had reached the point of telling store managers I was missing. Grocery workers joined them looking under counters, inside walk-in refrigerators, and in the stockroom at the back of the store. My mother was bordering on hysteria when my father suggested they call the police.

Patrolman Howard B. Taft of the Elyria Police Department arrived a few minutes later. After quickly ascertaining that I was not in the store, he led my parents to his patrol car to start a slow search of the streets around the store.

By then, however, I had been walking steadily west, crossed

the Black River Bridge, and was now making my way towards the western edge of Elyria. Taft and my parents focused their search on Ely Park and the center of town.

Not spotting me on the street, Taft led my parents into the Rivoli Theater, which was showing an action-adventure feature movie. He convinced the projectionist to stop the film and turn up the house lights so they could scan the crowd of youngsters for me.

I was near the intersection of West River Road and West Bridge Street, sobbing as I kept walking. A group of ragged-looking boys across the street watched me. They began to shout and tease me about my crying, and then threw dirty snowballs packed from the gray slush lining the street. I ducked the snowballs and started to run, crying even louder as I tried to put distance between myself and my tormentors.

This was less than ten years after the kidnapping of the Lindbergh baby, and by now my mother had convinced herself that I had been kidnapped from the grocery store. Patrolman Taft, in a soothing voice, reassured her over and over that young children wander off all the time and I was sure to turn up. He kept their hopes up as they continued to search the streets and alleys of downtown Elyria.

By this time I had walked nearly four miles from the grocery store and was wandering along the edge of the state highway called Telegraph Road. My nose was running and tears were streaming down my face as I passed a farm house where a kind looking lady was getting the mail from her mailbox.

"Little boy!" she called to me. "Is something wrong?"

"My parents ran off and left me," I sobbed, standing forlornly on the side of the road.

She told me her name was Mrs. Carrie Dellefield and asked what my name was. I told her. She suggested we go into her house and see if she couldn't help me get home.

After she brought me some milk and cookies, I sobbed out my story. I told Mrs. Dellefield I was headed for my grandparents' home in Henrietta. She asked for their phone number, and in a few moments I was telling my shocked Grandmother Currier what had happened. She was unaware I was missing, but she told me to stay where I was while she called the Elyria police to see what was going on.

Patrolman Taft's police cruiser pulled into the Dellefield yard a short while later, reuniting me with my parents. By then I realized that I was the one who had caused all the ruckus. But any fears of punishment evaporated when I saw my mother's tearful face and the big smiles on my father and Patrolman Taft. Taft told us that he and his wife had their first child, a son, only two months earlier, and that this day had given him a preview of what life would probably be like as his little boy grew up.

He gave me a little lecture on the ride back to our car in Elyria. When I thought my parents were gone, he said, I should have found a store official and asked him to call a policeman. I should not have left the store.

And that was how I ended up in the rear of an Elyria police cruiser on Valentine's Day of 1942.

Six months later, a bizarre chain of events gave the story a sad ending.

Early on the evening of August 19, 1942, Patrolman Taft, who had been on the force less than a year, was giving a ride home to a fellow rookie, Donald Andress. Andress, who'd been on the force only a month, was off-duty and not in uniform. A call came over the patrol car's radio dispatching Taft to a minor auto accident on East Bridge Street.

It looked like a routine fender-bender. But as Taft talked to one of the drivers, thirty-nine-year-old Nathanial Spuriel of Cleveland, he noticed that he appeared intoxicated. Upon explaining to the man that he was taking him to police headquarters, Taft got behind the wheel of the man's Cadillac coupe and ordered Spuriel to get in the passenger side. Andress would follow in the patrol car. But as Taft started to move, he discovered that the smashed fender hindered steering. He stopped, got out, and with Spuriel's help pulled the fender away from the wheel.

Witnesses' accounts are unclear about what happened next.

Andress, who was in the police car, told investigating officers that Spuriel yanked the car keys from the ignition and refused to give them to Taft.

Arthur DuReitz, a witness who lived nearby, told police that Taft spotted a gun on the floor when he started to get back into the Cadillac.

Both witnesses agreed that the officer and Spuriel grappled before Spuriel grabbed a gun from the car and fired, striking Taft three times. Taft slumped to the pavement, but from the ground he was able to empty his service revolver at his assailant. Three bullets hit Spuriel in the chest, killing him.

Taft was still breathing when Andress rushed him to Elyria Memorial Hospital several blocks away. But Taft died of his wounds at the hospital about an hour and a half later. Only twenty-nine years old, he was the first Elyria police officer to lose his life in the line of duty.

But the bloody evening was not over.

Police Captain C. E. Southam and Patrolman Kenneth Martin completed the journey to police headquarters with Spuriel's Cadillac. Searching the car at the station, they opened the trunk and found the body of twenty-eight-year-old Doris McConnell of Cleveland. She had been beaten to death, and her nude body was stuffed in the trunk with a considerable amount of stolen property.

Detectives later determined that Spuriel, who had a lengthy criminal record, had recently been arrested for operating a house of prostitution in Cleveland, and that Doris was one of his employees. Both had imminent court dates. Cleveland police theorized that Spuriel beat McConnell to death in an apartment on Cleveland's east side the night before and was looking for a place to dispose of her body when he was involved in the accident in Elyria.

Two days later, on Friday, August 21—in the darkest days of World War II, when gasoline rationing limited travel of any kind—hundreds of law enforcement officers from around Lorain

County and Greater Cleveland and the Ohio State Highway Patrol turned out to honor Patrolman Howard Taft as his body was escorted to its final resting place in Brookdale Cemetery in Elyria. Two trucks were needed just to haul all the flowers from the funeral home to the gravesite. It was considered the largest funeral in the city's history.

He would continue to be the only Elyria policeman killed in the line of duty until 2010, when popular Elyria patrolman James Kerstetter was killed in a tragic shooting.

Afterword

On a gray November day not long ago, Bonnie and I drove out to my hometown of Henrietta to shop at Apple Hill, a small fruit stand and bulk foods store near the top of Henrietta Hill.

I remained in the car as Bonnie went in the store to shop. My eyes drifted across the highway to the empty building on the corner of State Route 113 and Vermilion Road that was once my parents' store. Much of the gravel driveway that I used to pace as a daydreaming teenager has been replaced by a highway widening.

I could almost hear the bell on the side of the building, signaling a customer had pulled up to the gasoline pumps, now long gone.

Three windows on the second floor stared blankly at the autumn countryside while in my mind I heard the voices of my family. My father, mother, brother, and I crammed into those three tiny rooms above the store. This was our home.

A flood of memories surprised me and brought tears to my eyes. I blinked and quickly wiped them away, hoping to conceal from Bonnie the emotions this casual visit had suddenly triggered.

In 2000 I had reached my sixty-fifth birthday. I was still traveling fifty-two weeks a year doing One Tank Trips on Fox 8, but my health was declining. As I walked into the station one morning from the parking lot in back, I found myself stopping every few feet to rest and catch my breath. All that day, even walking across the room was difficult. That night I had a speech in Shaker

Heights. Much to my surprise, I couldn't stand through the whole talk, and had to sit down to finish.

The next morning we visited my cardiologist, Praful Maroo, chief of cardiology at Fairview Hospital. He took a look at me, checked some vital signs, and immediately had me admitted to the coronary care unit. From that point on, things seemed to go downhill. The next few days are a blur. I remember being in the intensive care unit with a technician screaming for someone to get a tube to force down my throat when I stopped breathing. Another time I hallucinated that I was in an Old West saloon and the nurses were bar girls. I began to realize how serious my situation was when my daughters drove in from their homes in Cincinnati and Dayton. I later learned Bonnie had called them and told them I was seriously ill. It was a week before I left the ICU, and Dr. Maroo later told me he was surprised I was still alive.

I knew things were not good the morning that Maroo and Dr. Neal Chadwick, a pulmonologist, came to see me in the hospital. As gently as they could, they said it might be time to retire and change my lifestyle. Dr. Chadwick told me that I probably would have to be on oxygen for the rest of my life, and suggested that I no longer drive.

It was one of the bitterest days I can recall. I loved my job and certainly didn't want it to end this way. And how could I enjoy life tethered to an oxygen tank, unable to jump in a car and go where and when I wanted?

I went home to recuperate. A large oxygen-making machine was installed in the house. Long coils of clear plastic tubing that ran from the machine allowed me to wander through my home, wearing an oxygen mask. I could go out for an hour or two carrying a steel tank of oxygen on a small cart. But Bonnie had to drive. I found myself sinking into dark depression.

Bonnie, a recently retired RN, didn't agree with the doctors' assessment of my condition. She thought I was showing signs of improvement. So, without telling me, she slightly reduced the amount of oxygen I was getting each day and watched closely for any noticeable effects. She did this for a week or so until she had turned the oxygen completely off. I was totally unaware. Then she insisted I make an appointment with Dr. Chadwick to see what he thought. He checked my oxygen levels, found they were near normal, and gave me the happy news that I could stop the oxygen treatment and drive a car again.

In her wisdom, Bonnie had given me back my life.

I soon returned to the road and Fox 8 Television. In 2004, however, forty-two years after I started as a freelance reporter for WJW, the station decided not to renew my contract. Since I was approaching seventy years of age, I decided it was time to retire from TV but not from writing. I had been a regular columnist for the *Ohio Motorist* magazine since the late 1990s, and I continued to travel and write a column for them for five more years. In 2006 I completed a new travel book, *Ohio Road Trips*, published by Gray & Company Shortly after publication, I was contacted by the *Cleveland Plain Dealer* and asked to write a column every other Saturday based on the new book. At this writing, I am still doing the travel features for the *PD*.

It has been a wonderful life filled with adventure. As for regrets, as the song says, "I've had a few." I deeply wish I had been a better parent to my children. I truly hope they understand that I always loved them unconditionally and that I am so proud of the adults they have become and their achievements.

As for my wife, Bonnie, she is the love of my life, and I only wish that we could spend another lifetime together.

On that gray November day as we drove away on State Route 113, I looked in the rearview mirror and saw the little country crossroads of Henrietta fading in the distance. It was the place where I used to watch cars go past and wonder where they were going. Now, a lifetime later, I think I know.

They were probably people just like me, on their way to find their future. We all discovered it was a far longer and bigger adventure than we could ever find on just a One Tank Trip.

Acknowledgments

Being raised in the tiny community of Henrietta was, in many ways, like growing up in a big family.

As I wrote early on, no one played a greater role in shaping my life than my mother's parents, Canarius and Caroline Currier, with whom we lived.

My first babysitters, friends, and playmates were my cousins Jean, Bud, Gerald, Joyce, and Nancy Currier, who lived just down the road. Also Jim, Ruth, Madge, Richard, and Tom Currier, more cousins who lived just a mile or so away.

My first grade teacher at Henrietta School was longtime family friend Mae Mahan. My teacher in the third and fourth grades was my aunt, Ada Berger, who knew me from birth. The cook in the school cafeteria was my aunt Helen Currier, wife of my mother's brother, Leon.

My graduating class from Henrietta High School in 1953 had just eight students: Marcella Horvath, Rachel Howe, Wilma Bursley, Dale Morrow, Jack Dodd, Dennis Brill, Wayne Gerber, and me.

One of my favorite teachers was Patricia Penton Leimbach, who tried mightily to impart writing discipline and knowledge to me. I wish I could say I responded well to her efforts, but that would not be true. I was a lackadaisical student who was inattentive and not motivated by grades.

The point I am trying to make is that acknowledging the contributions of people who played a role in my life is a huge undertaking. I could tell stories about every person listed here. No matter how hard I try to recall each of their names, there are hundreds of people I owe so much to, and age and time ensure that there is no way that I am going to remember every one. To those I inadvertently overlooked, my apologies. Please know that the oversight of your name and contribution in this book is simply the result of advancing age and the death of some brain cells.

Let me start by thanking Brad Williams, former editor of the *Oberlin News-Tribune,* for hiring me in my first news job. Paul Nakel of WEOL in Elyria for giving me my break in broadcasting. Walt Glendenning for talking me into learning how to use a movie camera and encouraging me to work as a freelancer for television news. Ray Goll, who also taught me the ins and outs of news photography. Norm Wagy, who gave me my first job in television and became a friend as well as the first of eight news directors I worked for at WJW-TV. The others include Bill Feest, Virgil Dominic, Tony Ballew, Phyllis Quail, Grant Zalba, Kathy Williams, and Greg Easterly. Then there were my colleagues down through the years. The late Jim Fixx, who worked with me at the *Oberlin News-Tribune.* From WEOL there were John Christman, Todd Burke, Gary Short, Walter Harrell, Hugh Coburn, Bill Stipsits, Dick Barrett, Terry Boyson, Gerald Warner, Don Borlie, Doug Caldwell, Dick Conrad, Andy Butte, Doug Lillico, Chuck Blair, Bill Humphries, Buzz Tyler, and many others.

When I reached Cleveland television in the 1960s, I had the privilege and pleasure of working with some of the pioneers of television at WJW and other stations. I will always appreciate the advice and help I received from Doug Adair, Joel Daly, Harry Jones, Marty Ross, Murray Stewart, Jenny Crimm, Bob Huber, John Fitzgerald, Howard Hoffman, Ken Coleman, the legendary Dick Goddard, Neil "Mickey" Flanagan, Dan Hrvatin, Ron Bilek, Jim Cox, Pete Cary, Barbra Caffie, Bob Franken, Bill McKay, Teel Salon, Ed Bates, Jim Doney, Bob "Hoolihan" Wells, Chuck "Big Chuck" Schodowski, Sandford Sobul.

As the years went by, the faces changed, and I was allowed to work alongside a new generation of TV people like Tana Carli,

Loree Vick, Robin Swoboda, and Wilma Smith. There was Dick Russ, Bob Cerminara, Dave Buckel, Vince Cellini, Sandy Lesko, Kristy Steeves, Lori Taylor, Belinda Prinz, Mark Koontz, Jeff Maynor, and Jim Hale. Jan Jones, Jim Finerty, Kathy Brugette, Jacqui Bishop and Kelly O'Donnell, John Telich, Jim Mueller, Gary Stromberg, Carl Monday, Don Olson, Susan Howard, Mike Creagan, Anne Mulligan, Isabel Tener, Steve Bloomfield, Dan Coughlin, John "Lil John" Rinaldi, Joel Rose, the Hambrick Brothers, Judd at TV8, John at WEWS, Kevin Salyer, Chris Geiselman, Stephen Bellamy, Steve Goldurs.

In the later years of my career it was wonderful to work with talented young people like Wayne Dawson, Stefani Schaefer, Dave Nethers, Todd Meany, Bill Sheil, Tracy McCool, Andre Bernier, Scott Sabol, A. J. Colby, Bill Martin, Martin Savidge, Lou Maglio, Macy McGinnis, Kenny Crumpton, Robin Meade, Bob Kovach, Tony Harris, Stacey Bell, Tom Merriman, Stacy Frye, Lynne Zele, Margaret Daykin, Jaque Smith, Dan Jovic, Linda Norman, Tomi Toyama-Ambrose, Lisa March, Molly Randel, Tatyana Junkers, Bill Ward, Patti Braskie, Denise Dufala, Andre Bernier, John Loufman, Margaret Daykin.

Probably the people I was closest to at WJW-TV were its many talented photographers, some of the best in the business. People like Ali Ghanbari, Ron Mounts, Bill Wolfe, Bill West, Jim Pijor, Jim Holloway, Mark Saksa, Loren Kruse, Ralph Tarsitano, Peter Miller, Gary Korb, Bob Begany, Cook Goodwin, Dave Williams, Terry Patti, Lynn Chambers, Greg Lockhard, Chuck Sanders, Roger Powell, Bob Kasarda, Herb Thomas, Dave Almond, John Paustian, Russ Herbruck, Dave Hollis, Bob Wilkinson, John Yuhas, Cragg Eichman.

There were colleagues from the other stations in town that became friends, like Ted Ocepek, Bob Dale, Paul Wilcox, Dave Patterson, Nev Chandler, Leon Bibb, Fred Griffith, Bill Jacocks, Bob Howick, Linn Sheldon, Alice Weston.

At WVIZ, Betty Cope, Kent Geist, Dee Perry.

WKYC, Tom Beres, Mike O'Mara, Betsy Kling, Paul Thomas,

Paul Sciria, Rita Andolsen, Dave Summers, Del Donahoo, Mike Greene, Ed Verba.

From my youth there were Joe and Alice Velasquez, Marv and Margaret Barr, Doris Barr, Bob Hartle, Dave Harper, Parker Miller, Ed Hale, Charley Bulger, Don Ward, Jim Mertz, Marv Reising, Gary and Bob Rice, John Tarr, Elizabeth Riscatti, Allison Blair, Maria Martin, Scotty and Nellie Blair, John Gullo, Lisa Tarr, Carl Crapo, John Lehman, Jack and Marilyn "Suki" Zagrans, Eric and Maura Zagrans, Marion and Anson Russell, Tom Porter, Char and Gene Lautzenheiser, Gary Pelger, Bill and Bonnie Cutcher, Jim and Kim Zucker, Joseph Velasquez, Karen Velasquez Clark, David Clark, Ted and Karen Driscol, Jim and Peg Sands, Jason and Katy Sands, JoAnn Hershberger, George and Janet Voinovich, Jody Wilson, Susan Nager, Christa Luttmann, Tony Aringer, Jimbo Thompson, George Condon, George Kilburg, Cindy and Kevin Ruic, Jerry McKenna, Linda Feagler, Michael von Glahn, Thomas W. Porter, Gary Carrothers, Ralph Paul.

A special thank you to all the area librarians who answered countless questions and assisted me in looking up dates and facts, especially to Dorene Paul of the Sandusky Public Library for her assistance and suggestions.

My publisher, David Gray, marketing director Chris Andrikanich, publicity director Jane Lassar, and my editor, Rob Lucas. Also thanks to Tom Feran, Linda Cuckovich, and Pat Fernberg for their editorial skills as well.

My former wife, Gay Zurcher.

My step-mother, Edna Zurcher. My brother and sister-in-law, Noel and Linda Zurcher. My sister and brother-in-law, Caroline and David Powley. My stepbrother, Jim Birrell, and his wife, Diane, my stepsister, Janet Travers, and her husband, Phil Gray. My sister-in-law Susan Nager.

My family, my daughters and sons-in law, Melody and Ernie McCallister, Melissa and Peter Luttmann.

My son, Craig Zurcher.

My grandchildren, Allison and Bryan McCallister, Ryan and Jason Luttmann.

And last, but certainly not least, my wife and friend, Bonnie Adamson Zurcher.

Everyone I have mentioned on these pages has played a role in my life, and I have a story to tell about each of them. For some it is a major part, while for others it might be just a walk-on. In either case their presence in my life was so strong that I have always remembered them. As to those whom a faulty memory has overlooked, my deep apologies again.

Once more, to everyone, thank you.

— Neil Zurcher,
Bay Village, Ohio

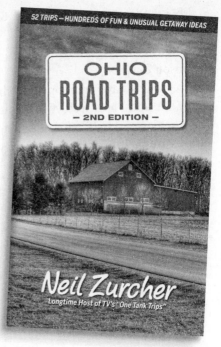

The Buckeye State has no shortage of strange, silly, goofy, quirky, eccentric, and just plain weird places, people, and things—if you know where to look . . .

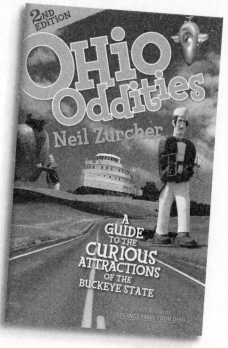

- **REALLY BIG THINGS**. Like the World's Largest Basket . . . Gathering of Twins . . . Cuckoo Clock . . . Crystal ball . . .

- **MYSTERIES**. Like the "bottomless" Blue Hole of Castalia and Delaware's haunted observatory.

- **STRANGE COLLECTIONS**. Like the objects swallowed by citizens of Lima, the nation's only vacuum cleaner museum, and the world's largest collection of popcorn poppers.

- **PECULIAR CLAIMS TO FAME**. Like the "Oldest concrete road in America," and the "World's fastest pumpkin carver."

- **EXTRAORDINARY CITIZENS**. Like Balto the Wonder dog, firewalking Komar the Magnificent, Napoleon's horse, and Chic Chic—the chicken who bought his own lunch.

- **THE JUST-HARD-TO-EXPLAIN**. Like the Wellington ATM shaped like a Victorian horse and buggy or Ohio's strange attachment to the bathtub from the U.S.S. Maine.

- Why the most popular resident during his term in the White House was not Marion native President Warren G. Harding but **HIS DOG, LADDIE BOY**.

- **AND LOTS MORE!**

OHIO ODDITIES by Neil Zurcher
$14.95 / paperback / 240 pages / 56 photos

AVAILABLE AT BOOKSTORES
FOR MORE INFO VISIT **WWW.GRAYCO.COM**